An objective of *The ABCs of Strategic Communication* and this *supplement* is to assist communication practitioners – no matter the discipline – in achieving *their* goals. To do that, dissect the author's "informal" definition of *public relations*:

Public relations is as simple as a thank-you note and as complicated as a four-color brochure.

It's as specific as writing a news release and as general as sensing community attitudes.

It's as inexpensive as a phone call to an editor or as costly as a full-page advertisement.

It's as direct as a conversation, text or email between two people and as broad as a radio or television program, or social media, reaching thousands of listeners or millions of viewers.

It's as visual as a poster and as literal as a speech.

HERE, MY FRIENDS, IS THE BIG QUESTION:
What IS *public relations*?

It is a term often used – seldom defined!

In its broadest sense, **public relations** is "good work, publicly recognized."

Believe me, there are no secret formulas. **Public relations** is simply: the group itself saying –

- "This is who we are
- What we think about ourselves
- What we want to do – and
- Why we deserve your support."

M. Larry Litwin and Ralph Burgio © 1971; © 1999; © 2013

**For information, updates and additions, visit:
www.larrylitwin.com**

More ABCs of Strategic Communication
Thousands of terms, tips and techniques that define the professions

Supplement to the Second Edition

by M. Larry Litwin, APR, Fellow PRSA
Rowan (NJ) University
Parsons (Iowa) College

AuthorHouse™
1663 Liberty Drive
Bloomington, IN 47403
www.authorhouse.com
Phone: 1 (800) 839-8640

© 2015 M. Larry Litwin, APR, Fellow PRSA. All rights reserved.

No part of this book may be reproduced, stored in a retrieval system, or transmitted by any means without the written permission of the author.

Published by AuthorHouse   09/22/2015

ISBN: 978-1-5049-2741-3 (sc)
ISBN: 978-1-5049-2740-6 (hc)
ISBN: 978-1-5049-2742-0 (e)

Library of Congress Control Number: 2015912434

Print information available on the last page.

Any people depicted in stock imagery provided by Thinkstock are models, and such images are being used for illustrative purposes only.
Certain stock imagery © Thinkstock.

This book is printed on acid-free paper.

Because of the dynamic nature of the Internet, any web addresses or links contained in this book may have changed since publication and may no longer be valid. The views expressed in this work are solely those of the author and do not necessarily reflect the views of the publisher, and the publisher hereby disclaims any responsibility for them.

Dedication

More ABCs of Strategic Communication is dedicated to the memories of my and Nancy's parents, Jean and Eddie Litwin and Janet and Lionel Perris. Their support has always been unconditional. I would be remiss if I didn't mention my mother, in particular. Jeanie was always known for her "isms"– thoughts and expressions – which she passed onto her children, grandchildren and great grandchildren. Two of our favorites: "Never say I *can't* as in 'I *can't* do it.' *Can't* should never be part of your vocabulary"and "If you dream it, you can achieve it."

Because any book I write also has to be dedicated to the thousands of students who have passed through my classes, here are a couple of Eddie Litwin's "isms" for *them* – "Always strive to be the best that you can be." And, "Never be afraid to ask questions. Questions are a sign of strength, not weakness." For those who didn't know him, Eddie Litwin was truly bigger than life. And, he seemed to always have the right answer.

M. Larry Litwin, APR, Fellow PRSA

M. Larry Litwin, APR, Fellow PRSA, was born in South Philadelphia, raised in Camden and Pennsauken, New Jersey, lived in rural Iowa for three years, suburban North Jersey for two years and now resides in Berlin, N.J. after living in Cherry Hill, N.J. for 35 years.

Litwin is an established strategic adviser, teacher, mentor, role model and ethicist, and an award-winning public relations counselor and broadcast journalist, who has left a lasting impression on thousands of students and professionals.

He spent 42 years as an adjunct and full-time faculty member at Rowan (N.J.) University before retiring as associate professor to guest lecture at other universities in public relations, advertising, radio and television. His classroom is considered a "laboratory for practical knowledge" where he implements "edutainment" to motivate his students.

He is a graduate of Parsons (Iowa) College with a bachelor's degree in business where, in 2013, he was inducted as a member of its Wall of Honor joining 48 others. He received his master's in communication – educational public relations – from Glassboro (N.J.) State College. In 2002, he earned his APR (Accredited in Public Relations) from the Public Relations Society of America (PRSA). In 2007, Litwin was inducted into PRSA's College of Fellows – one of fewer than 445 members at the time.

During his nearly 50 years in the communication profession, Litwin has worked as a public relations director for two school districts and as a radio and TV reporter, editor and anchor for ABC News in New York and KYW in Philadelphia. He was education reporter at KYW Newsradio for 10 years. He spent nearly two years in the U.S. Department of Labor as a deputy regional director of information and public affairs during Elizabeth Dole's tenure as labor secretary. He has also served as a strategic counselor, and public relations and advertising consultant.

Litwin was a governor's appointee to serve as chair of the New Jersey Open Public Records Act Privacy Study Commission, which recommended cutting-edge legislation to assure government records would be available to the public without exposing personal information – such as home addresses and telephone numbers – that should remain private and out of the public domain.

He is treasurer of the Philadelphia Sports Writers Association after serving as secretary for nearly 45 years. He chairs the board of trustees of the South Jersey Baseball Hall of Fame (SJBHoF) and was a member of the Cherry Hill Public Library Board of Trustees. He served on the Cherry Hill Economic Development Council and as president of the Township's Alliance on Drug and Alcohol Abuse. Litwin was a member of the South Jersey Scholar-Athlete Committee sponsored by the *Courier-Post* and *Coca-Cola*. In 2011, he was inducted into the SJBHoF.

Litwin has authored three books in addition to *More ABCs: The Public Relations Practitioner's Playbook for (all) Strategic Communicators – A Synergized Approach to Effective Two-Way Communication* (AuthorHouse – 2013), *The ABCs of Strategic Communication – Thousands of terms, tips and techniques that define the professions* (AuthorHouse – 2008); and *Broadcast Journalism — A Potpourri* (Burwyn Associates — 1972). *The PR Playbook's* third edition was considered for the 2009 Pulitzer Prize. He is a contributor to several college textbooks and has written many articles for national magazines.

In 2012, Rowan University presented Litwin with its prestigious "Gary Hunter Excellence in Mentoring Award," its "Adviser of the Year Leadership Award for Exemplary Advising" (of a student organization), and named him to the Rowan University Faculty Wall of Fame and its Adviser Wall of Fame.

He is the 2006 recipient of the National School Public Relations Association's *Lifetime Professional Achievement Award* for "his excellence in the field of educational public relations, leadership and contributions to NJSPRA (New Jersey chapter) and PenSPRA (Pennsylvania chapter), dedication to NSPRA and the (public relations) profession, and advocacy for students and our nation's public schools." He has also been awarded the Sigma Delta Chi (Society of Professional Journalists) *Bronze Medallion for Distinguished Service in Journalism* and the first ever *Grand Award* presented by the International Radio Festival of New York.

In 2002, the Philadelphia chapter of PRSA honored Litwin with its *Anthony J. Fulginiti Award* for "Outstanding Contributions to Public Relations Education" – which recognizes a person who excels in education, either through their mentoring/teaching, their efforts to help shape the careers of future PR professionals or their contributions to PRSSA (student organization). Philadelphia PRSA awarded Rowan University's PRSSA chapter its *Pepperpot* for "Excellence in Public Relations" in 2004 and 2006, the only non-professional organization or agency to ever be so honored. Litwin served as chapter adviser. In 2008, he received National PRSSA's "Outstanding Faculty Adviser" Award.

Larry and his wife Nancy have two children, Julie and Adam Seth. Julie is a second grade teacher in Atlanta. She and husband Billy Kramer have a daughter Alana and son Aidan.

Adam is associate professor of industrial and labor relations (ILR) in the Cornell University School of ILR after earning his Ph.D. as a Fellow at Sloan School of Management, Massachusetts Institute of Technology (MIT). He and wife Claire Schwartz Litwin have a daughter Beatrix Grace and son Hugo Pi.

Foreword

Communications is a large and diverse industry with many facets. Advertisers, public relations practitioners, marketers, researchers, journalists and professionals in myriad other related or ancillary disciplines all have their own languages or jargon. *The ABCs of Strategic Communication* — with this *supplement* — is a veritable Rosetta Stone for the entire field.

The ABCs of Strategic Communication and *More ABCs* are treasure troves of easy-to-understand definitions for more than 8,000 communications terms, phrases, acronyms and abbreviations. They will prove invaluable to anyone who works in the communications business or has to work with someone who does.

Reading these books can help even the complete communications neophyte become conversant in the field. No one will ever have to be in the dark again, wondering what a particular term means. Aspiring young communicators who study the books will be rewarded as well. They will learn practical tips – the little things – that count toward success and will help them thrive in the business world.

For students, *The ABCs of Strategic Communication* is the *Cliffs Notes* of the language of communication. But even seasoned pros will want to keep these books close at hand for easy reference – right next to their *Associated Press Stylebook*.

Larry Litwin and his present and former Rowan University students who helped put *The ABCs* and *More ABCs* together deserve our thanks and our applause. They have given us recipes for success. As we learn to use the common language of communication, we are learning life's lessons of business.

Anne Sceia Klein, APR, Fellow PRSA
Founder and Co-owner, Anne Klein Communications Group Public Relations Counselors
Marlton, New Jersey

Preface and Acknowledgements

More ABCs of Strategic Communication – A Supplement and *The ABCs of Strategic Communication* (AuthorHouse – 2008) *are* prime examples of quintessential teamwork. The two books quickly became the go-to sources for marketing, sports, medical and other strategic communication terms.

Like its companion *The Public Relations Practitioner's Playbook for (all) Strategic Communicators* (AuthorHouse – 2013), *The ABCs* and its *Supplement* are jargon free and jam packed with communication ideas that work. What started as a 48-page booklet has grown to a combined more than 1,000 pages because the communication professions are so integrated and dependent on one another. More than 8,000 words, terms, tips and proven techniques are an aggregation of many sources – verbal (personal and professional), printed and online.

The ABCs books represent the accomplishments of an incredibly talented team of outstanding strategic communication practitioners and counselors led by the commitment and dedication of senior editor Amy Ovsiew. Amy, a corporate strategic counselor, headed a team of nose-to-the-grindstone researchers, persuasive strategic writers, and an award-winning graphics specialist. Together, we took a concept, honed it and produced a major desk-top reference reviewers believe is a standard for the industry – the many disciplines that comprise the strategic communication professions.

It all began when the first edition's editor Katie Hardesty raised the question, "Wouldn't it be great if there were a book of terms all communicators would find valuable?" That "outside-the-circle" thinking, which included the unique approach of interspersing relationship marketing tips and techniques throughout, has evolved into *The ABCs of Strategic Communication* and *More ABCs*.

The finished products could never have been accomplished without six other colleagues who took a concept, ran with it and motivated me every step of the way: Michael Gross served as senior editor and operations manager of the inaugural edition; Mark Marmur, researcher and first reader; Linda Alexander, Tara Lhulier and Arianna Stefanoni Sherlock, editors; and Stephanie Biddle, graphic designer. Michael is an agency executive; Linda, Mark and Arianna, corporate PR executives; Tara, an educator; and Stephanie, designer and owner of *Corporate Imagination*.

All of us appreciate one of their mentors and my colleague, Professor Claudia Cuddy, ELS, for providing publications terms from her book *Communicating With QuarkXPress* (Kendall/Hunt). Thank you to Frank Hogan, former Rowan University professor and general manager of its award-winning radio station WGLS-FM, for many of the electronic media terms used in *The ABCs*.

A personal thanks to Anne Sceia Klein, APR, Fellow PRSA, and her husband Jerry Klein, Esq. – Anne for crafting and writing the foreword and Jerry for his wisdom and advice. The Philadelphia-area firm *Anne Klein Communications Group* is among the most respected in the United States and internationally, where *AKCG* is an active member and participant in *IPREX* – Global Public Relations and Communication.

Special kudos and a tip of the editor's "green eye shade visor" go to my wife Nancy. She stuck with me and helped turn stumbling blocks into stepping stones and challenges into accomplishments. As deadlines approached, Nancy rolled up her sleeves, grabbed a red pen and joined the others at the editors' desk to help complete this and other massive projects.

No acknowledgement would be complete without mention of my late long-time friend, colleague and business partner Ralph Burgio. His influence is woven into so many of my strategic decisions. For all intents and purposes, Ralph invented the rounded-corner boxes used in this book and the term "blurb" – at least in my mind.

And, what kind of father would I be if I didn't recognize the patience of my "grown" children (Julie Beth and husband Billy, and son Adam Seth and wife Claire) and grandchildren, Alana, Aidan and Beatrix Grace (Trixie), for putting up with my "neglect" and wondering: "Does it have to be 'all book, all the time?'"

As a small boy, I was taught: "If you dream it, you can achieve it."

The ABCs was a dream that did, indeed, come true – thanks to the efforts and perseverance of so many. There is no way to fully express my gratitude.

M. Larry Litwin, APR, Fellow PRSA
July 2015
www.larrylitwin.com

Contents

A	1		**N**	27
B	3		**O**	29
C	6		**P**	30
D	10		**Q**	34
E	13		**R**	35
F	14		**S**	38
G	17		**T**	45
H	18		**U**	47
I	20		**V**	48
J	21		**W**	49
K	22		**X**	51
L	22		**Y**	51
M	24		**Z**	51

Abbreviations and Acronyms 53
Index 261

Tips and Techniques to Succeed

1	Leaders make the best teachers	65
2	Phone etiquette	65
3	Be interview ready	67
4	Resolving client reluctance	67
5	Know your audiences	68
6	Be a team player	68
7	Know where you are headed	68
8	Online resources can improve writing	69
9	A user-friendly website	69
10	Economical business trips	70
11	Five C's of Credit for business loans	71
12	Making a good first impression	71
13	Ad placement matters on the Web	73

14	Make the most of your ads	74
15	Six tips for keeping PR pitches out of newsroom recycle bins	74
16	Budgeting – beyond the basics	76
17	Business dining: Dos and don'ts	77
18	Business angels – bearing cash for business	77
19	When you think branding – think:	78
20	The basics of budgeting – for business or personal	79
21	Establishing a consistent image – building a brand	79
22	Healthier business travel by car	80
23	Helpful budgeting guidelines	80
24	Belt and suspenders	80
25	The benefits of hiring a public relations or advertising agency	81
26	A lasting behavioral change	81
27	Annual Reports – Reading ease	82
28	Bad with names?	82
29	Be a better manager	83
30	Know your etiquette in business settings	83
31	Boost a small firm's image	84
32	The communication audit	85
33	Cell phone etiquette	86
34	Credit Card Act protects you	86
35	Credit cards – read those notices	87
36	Understanding your credit report	88
37	"Credit Killers"– 5 common mistakes that can ruin a credit score	88
38	Convince vs. persuade	89
39	Increase business by cold calling	89
40	Cover letters: Get to the point	90
41	Knowing how to correspond	91
42	In front of the camera	92
43	Dollar Bill Test	92
44	Communicating with older people	93
45	When a crisis strikes – communicate early and often	93
46	When a crisis strikes – learn from the best	94
47	Bill Jones' 10 Commandments of Crisis Communication	94
48	David Ogilvy's Advertising Tenets	95
49	Credit Report vs. Consumer Report	95

50	Cracked Egg Persuasion Model	96
51	Stretching your cash	96
52	Get yourself ready for a career move	97
53	Cell phone guidelines	97
54	Businesses can learn through osmosis	98
55	One expert's "New 4 P's of Marketing"	99
56	Getting a handle on debt	100
57	Business dining etiquette	100
58	Help your employees get the most from their doctor visits	101
59	Address the mess: A clean desk clears the working mind *and* the working area	102
60	How to safeguard your debit card – from "phishing" and "skimming"	103
61	Karl Rove's 3 D's	103
62	Drip-Drip-Drip	104
63	Call it "reverse psychology"	104
64	The Double Bottom Line Public Relations Theory	105
65	Be alert for workplace problems	105
66	Choosing the correct coach	106
67	College seniors preparing to jump into the job market	107
68	Improve your credit score	107
69	Store-brand goods rival national names	108
70	Renew your work place enthusiasm	108
71	PR practitioners don't make excuses	109
72	Getting on the air	109
73	For those who commit industrial or corporate espionage	109
74	Shaping *your* life	110
75	Reducing stress at work	110
76	Work etiquette	111
77	How to improve *your* customer relations	112
78	Customer satisfaction – Make it an experience	112
79	Achieving goals takes planning	113
80	Retaining talented employees	113
81	From the late Frank Perdue – 'Not all chickens are alike!' – or *fronting* your brand	114
82	If you think you'll be fired	114

83	The right way to get a favor	116
84	View your failures as a learning experience – or – turning a stumbling block into a stepping stone	117
85	Family businesses need to have rules, too	118
86	Terminology of mutual funds	119
87	Try a charette design	120
88	You are hired for a reason	121
89	Workplace relationships	121
90	Dressing for work	122
91	Dress up to move up	123
92	Sculpt email to make it stand out	124
93	Fashion choices for workplace	125
94	Advice from Google®	125
95	Chicken soup for the investor	126
96	Doing business with government	127
97	Stress and anxiety	128
98	Beware of office gossip – it will come back to 'getcha'	129
99	Know the branches of government	129
100	Gunning Fog Index	130
101	De-clutter your space	131
102	Demand attention in cover letter	131
103	Bookkeeping – Don't get overwhelmed	132
104	Make your email effective	132
105	Burnout busters	133
106	Home entertaining for business	134
107	Update HR policies to avoid lawsuits	135
108	The proper business handshake	136
109	Impress the boss – know the difference between *home in* and *hone*	137
110	Look for errors in handbooks	138
111	Avoiding holiday office party overload	139
112	Hosting a business dinner	140
113	Customer Service – Practice the 'Customer Delight Principle'	141
114	The elevator 'speech'	143
115	Internet security: Password creation takes homework and creativity	144

116	Perfecting business letters	144
117	Product placement	145
118	Just what does APR stand for?	145
119	Be proactive to keep identity secure	146
120	Audience Segmentation/Fragmentation	146
121	Keeping sane when stressed by *client* or *co-worker*	147
122	Make investing work	148
123	Looking for a job: These tips should help	148
124	The telephone: Friend or foe	150
125	Just what is *integrated marketing communication – synergy*	151
126	Why information campaigns fail	151
127	The on-camera interview	152
128	Calming those interview butterflies	153
129	Prepare for interview with questions	153
130	Slash your phone bills	154
131	Have right goals and strategy for job hunt	154
132	Getting a job after graduation	156
133	'An applicant statement'	157
134	Choosing good restaurants	157
135	Send positive vibes to your co-workers	158
136	Pre-business plan for small business	158
137	Meeting people	159
138	PRSA's Code of Ethics	160
139	Make your customers your friends	161
140	Are you a new leader?	162
141	Leadership	162
142	Often-made loan mistakes – beware	162
143	Building *relationships* leads to *leadership*	163
144	Leadership development	164
145	Communication and leadership	164
146	Pointers for Fridays before holidays	165
147	The plan is nothing – planning is everything	165
148	Keep holiday cards professional	166
149	Litwin's 9 P's of Marketing	166
150	Some reasons to earn an MBA degree	167
151	Think twice before challenging the media	167

152	Key elements of a mission statement	167
153	14 ways public relations practitioners should *deal* with the media	168
154	Top 10 list of media relations mistakes	168
155	Understanding reporters and editors	169
156	Media interviews: Dos and don'ts	170
157	Ways to meet on the job	171
158	A "5th" P of marketing	172
159	Don't blame the reporter	172
160	The basics of conducting a scientific survey	172
161	iPod® etiquette	173
162	Be specific when giving presentations	173
163	Recovering from a crisis	174
164	Wanted: A strategic adviser (communicator) with a deep understanding of the process	174
165	The right way to get a favor – networking	175
166	Hiring an accountant takes research	176
167	Meet the new boss with open mind	177
168	Organize better for networking	178
169	Networking at non-networking events	179
170	Talk and drive? How to survive	180
171	20 ways to rate your website©	181
172	Practice organizational learning	182
173	On and off the record	182
174	Getting *you* out there	183
175	Encourage thinking outside the box	184
176	Take stock when traveling	184
177	A personal *Code of Ethics*	185
178	Making the best impression on your audience	185
179	Take the time for workspace spring cleaning	186
180	Reaching the desired outcome	187
181	Big 12 Dining Etiquette Rules	188
182	It's all about preparation	189
183	You are what you wear	190
184	Staying positive: Smile	191
185	ABCs of strategic public relations	192

186	CBAs of strategic public relations	192
187	Know your audiences	193
188	Grunig's *Four Models of Public Relations*	194
189	Like artists, public relations practitioners should see the whole apple before painting it	195
190	Turning the 'green' handshake into the 'confident' handshake	195
191	Newsome's Principles of Persuasion	196
192	Recency-Primacy – try it; it works	196
193	A picture is worth 1,000 words – scoring more coverage with newsworthy photo opps	197
194	Getting 'pinged'	198
195	How pay-to-play works	198
196	Punctuality – important in the U.S	199
197	Public relations practitioners	199
198	An effective public relations planning rule	199
199	When it came to planning, the general knew	200
200	Plan before you publish	200
201	Maslow's Theory of Motivation	201
202	A dozen tips to produce top publications	201
203	Planning ahead	202
204	Fly with less 'turbulence'	202
205	The power of the personal note	204
206	Political Advertising	205
207	Pricing Strategies	206
208	Being boss and friend – but be careful	207
209	They call it – Workplace politics	207
210	Don't get caught – Quid Pro Quo	208
211	Want to sit at the corporate table?	208
212	How to make an editor angry	209
213	10 essential tips to ensure your news release makes the news	210
214	Crafting your resume	211
215	Maintaining a strong professional relationship	212
216	The power of the referral	212
217	Using a boilerplate	212
218	Office romances and workplace efficiency	213
219	A good reputation sells *itself*	213

220	The art of rhetoric – learning how to use the three main rhetorical styles	214
221	25 words that hurt your resume	215
222	Make resume point quickly, but don't stop short – one page may not be enough	216
223	PR counselors are heard, but not seen	217
224	Ease those public speaking jitters	218
225	A publisher's view of journalism	218
226	When output = outcome *synergy* is achieved	219
227	Job hunting – consider using an agency	219
228	For entrepreneurs pondering a change	220
229	What amount of success is satisfying?	221
230	Assertiveness skills help you de-stress	222
231	Speaking helps maximize growth	223
232	The basics of conducting a scientific survey	224
233	Rather be somewhere else? Your customers will too!	225
234	Juggling at work? How to stay sane	226
235	10 steps to shamefully successful self-promotion	227
236	The dreaded social kiss	228
237	Speaking in front of groups	229
238	For the self-employed or soon to be	230
239	Rules followed by the best writers	231
240	The 30-3-30 Principle	232
241	Writers should use their heart *and* their soul	232
242	Marketing yourself online	232
243	Public relations practitioners	233
244	Survival of the fittest	233
245	25 Unwritten Rules of Management	233
246	Speaking in front of groups	235
247	Trade show prep	236
248	10 Tips from 'The Donald'	237
249	Pack without wrinkles	238
250	Don't overlook top workers	239
251	The importance of *thank you* notes	240
252	That all important *thank you* note	241
253	A proven, simple, two-way communication model	242

254	Teamwork – a key to success	242
255	Tips for tipping = To Improve Service	243
256	Preventing identity theft	243
257	The 3-minute drill	244
258	Consistency	244
259	Six career secrets you won't learn in school – to help you win at the business world's game:	245
260	Effort-Benefit Ratio	246
261	Know the Product Life Cycle	247
262	Achieve the 6 C's (Assess your writing)	247
263	Reaching new heights	247
264	More on business dining	248
265	As a public relations counselor…	249
266	If the problem is *you*, climb out of that work rut	249
267	Be skeptical of venture ads	250
268	Leaving phone messages on voice mail	251
269	Using visual aids	251
270	Balance your life	252
271	(Jim) Lehrer writing approach	252
272	Better writing through self-editing	253
273	Enroute to *synergy*	254
274	Make your website 'pop'	254
275	Maximizing your workers' potential	255
276	Moderating a focus panel	255
277	Starting or expanding *your* own business	257
278	Do for yourself	257
279	Take time to smell the roses	258
280	Beefing up your credit report	258
281	Event Planning – 10 key points	259
282	Do you have a brand? – Evaluate *your* 5 P's	259

> **All Tips and Techniques are on the Companion CD available at www.larrylitwin.com.**

(a)cross – An *extra* (actor) – background artist – seen walking across the screen (for many actors, a difficult technique to master).

A-frame kiss/hug (stance) – Only the lips touch. Hips are far apart with the two bodies forming the letter A. See *Technique 236*.

a la carte services – Rather than provide all advertising services for one price, an agency may provide only the services a client wishes to purchase. *Boutique* or *niche agencies* are in and of themselves, *a la carte service* providers. Also, cable television providers who offer subscribers personal channel choices at a pay per channel rate. See *boutique; niche agency*.

abandomenium – An abandoned house, apartment or condo taken over by squatters.

(absolutely) pukka – A slang British term for absolute first class, genuine or correct.

actionable information – Immediately available information or data that can be used to make specific (business) decisions. *Actionable information* is specific, consistent and credible.

actuality/cut – A radio interview in which the voice of the interviewee is heard. It can be incorporated into a radio *copy story/reader* or a *voicer*. If the *actuality* is incorporated into a radio *copy story/reader*, then the end product is called a cut and copy. If the *actuality* is incorporated into a *voicer*, then the end product is called a *wrap* or *wrap around* (Pages 6 and 660 in *The ABCs*).

adjacent products – Products that complement each other are grouped together on store shelves or on the same page in an online store. Known as *tie-ins*, the strategy is that the purchase of one of the products will lead to the purchase of the other (e.g. big screen televisions and stands; digital tablets and protective cases; peanut butter and jelly; bread and rolls near the deli counter; Danish and other sweets near freshly brewed coffee (Dunkin Donuts®; Starbucks® etc.).

age-specific investments – Investments with a target date for maturity and an interest payoff (e.g. a college fund targeted toward a child's college start; investment funds aimed at supplemented retirement income).

aggregator – A website (Google®, Bing®) that gathers Web content from online sources for reuse or resale. Many *aggregators* are *search engines* – used for research. See *search engine; secondary research*.

algorithm – In mathematics and computer science, it is a step-by-step procedure for calculations – used in problem solving. An algorithm is often referred to as a (computer) *cookie* or *pixel* – a small amount of data generated by a website and saved on the Web browser. Its purpose is to remember information about you, similar to a preference file created by a software application. See *cookie; pixel*.

alternative universe – American-made products more popular in other countries than in the United States. For example, General Motors® cars and Fords® are more popular in China, India and elsewhere, than they are in the U.S.

ambush (reporter/news media) – The act of a reporter(s) lying in wait to surprise a newsmaker.

anthropology-experienced based business – Provide more than just shopping. Businesses that want their customers to experience a good feeling.

anticipatory shipping – Amazon.com® has developed the process that moves items from its fulfillment center to a shipping hub close to the customer in anticipation of an eventual purchase based on a customer's buying habits and previous purchases. See *behavior targeting*.

app – Common term for applications downloaded on smartphones, digital tablets and other mobile devices. Single-purpose programs that allow users to do everything from read the news to play musical instruments.

Apple® picking – Term coined by police to refer to iPhone® and other smartphone thefts.

athleisurewear – Athletic-type clothing that can be worn away from the gym and has become acceptable as casualwear.

augmented reality – A technology using a smartphone or other digital device that supplements (augments) a "live" real-world environment using computer-generated (digitally manipulated) sensory input such as sound, video, graphics or GPS (global positioning system) data. It bridges the gap between real (physical) and virtual.

automatic content recognition (ACR) – This term is best defined this way: Imagine a TV viewer watching a television program while using a smartphone, iPad® or other digital device, which is synchronized with the TV. Real-time information about the TV program, related programs and targeted commercials can be sent to the device. ACR enables programmers to know their content was consumed on both devices simultaneously. See *split concentration*.

B-roll – Film or video recording used as background – or extra "footage" – for a TV news story that plays while an announcer speaks over it. See *talent reader* (Page 596 in *The ABCs*).

baby boomer – Born 1946 to 1964. (Page 31 in *The ABCs*.)

baby bump – The rounded belly that shows on a pregnant woman.

back story – Another term for the "real" story.

backchannel – Generally refers to an online conversation (tweeting) about an ongoing conference topic, speaker, television program or event. Also, the practice of using networked computers to maintain a real-time online conversation alongside a primary group activity or live spoken remarks.

backhauling – Companies that deliver to remote or out of the way locations offer truck space to haul other companies' goods. Also, one truck pulling two trailers, (piggybacking). See *piggyback survey* (Page 431 in *The ABCs*).

backwards classroom – A form of blended learning where students learn new content online – rather than in the classroom – by watching video lectures and reading assignments and other material, usually at home or location other than the classroom. What was once homework (assigned problems, etc.) is now done in class with teachers offering more personalized guidance and interaction with students, instead of lecturing. This is also known as *"teaching naked"* – without classroom technology – or as a *flipped classroom, inverted classroom* and *reverse teaching*.

BANANA Republic – Build absolutely nothing anywhere near anything.

banana (second) – Someone who is not as important or as powerful as another person. Also, a comedian who plays a supporting role to a "top banana."

bandit sign – Unauthorized posters or small signs usually seen on the roadside, lawns or utility poles, and bulletin boards for local advertising, political campaigns, etc. Not unlike "spam" emails or "spam" faxes.

behavior observable actions – See *anecdotal research* (Page 17 in *The ABCs*).

behavior targeting – A technique used by online publishers and advertisers to increase the effectiveness of their campaigns through information collected (*cookies*) on an individual's Web-browsing behavior – such as sites and pages they have visited or searches they have made – to select which advertisements to display to that individual. *Behavior targeting* helps deliver (target) online advertisements to the users who will be the most interested in them. Behavioral data can also be combined with other user information, such as purchase history, to create a more complete user profile. Visit http://www.bluefountainmedia.com/glossary/behavioral-targeting/. See *hyper targeting*; *niche marketing* (Page 386 in *The ABCs*).

behavioral research – See *anecdotal research* (Page 17 in *The ABCs*).

beauty – A strategy for survival.

belt and suspenders – A man (person) who goes to great lengths to avoid risk or embarrassment – if the belt should break, the suspenders will keep his pants up (e.g. a reporter who carries pens and a notebook in addition to a digital tablet and recorder is practicing *belt and suspenders* – taking precautions against failure).

bench scientist – A person who helps scientific researchers with the research work. The person performs no laboratory work, but does the recording, writing and editing.

benchmark – A point of reference – baseline. (A person or organization that others aspire to match or exceed.) A standard for comparing similar items such as research findings, the creative elements of a campaign, advertising results, etc. A standard for comparing products to determine competitors' costs and quality with one's own. Many times, one organization will refer to another as "the benchmark" it wants to emulate or surpass.

binge watching (viewing) – Watching many episodes of a single television program at one sitting – sometimes an entire season's worth of programs.

Bitcoin – A software-driven payment system – with no central authority or banks managing transactions – where payments and revenue are recorded in an electronic public ledger using its own accounting unit. Payments work peer-to-peer without a central repository and no single administrator. The concept has led the U.S. Treasury to call Bitcoin a decentralized virtual currency. Also called crypto currency or digital currency.

blackground – Using a black screen – or green screen – that shows black to emphasize the person(s) sitting in the forefront. Directors like the technique, which is similar to a *superstitial*. See *superstitial* (Page 583 in *The ABCs*).

blast email – An email sent to many recipients simultaneously. It is recommended it be sent as a bc (blind copy) rather than identifying recipients.

boat check - See *compensated absence liability.*

booker – A television news program staffer responsible for scheduling "talking heads" and other guests.

boomed out – When there is no work locally, skilled laborers will go to other regions – where the work is.

boomerang method – A selling technique where the salesperson turns around customer objections into reasons for making an immediate purchase. Changing one's mind.

boots on the ground – Slang term for going door-to-door (face-to-face) to persuade voters to support (or oppose) a political candidate, organization or an issue. See *get out the vote (GOTV)* (Page 229 in *The ABCs*).

brand ambassador – See *icon; trade character* (Page 614 in *The ABCs*).

breastaurant – Restaurants whose servers are scantily clad girls or young women (e.g. Hooters®-type restaurants).

bricks and clicks – A business model where a retail store shows its products online and offers consumers the service of buying online and picking up the product in one of its retail stores. See *bricks and mortar* (Page 54 in *The ABCs*)

bridge job – A full- or part-time job designed to ease/transition a worker into retirement.

brokered convention – A situation in United States politics where there are not enough delegates won during the presidential primary and caucus elections for a single candidate to have a pre-existing majority. Once it appears the convention is deadlocked, the nomination is decided after negotiations and "tradeoffs" between the candidates and their delegates. See *compromise candidate; deadlocked convention.*

bromance – A close non-romantic relationship between two (or more) men.

bubble – Used in comics (print cartoons) to show *dialogue.* Sometimes called a *dialogue balloon* or *callout* (Page 66 in *The ABCs*).

bucket list – A list of "things" a person wants to see or accomplish in their lifetime (before they die) – especially after learning they may have a terminal illness.

budget meeting – Editorial planning meeting. Also called *budgeting meeting*; *log meeting* (Page 325 in *The ABCs*).

butt call – Also called pocket dialing. It is an accidental cell or smartphone call when the phone is in the caller's (back) pocket.

buttoned up – Term used during new home construction, after windows, doors and garage doors are installed, and house can be locked during final construction phases.

buzzkill – Something or someone who spoils an otherwise enjoyable or successful event – has a negative effect.

carajo – Slang for "get out of here" or "get lost."

case-bound (cover) book – A hard bound book that uses a self-contained cover featuring the title, artwork, author's name, etc. rather than having a dust cover (heavy paper) draped around a blank hard cover.

casting director – When producing video news releases or other strategic videos, the person responsible for matching character and personality to a "part" being played.

casual fast food (cuisine) – A restaurant that does not offer full table service, but offers a higher food quality and atmosphere than stereotypical fast-food restaurants. The concept is viewed as between fast food and casual full-service dining.

cattle call – A casting call open to almost anyone who wants to show up and audition. See *gang bang*.

cell phone only – Families or individuals who do not have a landline phone at their home.

cellphone lot – A parking lot, near an airport, where drivers waiting to pick up arriving passengers may legally park.

center button – Phrase coined when car and truck radios had only five buttons. Such radio stations as KYW (1060 AM), Philadelphia, and WINS, (1010 AM), New York, encourage listeners to "set the 'center button' " to their frequency. It is a "set to forget" strategy. WHYY, Philadelphia (90.9 FM), uses a "first button" promotion. See *first button*.

changing landscape – In communication terms, it would be a cultural, environmental, image change, or a philosophical change in approach. In this case, the landscape change may not be visible, but felt.

character – What you do when people are not watching. It is what you are (*identity*). *Reputation* is how you are perceived (*image*) (Pages 264 and 265 in *The ABCs*).

chargemaster (charge master) – At a hospital, the person responsible for establishing a hospital's rates or the master billing file itself – a comprehensive listing of items billable to a hospital patient or a patient's health insurance provider.

cheater – Product placement or product integration in video games. (Page 463 in *The ABCs*).

cheerleader – A one-sided news story usually praising someone or something with no negatives or downsides. The story lacks objectivity.

cicerone – A certified beer server. One who ensures that consumers receive the best possible beer and enjoy its flavor to the greatest extent possible. Also, a guide (museums, galleries, etc.) who explains antiquities and other historic items of interest.

circular – A large *flier* used for advertising – many times the size of a *broadsheet*. See *advertising; broadsheet* (Page 56 in *The ABCs*).

Citjo – Citizen journalism. Citizens playing an active role in the process of gathering and reporting news and information – using still and video cameras, other recorders and cell phones. See *iReporter*. Also called *participatory journalism* (Page 417 in *The ABCs*).

closely-held (company) – The Internal Revenue Service defines a closely-held company as a corporation that has more than 50 percent of the value of its outstanding stock directly or indirectly owned by five or fewer individuals at any time during the last half of the tax year. It also cannot be a personal-service corporation.

cloud distance data center (The Cloud) – Facility (well protected), which stores computer files at remote locations and backup files at other off-site locations.

command center – See *situation room*.

commentariat – A commentator who takes on advocacy journalism (e.g. Oprah Winfrey).

compensated absence liability – The amount municipalities expect to pay when public employees cash out their unused sick days. Using a slang term, the money is issued on what is referred to as a *"boat check."*

It is based on the number and pay of employees, not the number retiring in a given year, and depending on the town's size and the generosity of labor contract agreements, these IOUs can range from zero to the millions. Also, expected payments to employees who miss work because of illness, vacation or holidays. See *boat checks*.

compromise candidate – See *brokered convention; deadlocked convention*.

computerized trading – Also called high frequency trading. A program-trading platform that uses powerful computers to transact a large number of orders at very fast speeds. A criticism is that traders with the fastest execution speeds will be more profitable than traders with slower execution speeds. See *flash crash; high frequency trading; price maker*.

conscious uncoupling – An amicable divorce. See *reciprocal engagement*.

consumer package goods (CPG) – An advertising category or sector – cereal, shampoo, soup. In some cases, many may be from same manufacturer: Proctor & Gamble®, Kellogg's®, General Mills®, Campbell's Soup®. See *corporate advertising*.

consumer power – Consumers' ability to ignore, resist and adapt to societal changes or negative comments by the opposition – including "assaults" by various segments of the news media.

content meeting – Editorial planning sessions at newspapers and radio and television news departments. See *budget meeting; editorial content meeting; log meeting*.

conversation pit – An architectural feature incorporating built-in seating into a depressed section of flooring within a larger room – usually with a large table in the center. The seats typically face each other in a centrally focused fashion, bringing the occupants closer together than would free-standing tables and chairs. The design removes artificial (or real) barriers and encourages discussion.

conversion therapy – Also known as reparative therapy. It is a range of treatments to change sexual orientation from homosexual to heterosexual. See gender reassignment.

cook the books – Fraudulent activities performed by businesses to falsify financial statements. Many times, *cooking the books* involves augmenting financial data to yield previously non-existent earnings.

copy story/reader – In radio or television, this is a story told strictly in words, without *actualities* (taken from radio interviews) or *soundbites* (television interviews or video).

corporate (tax) inversion – Re-incorporating a company overseas to reduce its U.S. tax burden. According to CNBC, "It is basically (a corporation) moving its legal address outside of the U.S. simply for tax purposes. Nothing else moves. It is business as usual for its American operations, employees and customers."

cosmeceutical – A combination cosmetic and pharmaceutical. A cosmetic claiming to have medicinal benefits. *Cosmeceuticals* are usually topically applied – lotions, creams and ointments. See *nutricosmetic*.

cost certainty – Used to help a client budget for a service, which may be adjusted downward. Clients prefer *cost certainty* rather than estimates in their (yearly) planning process. If the agreed upon (annual) rate were lower or higher, it would be adjusted in the next year's budget.

coupon stacking – Not to be confused with a coupon that receives double or triple the face value. Rather, it is the combining of coupons, where accepted, such as a store coupon and a manufacturer's "couple". Many stores allow *coupon stacking*, but store policies must be followed.

cover band – A band that plays mostly or exclusively cover songs – songs made popular (and recorded) by someone else.

cover song – A song performed by an artist after being made popular (and recorded) by someone else.

coyote – A person who sells his/her services to help smuggle humans across a border into the United States. Also, a person(s) who robs a driver stuck in traffic. Often, it is a smash (window) and grab or open passenger door where the thief grabs a handbag, backpack, etc.

cramming – The illegal practice of adding charges to a cell or landline phone bill for (premium) services not ordered – e.g. horoscopes, quirky ringtones, map services, etc. See *slamming*.

creative – In the advertising profession, the specialty where ideas are carried through into strategic messages and eventually an ad (print, Internet, billboard or other outdoor, etc.) or commercial (broadcast).

creative architect – An advertising copywriter – a member of the creative team.

creative briefs – A document or "script" containing the *creative strategy* and the key execution details – similar to a *situation analysis* (Page 551 in *The ABCs*).

critter stories – Stories about animals.

cross fit – A strength and conditioning program aimed at improving cardiovascular/respiratory endurance, stamina, strength, flexibility, power, speed, coordination, agility, balance and accuracy. It is usually a mix of aerobic exercise, gymnastics (body weight exercises) and Olympic weight lifting.

cross-selling – Sometime called cross-over advertising. It is the strategy of pushing new products to current (loyal) customers based on their past purchases. *Cross-selling* is designed to widen the customer's reliance on the company and decrease the likelihood of the customer switching to a competitor.

crossover vehicle – A vehicle built on a car platform and combining the features of a sport utility vehicle (SUV) with features from a passenger vehicle – similar to a station wagon or hatchback.

crowd funding – Using social media or other Internet site (e.g. kickstarter®) to raise money for charities, starting a business or other "legitimate project or venture.

curb alert – An announcement – usually through a "list host" or website (e.g. Craigslist) – announcing the presence of "stuff" (e.g. furniture, appliances, toys, etc.) left outside a residence and free for the taking. See *flash mob* (Page 201 in *The ABCs*).

custom market mail (CMM) – An option for mailing nonrectangular and irregular-shaped envelopes or postcards.

Cyber Monday – Busiest shopping day of the year on the Internet. It is traditionally the Monday *after* Thanksgiving. See *Black Friday* (Page 42 in *The ABCs*).

dark website – A fully functional website kept offline until it is needed. Many organizations have *dark websites* that would not go live unless and until the organization experiences a crisis.

daymare – A nightmare (hallucinatory condition) one experiences during the day while awake that can be just as frightening or unsettling. See *nightmare*.

deadlocked convention – See *brokered convention; compromise candidate*.

deer in headlights – The look of fear, panic, surprise or confusion. See *lizard look*.

dialogue balloon – Used in comics (print cartoons) to show *dialogue*. Sometimes called a *bubble* or *callout* (Page 66 in *The ABCs*).

digital content center(s) – Newsroom conversion – behind-the-scene staffers going from writer, producer and editor to becoming daypart managers, content producers and platform managers. Television stations have transformed to *DCCs* to "beef up" their presence on other platforms, including the Web. *DCCs* are also websites for emerging software, e-books, articles, CDs, DVDs, music and any form of digital media available (for purchase or otherwise) on one convenient website.

digital inheritance legacy – Information stored on a computer and/or *Cloud* passed on to survivors when the information's owner/account holder dies. Digital assets might include websites, documents, software, downloaded content, online gaming IDs, social media accounts, pictures and emails. Value doesn't always lie in the monetary value of items. Content could be lost forever – or inaccessible – to anyone but the account holder – who dies – unless passwords are left in a will.

digital printing – Such printing methods such as laser and ink-jet printing. In *digital printing*, an image is sent directly to the printer using digital files such as PDFs and those from graphics software such as Illustrator®, InDesign® and Quark®. This method eliminates the need for negatives and printing plates, which are used in offset printing. It saves time and money. Unlike offset printing, as few as one copy can be printed. Using offset, the cost would be prohibitive. See *letterpress; offset printing* (Page 395 in *The ABCs*).

dilettante – A person who takes up an activity or subject merely for amusement – a dabbler. See *renaissance*.

disruptive technology – Technology that interferes with a person's everyday activities. "Breakthrough" technology has improved our lives in ways not anticipated. However, use of that technology – smartphones, iPads®, tablets and other digital devices, can interfere and be distracting when we should be paying attention to something or someone else.

distance (education) learning – Delivering education/instruction to a student or students not physically present in a traditional classroom, but rather via the Web. The student could be one person using a computer or a class using a large video screen. See *MOOC*.

doorstep reporting – A reporter who knocks on a newsmaker's door for an interview or comment and then reports with the door, house or building as background.

double driveway moment – See *driveway moment*.

downshifting – A behavior or trend where individuals live simpler lives to improve balance between work and leisure, which helps focus life goals on personal fulfillment and relationship building rather than the all-consuming pursuit of economic success. *Downshifting* historically refers to reducing the gear of a manual transmission motor vehicle while driving (e.g. third to second gear). See *work and income*.

Dracula sneeze – A technique for covering up a sneeze to help prevent the spread of germs. It is holding your arm up over your face (burying your face) in a position similar to Dracula holding up his cape and then sneezing into your elbow.

dramedy – Drama-comedy (Grey's anatomy).

Dri FIT® (dry fit) – A high-performance, microfiber, polyester fabric that moves sweat away from the body and to the fabric surface, where it evaporates. As a result, *Dri-FIT®* keeps athletes dry and comfortable.

drink rail – A counter attached to a fence or railing for spectator convenience at athletic and concert venues to "rest" a beverage (bottle or cup) or food. Drink rails are now commonplace in homes, as well.

drip marketing – Limited expenditure on advertising, public relations and other strategic communication over a relatively long period of time. See *burst advertising expenditure; drip advertising; drip-drip-drip method* (Page 163 in *The ABCs*).

driveway moment – Listening to a story on the radio that is so compelling you just can't get out of your car when you reach your destination. If your neighbor is also experiencing a *driveway moment* it is called a *double driveway moment*.

drug mule – A person who illegally carries (smuggles) drugs across the border – as much as 75 to 100 pounds of drugs strapped to their back.

dry-erase board – Also known as *white board*. A board with a glossy white surface, which began the next generation after chalk boards. The use of non-permanent markers allows the dry ink to come off with an eraser or dry cloth. See *Smart Board®*.

dry fit (Dri FIT®) – See Dri FIT®.

duality – Acting one way in public, but another in private. Many times politicians and other public figures practice this approach. While unethical, they view it as a strategy to accomplish their objectives and eventually a goal.

e-reader – A digital device – iPad®, Kindle®, Nook®, smartphone, etc. – designed primarily to read e-books, newspapers, magazines or other digital periodicals.

e-tailer – An online store or an individual (retailer) who does business only or primarily on the Internet. See *bricks and clicks*.

e-vertorial – A blog or other digital (social media) post that carries the writer's opinion. A commentary. See *op-ed* (Page 401 in *The ABCs*).

eating script – Eating by habit

EBIF (Enhanced TV Binary Interchange Format) – A common software platform or content format that enables cable television systems to deploy simple interactive applications using existing systems and "cable boxes." Its primary purpose is to add such features as caller ID, Web surfing, etc. to an interactive (SMART) TV.

editorial content meeting – Editorial planning meeting. Also called *budgeting meeting; log meeting* (Page 325 in *The ABCs*).

elbow grease – A person's physical effort or contribution to a project. See *sweat equity*.

end mark – The number 30, three hash marks (pound signs) or the word end, signifying a story written for publication is finished. If a story continues, the word **MORE** is used at the bottom of the page. Lore has it that 30 is used because an 8 ½ by 11 sheet of paper – double spaced (12 point font) – would contain 30 lines of copy.

energy vampire – Someone who talks so much about themselves and their problems it drains the energy from the listener or "sucks the blood" from the conversation.

enterprise content management – Commonly known as searchable digital (computer) storage.

evaluation – The final step in the public relations process *PR-pie – purpose, research, planning, information/implementation, evaluation* or *RACE –*

research, action, communication, evaluation. It is an examination of the strategic plan to determine if *objectives* have been met (*The Public Relations Practitioner's Playbook* – AuthorHouse – 2013 Chapter 7). See *measure success*.

evidence gathering – Research to support a hypothesis.

explorers – Usually women who believe in shopping rather than going directly to a counter or rack. See *hunters*.

externality – The cost or benefit that affects a person who did not choose to incur that cost or benefit. The effect of a transaction between two or more people when the interests of at least one of the involved parties was not taken into account.

extra – An actor also known as a backup artist. See *(a)cross; principal*.

eye wear – Glasses, which are now referred to as *face jewelry*. See *face jewelry*.

4444 A baseball player – A professional player better than Triple A who has made it to the major leagues, but gets sent back down to the minors and then gets recalled – and back and forth it goes.

5 (five) hole – Sports term used when a ball or puck goes through a defender's legs. That space is known as the 5-hole. See *5-point-5 hole*.

5.5 (five-point-five) hole – In baseball and softball, the space between the third baseman (defender number 5 for scoring purposes) and shortstop (number 6). Some batters try to "poke" the ball to that (left) side of the infield for a base hit. See *5 (five) hole*.

501(c)3 – A nonprofit tax exempt public charity, private foundation in the United States is exempt from federal income tax if it meets certain charitable and/or nonprofit criteria. See *501(c)4*.

501(c)4 – A politically active nonprofit civic organization or association in the United States exempt from federal income tax if it meets certain criteria related to promoting social or general welfare. These organizations may engage in political activity and unlimited lobbying so long as they pertain to the organization's mission. Political Action Committees (PACs) would fall under this category. Political spending for print, broadcast and other ads is permitted as long as the expenditures are independent of any candidate. *501(c)4s* are exempt from many of the federal election laws. See *Super PAC; 501(c)3*.

527 – A type of tax-exempt group organized under section 527 of the Internal Revenue Code created to raise money for such (political) activities as issue advocacy, and candidate support in federal, state or local elections.

face jewelry – Glasses or other eyewear worn to improve eyesight and to enhance one's appearance. Beads, piercings and other jewelry worn on a face would qualify as *face jewelry*.

fall back – Also called *slap back*. An echo some singers and other on-stage performers experience. Singers will sometimes lip sync to prevent confusion.

falling off the cliff – See sequester.

fascinator – A headpiece worn as an alternative to a hat. Great Britain's Princess Kate has re-popularized *fascinators*.

fat finger (syndrome) – Accidentally tapping the incorrect adjacent key on a computer keyboard.

feticide – The act of destroying a fetus or causing an abortion. See *gendercide*.

FFP – Fabrication, falsification, plagiarization. Too often, *FFP* are being used by researchers – and some writers, too.

first button – Phrase coined when car and truck radios had only five buttons. Such radio stations as WHYY (90.9 FM), Philadelphia, use a "first button" promotion. KYW (1060 AM), Philadelphia, and WINS, (1010 AM), New York, encourage their listeners to "set the *'center button'*" to their frequency. It is a "set to forget" strategy. See *center button*.

five major (strategic communication) media – Print, broadcast, Internet, face-to-face and special events. At one time, broadcast was referred to as electronic. With the advent of emerging media – Internet, social media, "word of mouse/mouse to mouse," broadcast became its own major medium, as did the Internet (World Wide Web).

flash crash – Computers causing dramatic, quick fluctuations of stock prices. See *computerized trading; high frequency trading; price maker*.

flipped classroom – A form of blended learning where students learn new content online – rather than in the classroom – by watching video lectures and reading assignments and other material, usually at home or location other than the classroom. What was once homework (assigned problems, etc.) is now done in class with teachers offering more personalized guidance and interaction with students, instead of lecturing. Also known as *"teaching naked"* – without classroom technology – or as a *backwards classroom, inverted classroom* and *reverse teaching*.

floor (boxes) – Boxes at bottom of a newspaper or magazine page – especially page one of a newspaper's section front. Also called *footer(s)* (Page 205 in *The ABCs*).

floor pitch – During the recording of a television program (before a live audience) – usually a situation comedy – a joke or scene may be modified or changed (from the "floor") to increase the laughter. See *live to tape*.

food desert – A neighborhood or community with no supermarkets.

forensic digitalologist – One who investigates digital technology – such as photoshopping pictures and other types of digital manipulation – for the legal system (a forensic expert on pixel comparisons). See *photo manipulation* (Page 428 in *The ABCs*).

fractional edition – Print publications (newspapers/magazines) targeted to a specific geographic region. This is commonplace among metropolitan-area newspapers and many major magazines to attract local advertising as well as national ads. Also called *regional edition* and *zone edition*.

frame grab – One frame of a (digital) video – usually from a commercial, but could be any video, news, motion picture, sports, etc. When shown, it looks no different than any other photo. In motion picture film, it would be one negative (celluloid) frame. See *image grab*.

fraternity effect – A phenomenon involving males who participate in an activity mostly with the same sex/gender – drink, watch sports, play sports, etc. While there is no term *sorority effect*, if there were, the same premise would hold true for females. See *bromance*.

freemium – An item that appears free, but in the end, may cost the "buyer." (e.g. *freemium apps* for smartphones are free until the user attempts to link to a landing site. Then, they have to pay.) See *app*.

frenemy – A combination of the words friend and enemy. It could be a friend who is a rival or an enemy pretending to be a friend. (Sometimes spelled frienemy.)

friendly rude – An acquaintance who says something offensive and may not realize it.

gain from loss – A lesson learned in defeat.

gang bang (media) – Slang term for a news availability or news conference that attracts dozens or hundreds of reporters and is difficult to control. See *cattle call; media scrum*.

gap year – Term used by many college graduates who take a year off between their commencement and when they begin their job search. Also, a year taken off by some high school graduates before they begin college.

gender reassignment – The surgical procedures by which a person's physical appearance and function of their existing sexual characteristics are altered to resemble that of the other sex. See *conversion therapy; reparative therapy*.

gendercide – The systematic killing of members of a specific sex – practiced by some countries. It is considered a population control strategy. See *feticide*.

Generation-X – Born 1965 to 1980. (Page 223 in *The ABCs* with this update.)

genericide – The process/evolution of a trademark that transforms into a generic word. Among the brands experiencing *genericide* are Baggies®, Jell-O®, Google®, Kleenex®, Plexiglas®, Rollerblade®, Xerox® and Walkman®. Some have transformed from noun to verb (e.g. googled [searched], Xeroxed [copied]). For more: Steven Pinker, *The Stuff of Thought* (Viking – 2007).

gently used – Used clothing, sports and other equipment, furniture, etc. in almost new condition.

Gonzo journalism – See *stunt journalism*.

grab and go – When disaster strikes – tornado, etc., "controlled returns" allow homeowners to be escorted back to their properties to retrieve valuables and other cherished items.

gridlock – Severe road congestion. Also, a situation when there is difficulty passing laws in a legislature because the votes for and against a proposed law are evenly divided, or where two legislative houses, or the executive branch and the legislature are controlled by different political parties and cannot agree.

gross vs. net – *Gross* refers to the total and *net* refers to the part of the total that really matters. For example, *net* income for a business is the profit after all expenses, overhead, taxes and interest payments are deducted from the *gross* income. Similarly, *gross* weight refers to the total weight of the goods and the container and packaging. On the other hand, *net* weight refers to only the weight of the goods in question. When it comes to earned income: *gross* income is before taxes and deductions, and *net* income is after taxes and other deductions.

grunt – A foot solder. Also, a sound similar to that made by a hog.

hard money – Donations made directly to a political candidate. *Hard money is* regulated by federal laws (Federal Election Commission) that limit the amount a person can donate to a candidate. See *501(c)3; 501(c)4; soft money.*

hard (grand) opening – The formal grand opening of a new retail store or other business. See *soft opening.*

hashtag – The # symbol, called a hashtag (some refer to it as a hash mark), is used to mark keywords or topics in a tweet. It was created by Twitter® users as a way to categorize messages – tweets – by keyword. Also, (on social-networking ebsites) a word or phrase preceded by a hashtag, used within a message to identify a keyword or topic of interest and facilitate a search for it (e.g. The hashtag #PRPractitioner'sPlaybook is used to help coordinate *tweets* about *The Public Relations Practitioner's Playbook for (all) Strategic Communicators.*)

hatchery – Space in a retail store offered to local entrepreneurs to "test" a product or an idea. The small "store within a store" concept could include a local micro-brewer, coffee roaster or specialty baker. Sometimes a small rental fee is charged.

hectoring – Term coined by comedian Bill Cosby from his popular television program about the Huxtable family. It is African Americans (Blacks) who take greater personal responsibility for their own lives.

high frequency trading – Also called *computerized trading.* A program-trading platform that uses powerful computers to transact a large number of orders at very fast speeds. A criticism is that traders with the fastest execution speeds will be more profitable than traders with slower execution speeds. See *computerized trading; flash crash; price maker.*

historical perspective – A way someone looks at something or an event taking into consideration everything that may have happened in the past – associated past events.

hobby horse – Media outlets, publications, reporters, etc. who ride a story and just won't let go.

holdback – The release day and date for a motion picture DVD. Also, a term used by car manufacturers and new car dealers. It is a percentage of either the manufacturer's suggested retail price (MSRP) or invoice price of a new vehicle (depending on the manufacturer) that is repaid to the dealer by the manufacturer. The holdback is designed to supplement the dealer's cash flow and indirectly reduce "variable sales expenses" (code words for sales commissions) by artificially elevating the dealership's paper cost. For example, many times when a dealer shows a prospective customer the paper invoice, it does not include the *holdback*, which the dealer eventually receives.

hometender – Someone who lives in an unoccupied house – usually for sale – to give a lived-in look.

hot stover (talk) – Talking baseball in the winter months.

house brand – Sometimes called a *private label*. A proprietary product brand sold by one retailer and often bearing the name of the retailer (e.g. Berkley & Jensen® [BJ's]; Candies®, Chaps® and Croft Barrow® [Kohl's]; Ed & Phil's [Litwin Bros. Superette]; Kenmore® and Craftsman® [Sears]). See *mezzanine marketing; private brand; sub-brand* (Page 453 in *The ABCs*).

human resources talent acquisition – Once known simply as human resources (personnel), many companies now merge their Human Resources and Public Relations Departments to form Talent-Acquisition Departments headed by talent-acquisition strategists – strategic communicators/public relations specialists with human resources-training. Experts view this as an emerging trend.

human trafficking – Recruiting or harboring someone by threat or deception and controlling them for exploitation.

hunters – Usually men – who know their sizes, wants, etc. and go right to *that* "rack" or counter. See *explorers*.

hybrid creep – The quiet ride or operation, for example, of a car or other motor vehicle that can pose risks for unsuspecting pedestrians and the blind – who use sound cues. Derived from hybrid vehicles. Experts say, in this case, "silence is not golden."

hyper local (news coverage) – Media outlets whose primary focus is nearby residents (well-defined community). As emerging media evolve, online sites (newspapers, radio and television stations, bloggers, etc.) have concentrated on "focused" local coverage.

hyper targeting – Delivering advertising content to specific interest-based audience segments/fragments – even smaller than a niche market. See *concentrated marketing; niche marketing* (Page 386 in *The ABCs*).

ice breaker(s) – Sometimes called thought starter – to warm up the person or audience you are addressing or kick off a conversation. *Ice breakers* include open-ended questions, short games, simple visuals, etc. See *thought starter(s)*.

icon – A symbol or likeness that represents a product, brand, etc. Many times, *icons* are registered trademarks (e.g. the Geico® gecko, Ronald McDonald®, Aflac® duck, Charlie the Tuna® (Star-Kist®). Also known as *brand ambassador*. See *trade character* (Page 614 in *The ABCs*).

image gallery – Web-based photo album – many times interactive.

image grab – A single digital video frame (individual picture) converted to a "still" shot as if it were taken by a "still" camera. A number of video camera brands have this as a built-in feature. See *frame grab*.

immersion journalism – See *stunt journalism*.

indirect grilling – A barbecue cooking technique where the food is placed to the side of the heat source instead of directly over the flame as is more common. This can be achieved by igniting only some burners on a gas barbecue or by piling coals to one side of a charcoal pit. On a gas grill, some place the food in the grill's center and light only the burners to the sides and not underneath.

infotainment – Television or radio newscasts that deliver the (hard) news in an entertaining fashion – use of music and increased production. Pure journalists oppose this approach. See *vampire creativity; yellow journalism* (Page 638 in *The ABCs*).

inline attachment – An email attachment that appears in the email as soon as the reader opens it – rather than as an attachment. Many times it is an ad, newsletter or photo. Among the companies and organizations using this tactic are Victoria's Secret®, Staples® and Cherry Hill (N.J.) Public Library.

institutional stock buys (trading) – Investors who buy and sell billions of dollars in stocks – controlling the markets and affecting publicly traded stock prices. See *computerized trading; high frequency trading*.

internal integrity – See *morals* (Page 366 in *The ABCs*).

inversion (tax) – See *corporate inversion*.

inverted classroom – A form of blended learning where students learn new content online – rather than in the classroom – by watching video lectures and reading assignments and other material, usually at home or location other than the classroom. What was once homework (assigned problems, etc.) is now done in class with teachers offering more personalized guidance and interaction with students, instead of lecturing. Also known as "*teaching naked*" – without classroom technology – or as a *backwards classroom, flipped classroom* and *reverse teaching*.

iReporter – A citizen journalist who sends smartphone video or still pictures (fires, tornadoes, automobile accidents, etc.) to news outlets. See *citizen journalism* (Page 417 in *The ABCs*).

jaboya – The practice known colloquially in the Luo language of the Kenyan area, Jaboya. *Jaboya* is a woman who "sells" herself for sex so her family has food.

jailbreak – Jailbreaking is the name given to the process used to modify the operating system running on an iPhone®, iPod touch®, or iPad® to allow the user greater control over their device, including the ability to remove Apple-imposed restrictions and install apps obtained through means other than the official App Store (among the most prevalent of these alternative sources is Cydia). (Sam Costello – *About.com Guide*)

jawbone – An attempt to persuade or pressure others by the force of one's position of authority or possibly through Quid Pro Quo. See *quid pro quo* (Page 486 in *The ABCs*).

join – The point in a local radio or television broadcast when the announcer *joins* a network or other program. Sometimes referred to as hitting the "*post*." See *post*.

jolt – An attention grabber (graphic) on the screen/monitor – television, motion picture or computer (Internet website). A visual – with or without audio – to grab a viewer's attention.

journalism – Reporting, writing, editing, photographing and/or broadcasting news. It is a verification process. The unbiased transmission of information. Objective journalists via objective media may be the only voice the "little people have," according to retired Gannett editor Everett Landers, who stressed, "Never compromise on integrity." See *yellow journalism*.

jungle primary – Also called a *nonpartisan blanket primary* where all candidates for the same elected office, regardless of respective political party, run against each other at once, instead of being segregated by political party. It is possible that two candidates from the same party face each other in the general election. In some *jungle primaries*, the top vote getters from each party advance to the general election.

jury rig – Makeshift or temporary repairs using the tools and materials that happen to be on hand.

kiss and ride – Designated drop-off and pick-up areas at public transportation stops in such cities as Atlanta (Ga.) and Washington (D.C.).

knock and talk – Law enforcement practice where police *(pox)* visit someone to ask questions then request permission to conduct a search of that person's residence.

landing site – A single web page that appears in response to clicking on a word or phrase See *infosnacking* (Page 280 in *The ABCs*).

LEED (Leadership in Energy & Environmental Design) – A green (environmentally correct) building certification program that recognizes best-in-class building strategies and practices. See *carbon footprint*; *renewable energy*; *sustainable design*.

left brain vs. right brain (thinker) – According to the theory of left-brain or right-brain dominance, each side of the brain controls different types of thinking. Additionally, people are said to prefer one type of thinking over the other. A "*left-brained*" person is said to be more logical, analytical and objective, while a "*right-brained*" person is said to be more intuitive, thoughtful and subjective. See *lizard thinking*; *reptile brain*.

legacy media – Traditional media that existed before the Internet – newspapers, radio, television, magazines, etc.

Libor – London interbank offered rate. Used throughout the world to set interest rates for many forms of debt, including consumer credit cards.

line producer – The producer in charge of a television newscast.

listen line – In radio and television (video feed) station control rooms, newsrooms, etc. A "closed-circuit feed" – sound (audio) or video from a remote location or programming from another radio station or TV station.

live shot – In a live shot – the action being shown or heard is happening right now. When a reporter does a "live shot," he or she is on the scene at the moment they are speaking. They may lead into a recorded insert – an abbreviated "reporter package" prepared earlier – but the insert ends with the reporter live again, to wrap up the story with the latest developments. Live shots were initially used to cover stories from the field that continue to unfold as a newscast goes on the air or to break into programming when a big story has just reached a critical juncture. Then newsrooms began to use them to lend a sense of urgency to stories that were not breaking or evolving at the time of the newscast. So now many, if not most newsrooms go "live" just because they can. (Page 323 in *The ABCs*.)

live to tape – A recorded television program later aired (shown) without edits. At one time, it was the industry standard. Today, it is rare. See *join; floor pitch; post*.

lizard (reptile or reptilian) brain – Part of the brain that controls the body's vital functions. It is the part of the brain that rules by emotion rather than reason. It senses danger, where (natural) instincts and gut feelings originate. Subconscious or involuntary processes – cannot hide reactions. Term used to describe someone considered rigid and/or compulsive – we cannot resist because of the reptile in us.

lizard look – Also called the look of a "*deer in headlights*." The look of fear, panic, surprise or confusion. Also, stares of boredom when an audience doesn't understand or is not interested.

location manager(s) – Person who handles day-to-day motion picture and television show filming and video recording – might also be responsible for acquiring animals and "natural" scenery. They handle the entire site(s) during "shows" – including exteriors and interiors not shot in a studio. See *script supervisor (consultant)*.

location scout(s) – Person who finds locations/sites (facilities) that can be used for motion picture and TV shoots. See *location manager; script supervisor (consultant)*.

logo voice – A "voice" – announcer or otherwise – closely associated with a product or a radio or television station. Some refer to it as a *signature voice*. Its purpose is to evoke a *transfer effect*. See *signature voice; transfer effect; voice actor*.

logo (logotype) – A distinctive or unique mark, sign or symbol, group of letters, or a graphic version of a company's name or, used to identify and promote the company, its product or brand. For a logo to become a trademark, it must be registered with the United States Patent and Trademark Office.

logos – An appeal based on logic or reason.

lone wolf – A person who would rather spend his/her time alone rather than be in a group. One whose opinion differs from others. Some may refer to that person as one who lives alone on an island. See *outlier*.

lounge pants (shorts)/sleep pants – Look like full-length boxer shorts, but are actually pajamas. Many times, (female) college students wear them to classes as casualwear. See *lounge shorts; sleep pants*.

lounge (sleep) shorts – Look like boxer shorts, but usually a heavier fabric. They are actually pajamas. See *lounge pants; sleep pants*.

love child – A baby born out of wedlock.

love nest – A place (such as an apartment) where people who are having a love affair secretly meet with each other.

lower third – A graphic placed in the bottom area of a television monitor (screen). Lower thirds are most commonly found in television news productions and documentaries. Some lower thirds have animated backgrounds and text. See *interstitial; superstitial* (Page 583 in *The ABCs*).

luxury pricing – prestige pricing – A pricing strategy in which prices are set at a high level, recognizing that lower prices will inhibit sales rather than encourage them and that buyers will associate a high price for the product with superior quality. Also called *image pricing*. See *customary pricing; price lining; psychological pricing* (all in *The ABCs*). See *prestige pricing* (Page 447 in *The ABCs*).

man scrape – Removing body hair from a man usually through waxing or laser.

mapatite – A map – usually digital – that takes you directly to your requests and zooms into the neighborhood (e.g. Google® Maps and Google® Earth).

mass mail – See *blast email*.

McMansion – A large "luxury" house viewed as too large for the lot, parcel of land or neighborhood. Observers say the term was coined because such houses are mass produced and are generic in quality – not unlike fast food.

mean average – Mean, median and mode are three different kinds of statistical averages for a given set of numbers. *Mean*: The arithmetic average of a set of numbers. *Median*: The middlemost number in a set of numbers arranged in order. *Mode*: The value in a set of numbers that appears the most.

measure success – A more positive way to say evaluate. See *evaluation*.

media scrum – A hard to control news availability or informal news conference that attracts dozens or hundreds of reporters. See *gang bang*.

media value – Assessment of the market value of the particular space or time occupied by a (news) story placement. It captures story size, impressions and the perceived image or credibility of a media outlet. A formula reflects slant – if negative and/or positive values are used. It also reflects prominence since higher advertising rates tend to indicate more prominent placement. *Media value* is a recognized metric in marketing and advertising. See *ad value; publicity value* (Page 9 in *The ABCs*)

median average – Mean, median and mode are three different kinds of statistical averages for a given set of numbers. *Mean*: The arithmetic average of a set of numbers. *Median*: The middlemost number in a set of numbers arranged in order. *Mode*: The value in a set of numbers that appears the most.

metadata – Data about data – or data that provides information about other data.

microagression – A brief and commonplace verbal, behavioral or environmental indignity – intentional or unintentional – that communicates hostile, derogatory or negative slights and insults toward a person or groups of people.

mileage dudes – Frequent flyers.

mileage runners – Frequent flyers who have found impressive ways to rack up the most miles for the least amount of money – thus "beating" the system.

Millennials (millennial generation) – Born after 1980. (Page 360 in *The ABCs* with this update.)

misremember – Remember imperfectly or incorrectly. Failure to remember correctly. Some people who misstate facts or embellish (exaggerate) a story say they *misremembered* rather than lied. Some psychologists conclude when people recall stories over the years and misstate some of the facts or exaggerate, in their mind, those misremembrances (fuzzy-trace theory) become "fact."

mixed bag – See *potpourri*.

mobile journalist – Journalists who do more than write or report a story. They are multi-dimensional taking pictures, recording video and audio and usually filing podcasts and videocasts in addition to their normal reporting duties – writing print stories or recording voicers. See *voicer* (Page 648 in *The ABCs*).

mode average – Mean, median and mode are three different kinds of statistical averages for a given set of numbers. *Mean*: The arithmetic average of a set of numbers. *Median*: The middlemost number in a set of numbers arranged in order. *Mode*: The value in a set of numbers that appears the most.

monger – A person who sells a particular product (e.g. fish monger, rag monger – sells cloths, etc.). See *hawker; huckster* (Page 259 in *The ABCs*).

MOOC – Massive Open Online Course – An online course aimed at unlimited participation and open access via the Web. In addition to such traditional course materials as videos, readings and problem sets, MOOCs provide interactive user forums that help build a community for students, professors and teaching assistants (TAs). MOOCs are used in college and university distance (learning) education programs. See *Distance Learning* (Page 153 in *The ABCs*).

mortis head – A print or online headline (display type) printed over a photo or other illustration. Sometimes, they are not as legible – easy to read – as they should be. See *legibility* (Page 313 in *The ABCs*).

mouse-to-mouse – See *word-of-mouse* (Page 659 in *The ABCs*).

muck raking – Reform-minded journalism – often investigative reporting – aimed at exposing political or corporate corruption, or other scandal.

multigenerational (next generation) homes – Houses designed for three generations under one roof – grandparents, their children and their grandchildren. See *sandwich generation*.

narration track or track – This is the voiceover portion of a reporter *package*. It is different from a regular *voiceover* because it is first written, then recorded on what's called a track tape or digital file (a video or digital camera is used to record a reporter's narration). After it is recorded, the video editor electronically matches pictures from the reporter's field "tape" (scenes/soundbites recorded in the field as the story was being reported) to words on the track. The two, "matched" elements - audio and video – are electronically transferred to a third video or digital timeline to form the finished story.

natural, NAT or ambient sound – Natural sound is used in both radio and television stories. In radio, sometimes the anchor may use a natural sound cut i.e. cheering or music at a parade, as part of the reader. Or, the reporter may use it as background sound to a voicer or wrap. In a television reporter package or a VO/SOT, you may wish to use sound other than the interviews – i.e., honking horns during a traffic jam, animal noises, etc. Natural sound is just what it says – the sound of what you actually heard while reporting a story. At the beginning of a reporter package, or a voiceover story, you may want to call for natural sound under, so the honking sounds become a background sound over which the audience can hear the anchor's *voiceover* or the reporter's narration track.

Something to keep in mind: Natural sound should be used as often as possible at the beginning of radio or TV packages because it allows the listener or viewer to experience the situation before the VO (reporter) gets between them and being there. It is also a safety measure in case the recorded video/story is taken late you don't lose the first few words and thus are unable to make sense of what is being said. It's a good idea to use natural sound when transitioning from one location to another. Nat sound can also be used to create immediacy by breaking up the voice-over into smaller bites and therefore making the pacing more rapid. In other word, natural sound can be used to let the script breathe.

When doing radio reports, record the natural sound at the scene for 30 seconds to one minute. If you are doing a documentary, you would record more and usually a variety of sounds. You can always loop (repeat) the sound if more is needed. When doing a story for TV, remember to get plenty of "B" roll, which will be used to enhance your soundbites and illustrate the story. An overall reasonable shooting ratio (the proportion of footage shot to footage used) is 4:1 (four-to-one) or 6:1 (six-to-one). Shoot enough to tell the story, but do not shoot 45 minutes of video for a routine 1:30 story. *See B-roll* (Page 31 in *The ABCs*).

near field communication (NFC) – A set of standards for smartphones and other digital devices to establish communication with each other by touching them together or bringing them close to each other.

neighborhooding – Refers to grouping together similar cable channels, such as CNN, CNBC, Fox News and MSNBC, or Comcast Sports Net, ESPN, ESPN2 and Golf Channel, or various cooking channels, etc.

net vs. gross – *Gross* refers to the total and *net* refers to the part of the total that "really matters." For example, *net* income for a business is the profit after all expenses, overhead, taxes and interest payments are deducted from the *gross* income. Similarly, *gross* weight refers to the total weight of the goods and the container and packaging. On the other hand, *net* weight refers to only the weight of the goods in question. When it comes to earned income: *gross* income is before taxes and deductions, and *net* income is after taxes and other deductions.

netbook – Small, lightweight, lower cost, less powerful breed of laptop computers becoming increasingly popular among budget-conscious consumers primarily interested in surfing the Web.

news – Information of interest to a large number of people. It should be new, interesting *and* important. Also, information that might be unusual, unexpected, controversial, or of wide significance or interest to the audience of a publication (hard copy or online) or program. Does it matter? Never leave your audience wondering why. When dealing with the media, *news* is anything the *gatekeeper* (editor or news director) says is news.

news cycle – The amount of time that passes between the release of one edition of news from the media outlet and the follow up "edition." Originally associated with newspapers, the term now applies to all forms of news distribution – 24-hour all-news radio stations (24/7), cable channels, local and network television, magazines, etc. At one time, the most common example of a *news cycle* was the daily newspaper, which had multiple daily editions. All-news radio stations, cable and other TV channels have a variety of *news cycles*, in many cases, updating stories as warranted – either live on the air or on a related website.

news drop – News releases emailed to media outlets or hard copy, which may be delivered to a reporter's mailbox in a "press room."

next generation (multigenerational) homes – Houses designed for three generations under one roof – grandparents, their children and their grandchildren. See *sandwich generation*.

nightmare – An unpleasant dream that can cause a strong emotional response from the mind, typically fear or horror. See *daymare*.

non sequitur – An argument where the conclusion does not follow its premise(s). A disconnect between the premise and conclusion.

nutricosmetic – A nutritional supplement claiming to have medicinal skin benefits. See *cosmeceutical*.

obit call – When someone makes a mistake (or a major contribution) in life so unforgettable, it ends up in the first three paragraphs – the journalistic lead – of a person's obituary.

on camera stand-up – An introductory statement, summary or transition given by a reporter on camera. The *stand-up* can be done at the beginning of a story (O/C open), in the middle of the report (O/C bridge) or at the end of the story, to provide a conclusion (O/C close). The on camera stand up is digitally recorded and edited into the reporter package. Stand up opens are often used in conjunction with a stand up close to add urgency as a "look live" without calling it a live shot. A live, on camera stand up is done only as part of live reports (or live "shots") from the field.

one-to-one marketing – direct response/*narrowcasting* (Page 265 in *The ABCs*).

online chatter – Any "real time" communication/conversation over the Internet (tweets, texts, Facebook) that allows others in the conversation to quickly respond. Although online, it resembles a spoken conversation.

online image (persona) – A personality created through such social media as Facebook® or Twitter®.

online persona – Image created through such channels as your Facebook® page or Twitter®.

optics – How something looks on its surface – from the outside. See *image* (Page 373 in *The ABCs*).

original content – Online content – new, unique, created by the person posting it – usually written work or video not seen before in any form (media).

outlier – Someone or something different from all the rest. It lies outside a main body or geographic area, or a person who is outside of a group or has a difference of opinion. It could be a piece of a data (research) different from the rest. Also a distant observation point. Someone who lives an appreciable distance from his or her worksite. See *lone wolf*.

outside the circle – As in outside the box (interchangeable). *Outside-the-box thinking* requires openness to new ways of seeing the world and a willingness to explore. *Outside-the-box thinkers* know that new ideas need nurturing and support. They also know that having an idea is good but acting on it is more important. Results are what count. Read more at *www.canadaone.com/ezine/april02/out_of_the_box_thinking.html* (Page 410 in *The ABCs*).

park and bark – An entertainment term meaning a performer who stands – remains – in one place on stage while singing or delivering stand-up comedy rather than walking around.

parklet – A portable (temporary) park placed on several parking spaces – usually in a city's downtown area. It could be a small space serving as a sidewalk extension. It offers the illusion of green space and a comfortable setting. See *pop-up parks*.

pass-along rate – An advertising/marketing measure. The percentage of people who pass along a message or file. A measure of word-of-mouth (one-to-one) marketing. Vehicles/media/channels typically used include face-to-face, email, Web pages and multimedia files. Also, the number of times a received document (article, brochure, report, etc. – hardcopy or digital) is shared with others. See *one-to-one marketing; snowballing* (Page 399 in The *ABCs*).

pass-through cost – Offsetting increased (production) costs by raising prices.

pass-through release – A news release sent from one media relations specialist to another so the receiver may send it to his/her "mailing list." See *snowball survey*.

patch writing – Copying and pasting chunks of quotes or paraphrases that belong to other people – always attributing and/or citing to avoid plagiarizing.

Pathway of Honor – To honor military veterans – people line up on each side so the veteran(s) may walk down the center in recognition of service. Sometimes called "Path of Honor." Southwest® Airlines has perfected this customer service strategy.

pay per click (cost per click) – An Internet advertising method used to direct traffic to an advertiser's website (landing site). Rather than pay a flat advertising rate, the advertiser pays the publisher (wherever the ad appeared) for each unique click. Some call it "the amount spent to get an advertisement clicked." See *per inquiry* (Page 420 in *The ABCs*).

payday (lending) loan – According to Consumer Financial Protection Bureau, it is a cash advance or "check loan" – a short-term loan, generally for $500 or less, typically due on the borrower's next payday. According to the Center for Responsible Lending, some view *payday loans* as quick and easy, but annual interest rates have been known to be far higher than the market rate.

paywall – A system that restricts website access to paid subscribers only. Some newspapers, magazines and other media outlets have put their content behind a *paywall*. See *firewall* (Page 198 in *The ABCs*).

peer-to-peer (P2P) marketing (communication) – A marketing technique that encourages customers to promote their products and/ or services to one another – particularly on the Internet. *P2P* relies on social media to create a *buzz* – the viral spread of a strategic message that gets media and public attention for an organization, company, product or service. An example might be a website that offers users a discount on products in return for recruiting new customers to the site. See *buzz; snow ball survey (snowballing); viral marketing; mouse-to-mouse; word-of-mouth* (Page 659 in *The ABCs*).

performance-capture acting – A system of recording an actor's movements and then using the data to create a digital animation. Also called *motion capture*.

permalance – A permanent freelancer. A full-time part-timer. See *freelancer*.

permission or permission-based marketing – Tease the (target) audience, (but only if they have invited you in – with permission). Like the adage says, out of sight, out of mind. The pace of life today and the constant advertising clutter and "noise" make it difficult to focus. That means a manufacturer must identify effective ways to get its customers' attention. One of the most economical is *permission-based marketing*, a term coined by author Seth Godin. Two perfect examples of this form of marketing are e-newsletters and text-messaging services that ask (potential) customers to sign up for at a website. Your customers are essentially authorizing you to check back with them, and you can turn this into more sales in the future.

photo bomb – Someone who "crashes" a posed photograph by standing behind the intended subject(s) so they (crasher) are seen in the picture.

(physician) scribe – A person designated by a health care provider to transcribe a physician or surgeon's notes during an examination or surgery to help adhere to electronic medical record laws.

pixel – A single display element on an LCD screen. The more *pixels*, the higher the resolution and definition. Also, a picture element (single illuminated dot) on a computer monitor. The metric used to indicate the size of Internet ads. Also, (similar to an *algorithm* and *cookie*) in mathematics and computer science, it is a step-by-step procedure for calculations – used in problem solving. An algorithm is often referred to as a (computer) *cookie* or *pixel* – a small amount of data generated by a website and saved on the Web browser. Its purpose is to remember information about you, similar to a preference file created by a software application. See *algorithm; cookie* (Page 106 in *The ABCs*).

plating – Placing food on dinner, salad and other plates – food presentation – used by restaurants, caterers and other hosts. See *food stylist* (Page 205 in *The ABCs*).

pleb (plebian) – An ordinary person of low social status – commoner.

plunder – The violent and dishonest acquisition (wrongfully taking) of property – including intellectual property.

poach – The act of "stealing" an employee from a competitive organization.

pocket listing – A real estate term for a property under contract to a broker or agent who is trying to sell it, but has not yet advertised it or shared it with MLS (multiple listing service).

pop-up park(s) – Temporary or portable parks transported from place to place and set up for short periods of time usually within cities (downtowns) or other urban locations. *Pop-up park* kits are available. See *parklet*.

pop-up shopping – Edgy, trendy, shops where buying and selling often merge with art, education, performance and partying.

pop-up shower – "Surprise" rain storm usually unexpected and not in a forecast.

pop-up store – Usually a (seasonal) retail store – one that opens (in a high traffic area) a month or so before Halloween or Christmas selling costumes and decorations – with major retail sale implications.

porchtown – Spending your vacation week at home rather than traveling or at a resort.

pork barrel – The appropriation of government spending for localized projects secured solely or primarily to bring money to an elected representative's district – sometimes included as a bill's rider called an *earmark*. See *earmark* (Page 168 in *The ABCs*).

post – The first word, sound or piece of video in a radio or television program. When a broadcaster *joins* that program it is called "hitting the *post*." It is the point in a local radio or television broadcast when the announcer *joins* a network or other program. See *join*.

potpourri – Any mixture – especially of unrelated subjects. A *mixed bag*.

pre-roll – A commercial or promotional video that runs before a video brought up on the Internet via YouTube, a television network website, etc. Most pre-rolls cannot be skipped because that's how the provider earns its advertising dollars.

press proof – A proof made on a printing press that is usually the press on which the job is to be printed to show exactly how it will look – margins, colors, etc. See *blue line (proof); dylux* (Page 165 in *The ABCs*).

price maker – The strategy that a product is worth what a consumer is willing to pay. Also, a manufacturer who sets a product's price based on its exclusivity and perception of luxury. Also, a stockholder who controls a large number of shares and is able to affect the stock's price through selling or buying. See *computerized trading; flash crash; high frequency trading; new luxury; prestige pricing* (Page 447 in *The ABCs*).

principal – In addition to being a school's chief executive officer, a *principal* is also an actor whose face in a commercial is on the screen for several seconds – long enough that the actor is identified with the product and/or brand. Because of the *transfer effect*, the actor may not appear in a commercial for a similar product or brand. He/she would be compensated for being a *principal*. Some *voice actors* are considered *principals*. See *a cross; extra; logo voice; signature voice; voice actor*.

prock – A title for a professor who also holds a doctorate.

product integration (embedded advertising) – Also referred to as *brand* (product) integration when the product or brand name is said (verbalized) – *product placement* when the brand is only seen. Advertisers seamlessly blending their products with editorial content – both electronically and in print, which some view as a violation of "church and state" (so to speak). It is paying for the use of a product or service (easily distinguishable) within a television or radio program, a film or in a magazine article (hard copy or online). See *cheater; product placement* (Page 463 in *The ABCs*).

product placement (embedded advertising) – Also referred to as *brand* (product) placement when the product is seen – *product integration* when the brand is (verbally) mentioned only, but not seen. Advertisers seamlessly blending their products with editorial content – both electronically and in print, which some view as a violation of "church and state" (so to speak). It is paying for the use of a product or service (easily seen/distinguishable) within a television or radio program, a film or in a magazine article (hard copy or online). The placement may be visual (*product* placement) or verbal (*product integration*). A most visible example was seen in the motion picture "Cast Away," which featured FedEx®. See *cheater; product integration* (Page 463 in *The ABCs*).

propagation – A computer term meaning the process and time period for information to show across the Web (on the screen).

publicity (public relations) value – Multiplies media value by an arbitrary figure to account for the perceived third-party "credibility" of editorial copy over advertising. For example, arbitrary figures that a newspaper or magazine may use might be 1.982 readers per copy, which means that this one publication was read 1.982 different times for each copy sold and then those figures would be used to determine the *publicity value*. A similar approach is used for broadcasting. *Publicity value* of Internet publications is more precise because clicks can be more precisely measured – although more than one set of "eyeballs" may be viewing the screen. See *ad value; hit; impression; media value* (Page 268 in *The ABCs*).

pukka – A slang British term for absolute first class, genuine or correct.

punch in – When vocal and music tracks are recorded separately and merged. Some *punch ins* might include parts of recordings from different takes. With digital recordings, punch ins have become commonplace. See *mash up* (Page 348 in *The ABCs*).

push messaging/notifications – Highly targeted messages and/or alerts sent to landline phones (voice) or mobile devices (voice or text) on behalf of schools, colleges, municipalities or other organizations. Many organizations have made *push notifications* a major component of their emergency response procedure. Marketers (advertisers), charities and politicians use a similar *tactic* (Page 595 in *The ABCs*).

QR Code - Abbreviated from *Quick Response Code*. It is a matrix barcode, which originated in Japan. Smartphones and other digital devices offer apps that scan a barcode (for its imbedded information) and immediately link to a Web page or other landing site.

Quick Response Code – Also known by abbreviation *QR code*. It is a matrix barcode, which originated in Japan. Smartphones and other digital devices offer apps that scan a barcode (for its imbedded information) and immediately link to a Web page or other landing site.

quid pro quo – See *Tip 210*.

rainmaker – A public relations or advertising agency employee who brings in new business (new accounts). A person whose influence can change opinions and/or initiate progress. When someone is referred to as a rainmaker, they are considered successful in helping to contribute to their employer's financial bottom line.

range anxiety – Concern or worry about an electric vehicle (car) running out of power – having no "charge spot."

rate-based circulation – The circulation guaranteed to potential advertisers by a newspaper, magazine or other publication. See *Audit Bureau of Circulations* (Page 26 in *The ABCs*).

reciprocal engagement – Marriage. See *conscious uncoupling*.

red light syndrome – Red light on television studio camera to alert "talent" he/she is "on the air." Sometimes referred to as a *cue light* or *tally light*.

reefer – Boxed items at the top of a newspaper section or magazine cover promoting stories inside the newspaper or magazine. Also call *header*.

regional edition – Print publications (newspapers/magazines) targeted to a specific geographic region. This is commonplace among metropolitan-area newspapers and many major magazines to attract local advertising as well as national ads. Also called *fractional edition* and *zone edition*.

remnant buying – Last minute media advertising buys – purchasing leftover time (radio/television) or space inventory (newspapers, magazines, Web pages, etc.) – many times at a (major) discount. See *remnant space* (Page 504 in *The ABCs*).

renaissance (person) – A clever person with many skills, who cultivates an area of interest, such as the arts, without real commitment or knowledge. A *dilettante*.

renewable energy – Energy that comes from resources which are naturally replenished – sunlight, wind, rain, tides, waves and geothermal heat. *Renewable energy* replaces or supplements conventional fuels. See *carbon footprint*; *sustainable (design)*.

reparative therapy – Also known as *conversion therapy*. A range of treatments to change sexual orientation from homosexual to heterosexual. See *gender reassignment*.

reporter package with set tag – In some cases, when the edited reporter package airs, it ends with the reporter appearing live in the studio to "tag" or "wrap up" his/her story on the set, rather than ending with a recorded stand-up close and sign off ("This is Trixie Kramer reporting for Eyewitness News 7"). This technique can be used:

1. for visually unexciting stories, where there were limited opportunities for an effective stand-up

2. to provide an opportunity to omit incorrect information in a recorded stand-up – i.e., the corrected or updated information can be presented on the set

3. to allow for discussing a story – the anchor and reporter may have a question and answer (Q&A) exchange at the end of the report. This is sometimes called "crosstalk" or when it is superfluous, "happy talk." (Pages 413 and 660 in *The ABCs*.)

reporter package-field report – These terms refer to the same thing: a story reported, produced and written by a reporter who actually goes to the scene and gathers the facts. The reporter either shoots his or her own video or is accompanied by a camera person (videographer) who photographs the scenes and interviews involved in the story. It is different from the *voiceover*, the *copy story* and the *voiceover* with *soundbite (vo/sot)* and *soundbite* to *voiceover (SOT/VO)* formats, because the packaged story is recorded digitally or on video chip, rather than read live from the studio. While the package uses the same techniques as the *VOT*, *VO/SOT* and the *copy story*, the terminology changes somewhat, because of the editing process involved. (Pages 413 and 660 in *The ABCs*.)

reptile or reptilian brain – Term used to describe someone considered rigid and/or compulsive – we cannot resist because of the reptile (emotions) in us. See *lizard brain*.

reputation – How you are perceived (image). *Character* is what you are – what you do when people are not watching. (Pages 264 and 265 in *The ABCs*.)

research – evidence gathered.

rescue romance – One member (partner) of a couple who rescues/saves the other from possible self-destruction – heading toward a personal crash (drugs, embezzlement, etc.) – usually through professional help.

residual goodwill – The association that a consumer has between a trade mark or servicemark's original "owner" that may no longer be in use.

responsive design – Web design aimed at crafting websites to provide an optimal viewing experience – easy reading and navigation – no matter what type of device on which it appears – desktop monitor, smartphone, digital table, etc. The *smart design* – using proper software – adapts to whatever screen on which it appears.

restraint of trade – Any action (usually illegal), which damages in some way another's opportunity to carry on a business.

retention rate (advertising) – The percentage of those exposed to an advertising (strategic) message who remember it and can relate it to the brand. See *ad recall*; *sleeper effect*; *transfer effect* (Page 617 in *The ABCs*).

return monitor – Monitor (screen) usually placed above or below a studio camera during a remote interview so the interviewee at remote location can see the person asking the questions.

reverse teaching – A form of blended learning where students learn new content online – rather than in the classroom – by watching video lectures and reading assignments and other material, usually at home or location other than the classroom. What was once homework (assigned problems, etc.) is now done in class with teachers offering more personalized guidance and interaction with students, instead of lecturing. Also known as *"teaching naked"* – without classroom technology – or as a *backwards, flipped and inverted classroom*.

reward-based apps – Smartphone or other digital device apps that reward users who carry out certain tasks – watching television programs, critiquing motion pictures, grocery shopping, etc. Each "job" pays a fee.

right brain vs. left brain (thinker) – According to the theory of left-brain or right-brain dominance, each side of the brain controls different types of thinking. Additionally, people are said to prefer one type of thinking over the other. A "left-brained" person is said to be more logical, analytical and objective, while a "right-brained" person is said to be more intuitive, thoughtful and subjective. See *lizard brain*.

risk abatement agreement – A subsidy paid to encourage operators in a certain industry to "set up shop" by reducing their financial risk. It covers losses incurred (e.g. New Jersey [and other states] has subsidized airlines to fly into and out of their [smaller] airports to minimize or eliminate financial risk).

road warrior – A person who travels frequently especially on business.

roll in – Recorded video to drop into a television show.

rope line – People who line up awaiting a political candidate or celebrity in hopes of "pressing the flesh" (shaking hands). Politicians and successful CEOs "walk the rope line" in an attempt to break down barriers between themselves and their publics.

rush tickets – After a sellout, available tickets put on sale (online or elsewhere) – maybe standing room only.

salary cap – A rule that places a limit on the amount of money a team can spend on player salaries. The limit exists as a per-player limit or a total limit for a team's roster, or both. Several sports leagues have implemented salary caps to control costs and to ensure parity between teams so that wealthy teams cannot dominate by signing more top players than their less wealthy or small-market rivals.

sample video (reel) – Once referred to as "audition tape." Thanks to digital technology, *sample video* or *audio* is emailed as an easily downloadable attachment (its own file).

sandwich generation – The generation raising children and caring for parents at the same time. See *multigenerational (next generation) homes*.

score – During the folding process of a print job, it is an indentation made in the paper – especially heavier weight paper or card stock – to assure the fold is "crisp."

scratch kitchen – Usually an open (restaurant) kitchen where customers can see meals prepared individually from "scratch" or from the beginning. Better restaurants brag about their *scratch kitchen*.

scratch video – A video made by mixing together short clips into a single film with a synchronized soundtrack. *See mash up* (Page 348 in *The ABCs*).

script supervisor (consultant) – For motion pictures and recorded television programs, the person responsible for scene continuity – making certain video is consistent when the camera cuts from a scene and returns (e.g. if a beverage glass is half-full at the cut-away it should be half-full when the scene cuts back.) Many times, still (digital) cameras are used to assure the clothing, hair, scenery, etc. are consistent. One of their responsibilities is to work with *location scouts* to assure sites are consistent from day to day. See *location scout(s)*.

second banana – Someone who is not as important or as powerful as another person. Also, a comedian who plays a supporting role to a top banana.

self-publishing – The publication of any book or other media by the author without the involvement of an established publisher. A self-published physical/hard copy book is said to be *privately printed*. In *self-publishing*, the author is responsible and in control of the entire process including content, cover design, price, distribution, marketing and public relations. An author can do it all him/herself or outsource all or part of the process.

selfi – Taking a picture of yourself using a smartphone or other digital device.

selfie stick – An adjustable pole to take *selfi* pictures by positioning a smartphone or camera beyond the normal range of the arm. The metal sticks are typically extendable, with a handle on one end and an adjustable clamp on the other end to hold an iPhone® or other smartphone in place See *selfi*.

senatorial courtesy – In some states, an unwritten political custom where the governor consults a state senator before nominating a person for an appointment. In New Jersey, *senatorial courtesy* allows a single state senator to hold up or block a governor's nominee from that senator's home county without having to offer a reason. On the federal level, the president often consults the senior U.S. senator of his political party of a given state before nominating any person to a federal vacancy within that senator's state – federal district judges, U.S. attorneys, federal marshals, etc.

sequester – During the Obama Administration, the budget *sequestration* of 2013 referred to automatic (across the board) budget (spending) cuts during the budget stalemate. The Budget Control Act of 2011 dictated such policy. The *"sequestration"* is known as *"falling off the cliff."*

server – Guest service agent (waitress/waiter).

service gap – When retail sales people ignore customers because they are "interrupted" by a (personal) cell phone call and customers tire of waiting.

The reverse could also be true: customers making salespeople wait while they talk or text on their phone.

set-aside – Holdback of game, concert or other event tickets so they may be comped (given free) or sold to VIPs or other influential people including public office holders. Some professions consider *set-asides* unethical and in some cases illegal.

sexting – The practice of sending sexually explicit text messages, photos or videos via a cellphone, smartphone or other digital device.

shelter in place – Remain where you are when there is a threat – in your house, office, school or some other area where you are relatively safe – during a shooting, chemical spill, etc.

short sale – Sale of a house or other real estate for less than the amount owed on the mortgage or other loan. See *subprime mortgage*; underwater *(mortgage)*.

shovel ready – A construction project where planning, engineering and other preliminary work is complete. *Shovel ready* sites are attractive to prospective buyers. See *fast-tracking* (Page 192 in *The ABCs*).

showrooming – Examining merchandise in a traditional brick-and-mortar retail store without purchasing it, and then shopping online to find a lower/better price for the same item.

shutdown – In sports, when a team scores and then holds the opposition scoreless in the next inning (baseball and softball), the remainder of a quarter (football and basketball) or period (hockey, soccer, etc.). Would hold true for some other sports, as well.

Siamese twins of journalism – Context and accuracy are known as the *Siamese twins of journalism*.

side rail – Left side or right side column – usually on a newspaper's front page or section cover, a magazine cover or Web page. The column contains inside story summaries – teasers – to encourage readers to go to the inside.

signature voice – A "voice" – announcer or otherwise – closely associated with a product or radio station. Some refer to it as a *logo voice*. Its purpose is to evoke a *transfer effect*. Also, the voice an individual uses – other than his/her normal voice – during special presentations. Sometimes called a staged or broadcaster's voice. See *logo voice; transfer effect; voice actor* (Page 617 in *The ABCs*).

Silicon Alley – Such technology firms as Google® setting up "shop" – research, storage and other operations in a former warehouse building in major urban areas (e.g. Google in New York City).

singleton – Single people living alone.

situation analysis – The process of gathering and evaluating information on internal and external environments to assess a firm's current strengths, weaknesses, opportunities and threats (SWOT), and to guide its goals and objectives. It sets the table for public relations planners by detailing necessary information gathered through scientific and nonscientific research – identifying target audiences and determining the strategic direction the organization should take. Some public relations practitioners define *situation analysis* as a one-paragraph statement of the situation and refinement of problem definition based on research; a second paragraph identifies potential difficulties and related problems to be considered. See *Creative Brief* (Page 119 in *The* ABCs); SWOT *analysis* (Page 119 in *The ABCs*). (For examples, see *The Public Relations Practitioner's Playbook for (all Strategic Communicators* – AuthorHouse – 2013).

situation room – A room at a military headquarters or business used to plan operations or events – often used to provide centralized command for some purpose.. They are normally specially equipped with computers, charts, maps, etc.). Also called *command center; war room.*

slam clicking – Flight attendants who spend their time between flights "cocooning" in their hotel rooms because they need the time to eat, sleep and shower – even on long layovers.

slamming – The illegal practice (by a phone provider) of changing a customer's local or long distance telephone service without their permission. See *cramming.*

slap back – Also called *fall back*. An echo experienced by some singers and other on-stage performers. Singers will sometimes lip sync to prevent confusion.

sleep pants (shorts)/lounge pants – Look like full-length boxer shorts, but are actually pajamas. Many times, (female) college students wear them to classes as casualwear or *athleisurewear.*

sleep (lounge) shorts – Look like boxer shorts, but usually a heavier fabric. They are actually pajamas. See *athleisurewear; lounge pants; sleep pants.*

sleepunder – Showing PJ-clad kids the door at bedtime rather than have them stay overnight for a sleepover. Opposite of a *sleepover.*

slider(s) – Cute 3-ounce burgers (ham, turkey, chicken, etc. or mini-crab cakes), which have become all the rage. Campbell's® Pepperidge Farm® was the first to market slider-size burger buns.

smart design – Web design aimed at crafting websites to provide an optimal viewing experience – easy reading and navigation – no matter what type of device on which it appears – desktop monitor, smartphone, digital table, etc. The *responsive design*– using proper software – adapts to whatever screen on which it appears.

smart meter – An electronic device that records electric energy consumption and reports it back to the energy (utility) provider, which can adjust distribution during peak periods. Also provides utility with usage for billing purposes.

SMART system – Social media and traditional media measurement – Specific-Measurable-Attainable-Realistic-Timely or Tangible.

smart TV – An Internet-enabled television. A digital TV connected to the Internet. A TV, which also functions as a computer to enable video viewing streamed or downloaded from the Internet (Web) – most times in high definition.

smartphone – A cell phone that has so many functions, it serves as mini-computer (digital device) with a camera (e.g. iPhone®).

smash and grab – A particular type of robbery – characteristically committed with surprise and speed – usually smashing a display window or display case and making a quick getaway without regard for alarms.

snark – Comic – political cartoon – that deals more with "looks" than issues, but the satire leads to conversation.

snow ball survey (snowballing) – Passing along a message to as many people as you can and asking them to do the same. They in turn ask their recipients to do the same. While it may not be a scientific or targeted approach, it has proven successful. See *pass along* rate.

social marketing – Especially prevalent among non-profit organizations, government agencies, community-based organizations, private foundations, social/health/issue coalitions and any entity that wants to make social change. Also, the design, implementation and control of marketing activity intended to promote social causes or ideas within a target group in a society. A concept that requires balancing a firm or organization, consumer and public interests.

soft money – Donations made indirectly to a political candidate via a political action committee (PAC) or through some other type of donation. While *hard money* is regulated by federal laws (Federal Election Commission), *soft money* is not. This allows donors to contribute much larger amounts of money to a candidate's party than directly to the candidate. See *hard money; 501(c)3; 501(c)4*.

soft opening – The "informal" opening of a new retail store or other business prior to the celebrated and advertised grand opening. It gives the new business a chance to work out the "kinks." See *hard (grand) opening*.

sound art – "Beautiful (elevator) music. But what is beautiful to one person may not be to another. Thus, beauty is in the ear of the beholder.

spam – Unasked for emails.

spare geometrical style – A simple approach.

spiker – A public employee who works many overtime hours toward the end of his/her career to drive up his salary to increase his/her annual pension (in states where it is legal).

split concentration – Multitasking – particularly while listening or watching someone or something while at the same time interacting with a (lap top) computer, digital tablet, smartphone or other device. See *disruptive technology*.

split screen – Two or more "boxes" shown on a television screen usually during interviews or panel discussions. Some news programs have used 12 or more video boxes.

splurgeworthy – Tied to *prestige pricing*. Heard on the television program *Seinfeld*. The philosophy is you spend more for something of high quality or something you want because you "deserve it." See *prestige pricing* (Page 447 in *The ABCs*).

spoiler alert – A warning to viewer(s) or listener(s) that a crucial element of a movie, play, book, etc. is about to be revealed (i.e. the ending, character death, a plot twist, etc.)

spoofing ("caller ID spoofing") – A "shady" (fraudulent) practice where callers deliberately falsify the telephone number and/or name relayed as the Caller ID information to disguise the identity of the calling party. Also a practice used by some spammers who harvest an individual's email address from someone else's address book or who buy an electronic mailing list. The spoofer uses the individual's address to cover his/her tracks as he sends out his spam.

stack (a show) – The story order on a television or radio newscast. See *rundown* (Page 518 in *The ABCs*).

staging area – A controlled location where people, vehicles, equipment, etc. assemble before going into action. See *command center; situation room; war room*.

stinger – See *kicker* (Page 303 in *The ABCs*).

stove piping (stovepiping) – Raw intelligence information presented without proper context (or attribution) simply to give the impression that a problem is being solved. The lack of context may be due to the specialized nature, or security requirements within an organization.

strategic communication – A two-way – management supported communication process that builds mutually beneficial relationships between organizations and their publics. *Strategic communication* usually includes public relations, advertising, marketing, some forms of journalism, online communication (social and other emerging media), graphic design and sales promotion. Its ABCs are anticipation, being prepared (planning), communicating clearly, concisely, consistently, calculatingly, completely (specifically and simply) and correctly – always communicating in an *open, honest, thorough and valid* manner. *Strategic communicators* conceive with their head, believe in the heart and achieve with their hands (CBAs of *strategic communication*.)

stunt journalism – A form of journalism where the author – journalist – participates in an event or the everyday lives of those he/she is covering to gather first-hand information through observation (anecdotal research). An example dates back to Elizabeth Jane Cochran whose pen name was Nellie Bly. Bly wrote *Ten Days in a Mad-House* in 1887. In the book she gets herself committed to an asylum where she personally observes patient treatment and facility conditions. Bly went undercover to share the experience with other patients. Film, director John Waters' book *Carsick* is *stunt journalism*. Also called *Gonzo* and *immersion journalism*.

subprime (loan) mortgage(s) – Mortgages (loans) borrowers cannot afford. The house/property used as collateral has lost market value, which fell below the amount owed (known as *underwater*). Foreclosures could not generate enough money to cover the loans, which led to a financial crisis in 2007 and later. See *short sale*; *underwater (mortgage)*.

super PAC – Technically known as independent expenditure-only committees, *super PACs* may raise unlimited sums of money from corporations, unions, associations and individuals, then spend unlimited sums to advocate for or against political candidates. However, *super PACs* must report their donors to the Federal Election Commission on a monthly or quarterly basis – the super PAC's choice – just as a traditional PAC must. Unlike traditional *PACs*, *super PACs* are prohibited from donating money directly to political candidates and there are no limits on contributions. Read more at *www.opensecrets.org/pacs/superpacs.php*. See *501(c)3*; *501(c)4*.

sustainable (design) – A lifestyle that attempts to reduce the use of natural resources – reduce the carbon footprint. It makes the best use of renewable technologies considered environmentally correct. See *carbon footprint*; *renewable energy*.

sweat equity – A person's contribution to a project in the form of physical or mental effort. Sometimes called "*elbow grease*" when the effort is physical. See *elbow grease*.

swiftboating – An unfair, untrue or harsh political attack on an opponent. Derived from a type of United States Navy ship used during the Vietnam War.

synergistic – Of or relating to *synergy*. Producing or capable of producing *synergy* – the whole is greater than the sum of its parts.

synergy – Originally, a biological term. The principle in public relations and marketing that the whole is greater than the sum of the parts. Two or more "things" working together to achieve greater efficiency. Using as many of the *marketing mix* variables together in a way that achieves maximum effect. Ogilvy and Mather® refers to its *synergy* approach as 360 Degree Brand Stewardship® – a proprietary set of tools and techniques used to understand, develop and enhance the relationship between a consumer and a brand. See *marketing synergy* (Page 346 in *The ABCs*).

20-30-40 rule – In broadcast journalism, voice cuts, soundbites or actualities should run no longer than 20-seconds. Radio voicers (recorded reports) should run no longer than 40-seconds. See *actuality*, *soundbite (soundbyte)*, *voice cut*, *voicer* (Page 648 in *The ABCs*).

30 – See *end mark*.

3D printing – A "printing process" – technology that makes a three-dimensional object from a 3D printer or other electronic source using a process of successive layers of material laid down under computer control. Some refer to 3D printers as "industrial robots."

table read – A meeting where a television or Broadway show cast does its first run-through of the script – usually informal and fun.

tabula rasa – A blank (clean) slate (Philosopher John Locke). Also, "live the way that feels right to you."

take away(s) – The key message point(s) you want audience to remember.

take down "piece" – Something said or published (an article, blog, tweet, etc.) that has negative effects on a celebrity because its content is embarrassing.

talent-acquisition strategist – A human resource (director) practitioner. One who is responsible for placement, recruiting, compensation and team building.

TARP – Troubled Asset Relief Program designated by the federal government to assist economy during the Barack Obama presidential administration.

teaching naked – Teaching without classroom technology. A form of blended learning where students learn new content online – rather than in the classroom – by watching video lectures and reading assignments and other material, usually at home or location other than the classroom. What was once homework (assigned problems, etc.) is now done in class with teachers offering more personalized guidance and interaction with students, instead of lecturing. Also known as a *backwards classroom*, *flipped classroom* and *reverse teaching*.

televisiphonernetting – When a person is watching television, using the phone and surfing the Internet all at the same time.

thought starter(s) – Sometimes called *ice breakers*. They could be open-ended questions or other strategic messages to kick off a meeting or start a conversation. See *ice breaker*.

tick tock(s) – Chronologies or timelines often seen in newspapers, magazines and online stories. See *Gantt Chart* (Page 648 in *The ABCs*).

time ticks – Ticks represent the number of 100-nanosecond intervals. There are 10,000 ticks in a millisecond.

tip out – Part of a tip that servers (waitresses/waiters) give to runners, bus boys and others who assist them when waiting tables.

tool – If a tactic is a specific action that drives a strategy, a tool is the technique. For example, the tactic may be to get a story on a television newscast. The tool would be the *news release*, verbal *pitch* or *special event*. Tools and tactics have become interchangeable. See *tactic* (Page 595 in *The ABCs*).

trafficking (human) – Recruiting or harboring someone by threat or deception and controlling them for exploitation.

tramp stamp – Lower back tattoo – usually on a woman – sometimes accentuated by a cut-off top and low-rise jeans, slacks, shorts or bathing suit bottom.

transaction – An activity on an interactive website. Sending an email would be a transaction.

treed – An animal that has been chased up a tree by another animal. Could be related to a human who has been "cornered" by law enforcement or someone else.

tribute band – A musical group (or individual) who performs or impersonates specifically like a well-known band or vocal group – usually after the band group has disbanded or person is deceased.

triple truck – A three-page spread in a print publication, where the ad (editorial copy) runs across the gutters. It could be the center fold ("center spread") or any three full side-by-side pages (facing each other). If it prints across the gutters between the three pages, and if the pages are on the same sheet, rather than three adjacent sheets, it might be called a "true" *triple truck*. This name comes from the days when the heavy forms for newspaper pages, largely filled with lead type, were rolled around the composing room floor on heavy carts called trucks. Two pages for one project meant a double truck. See *double truck* (Page 160 in *The ABCs*); *gutter* (Page 239 in *The ABCs*)

Truth in Packaging – Known as the Fair Packaging and Labeling Act (FPLA) was created in 1966 to assure "all product packages and labels" provide accurate information. It continues to evolve and has seen many modifications. Packaging and labels are regulated by the Food and Drug Administration. Its purpose is to protect consumers by fully disclosing a product's ingredients, caloric and fat intake.

tweep – A person who uses Twitter®. One who tweets.

tweet – A Twitter® message.

twerking – A type of dancing where an individual (usually a female) dances to music in a sexually provocative manner involving thrusting hip movements and a low squatting stance.

under water – When the mortgage owed (debt) on a property is more than the property is worth. See *short sale; subprime*.

unregulated fun – Spontaneous. Enjoying oneself without structure. Not (pre) planned.

upcycle – The process of converting waste materials or useless products into new materials or products of better quality or a higher environmental value.

urinal cake – Scent cake inside a urinal.

vet (vetting) – To investigate someone or something thoroughly to determine if they (it) should be approved or accepted for a job.

video app ad – *Banner* – *header* or *footer* – advertisement at top or bottom of smartphone screen or other device – appearing when app is touched. It is usually interactive.

video boxes – Two or more "boxes" shown on a television screen usually during interviews or panel discussions. Some news programs have used 12 or more. See *split screen*.

video (app) scrolling – Moving text and/or graphics up, down or across a computer, smartphone or other digital device screen.

virtual advertising – Technique used by television. Banners or billboards electronically appear on the screen. Viewers at home see the ads while spectators inside the sports venue do not. Virtual ads can cover/replace a billboard that has been erected inside a sports stadium or arena – by first superimposing an electronic green screen over it and then the ad. (The yellow first-down line and direction arrows on football fields use the same technology to help entertain home audiences by making it easier to follow the game.) See *superimposition; superstitial* (Page 583 in *The ABCs*).

virtual tour – A panoramic view or video simulation of an existing location, usually composed of a sequence of video or still images. It may also use other multimedia elements such as sound effects, music, narration and text.

visual prosthetics – Use of a *green* or *blue screen* (*chroma key*) in motion pictures to change/import backgrounds or to change a character's appearance. Also used in venue advertising when a *green/blue screen* is superimposed over an ad (billboard) to replace it with an ad that "at home" viewers see, but venue spectators cannot. (Page 232 in *The ABCs*).

voice actor – A celebrity whose voice is used for cartoon-type characters. See *logo voice*.

voice microphone therapy – Nearly the same as *tally light* syndrome. No matter how badly one feels, once the light goes on or they are in front of a microphone, they set everything else aside and perform. See *cue light; red light syndrome; tally light* (Page 596 in *The ABCs*).

voiceover with soundbite or VO/SOT (voiceover video to sound-on-"tape") – In this case, the studio anchor reads copy live over video as in a "straight" *voiceover* story –but when the copy and pictures end, an interview (SOT) immediately comes up. Usually, a VO/SOT story ends with an on-camera (O/C) *tag* from the anchorperson, where the anchor offers a closing sentence or two that "wraps up" or concludes the story. When the closing sentence is read over video, it becomes a *voiceover tag*, creating a VO/SOT/VO format. Sometimes a SOT/VO (sound on "tape" to anchor/reporter voice over video on "tape") is used. It is often used in a newscast cold open or as a bumper (tease of a story that will run later in the newscast) leading to a commercial break. A *SOT/VO/SOT* is yet another possibility. (Page 647 in *The ABCs*.)

walk and talk – A distinctive storytelling-technique used in filmmaking and television production where a number of characters have a conversation en route to their destination. The most basic form of *walk and talk* involves a walking character joined by another character who engages in conversation in one continuous shot using a "Steadicam" camera. It was perfected by producer Aaron Sorkin on the television series "West Wing."

want – In journalism, it is a person (newsmaker) the reporter/anchor wants to interview. See *get*.

war room – See *situation room*.

wardrobing – The return of non-defective merchandise originally purchased ("borrowed") for a specific purpose. For example, people might purchase a "big screen" television for the Super Bowl – then return it a day or two after the game. Such a practice cuts into the store's profit margin because the product must be marked down for resale.

watch party – Gatherings of large groups to watch a special event on television – a big game, presidential speech, TV special, etc.

weapons of mass disruption – Not to be confused with weapons of mass destruction – "dirty" bombs. These WMDs would include computer viruses or other "hacking" that interferes with technology.

Web entry points – On a website, a link for parents, for teenagers, tweens, etc. – separate "links" to targeted landing sites.

Web page hotspot – A spot (icon or words) on a Web page (photo or words) that links viewer to a landing site. Also, visual or words of greatest interest on a Web page.

webenizing – Websites that have users log in with an email and possibly demographics and psychographics and then distribute that information – much like placing them on a listserve® or other mailing list (sharing personal information). The websites that sell the information are engaging in e-marketing.

white board – Also known as *dry-erase board*. See *dry-erase board; Smart Board®* (Page 554 in *The ABCs*).

white coat anxiety – When visiting a doctor, dentist or laboratory, anxiety sets in (e.g. blood pressure rises just before it is taken or patient gets nervous as he/she waits in a dentist's office or blood testing facility.)

woot woot – An expression one may utter in complete approval or joy. ("Woot Woot!" I said in agreement.)

words-eye picture – Radio play by play and other such descriptions. A reporter describing a scene in words that form pictures (ROSR – radio on scene report or TOSR – television on scene report). Technique was perfected by broadcast journalist Edward R. Murrow.

work and income – It is the philosophy that people work to live. See *downshifting*.

work-a-day actor – Sometimes called per diem performer – voice or on camera. He/she gets paid a daily rate rather than contract rate.

WOW (cart) – Wireless on Wheels. Schools and others use carts to transport wireless devices from room to room rather than have permanent classrooms or computer labs with desktops and other technology. Also, the electronic storing of a patient's medical records making them portable, i.e. physicians may access them on a laptop, iPad® or other portable device.

wrecking crew – A team of reporters who work together on a story usually to uncover wrongdoing – sometimes with an agenda and sometimes without. See *agenda* (Page 14 in *The ABCs*).

wrongfully attributed statement (WAS) – A famous quote spoken by one person and attributed to another. City University of New York Professor Corey Robin coined the phrase.

yellow journalism – Journalism based on exaggeration and sensationalism. Tabloid newspapers are sometimes accused of *yellow journalism*. See *journalism*; misremember; *tabloid* (Page 595 in *The ABCs*).

Abbreviations and Acronyms
Common to the Professions

AA = Average Audience
AAs = Author's Alterations
AAA = American Academy of Advertising
AAAA = American Association of Advertising Agencies
AASA = American Association of School Administrators
ABC = American Broadcasting Company
ABC = Audit Bureau of Circulations
ADI = Area of Dominant Influence
AIDA = Attention, Interest, Desire, Action
AIO = Attitudes, Interests, Opinions (Statements)
AMA = American Marketing Association
ANA = Association of National Advertisers
AP = Associated Press
APR = Accredited in Public Relations
ARF = Advertising Research Foundation
ARP = Address Resolution Protocol
ASBA = American School Boards Association
AUO = Administratively Uncontrolled Overtime
AV = Audiovisuals

B2B = Business to Business advertising
BANANA = Build absolutely nothing anywhere near anything
BANANA Republic = Build absolutely nothing anywhere near anything
BBB = Better Business Bureau
BBC = British Broadcasting Corporation
BCG = Boston Consulting Group
BDI = Brand Development Index
BHAG = Big Hairy Audacious Goal
Blog = Web log
BMI = Basal Mass Index
BMR = Basal Metabolic Rate
BOA = Behavior Observable Actions
BOGO = Buy One, Get One (free)
BPA – Border Patrol Agent
BUPPIE = Black Urban Professional

CARS = Car Assistance Rebate System
CARU = Children's Advertising Review Unit
CASS = Coding Accuracy Support System

CAT = Creative and Technology
CAVE = Citizens against virtually everything
CBBB = Council of Better Business Bureaus
CBD = Central Business District
CBS = Columbia Broadcasting System
CBSA = Core-Based Statistical Area
CCO = Chief Communication Officer
CGI = Computer Generated Imagery
CIO = Chief Information Officer
CIO = Chief Integrity Officer
CLV = Customer Lifetime Value
CMA = Cover My Ass
CMS = Content Management System
CMT = Crisis Management System
CMYK = Cyan-Magenta-Yellow-Black, and pronounced as separate letters C-M-Y-K
CNG = Compressed Natural Gas
COBRA = Consolidated Omnibus Budget Reconciliation Act
COGS = Certificate of Graduate Studies
COGS = Cost Of Goods Sold
CPA = Certified Public Accountant
CPA = Cost Per Action
CPA = Critical Path Analysis
CPC = Cost Per Click
CPC = Cost Per Customer
CPG = Consumer Package Goods
CPL = Cost Per Lead
CPM = Cost Per Thousand
CPO = Chief Privacy Officer
CPP = Cost Per Rating Point
CPS = Cost Per Sale
CPT = Consider, Ponder, Think
CPT = Cost Per Transaction
CPTM = Cost Per Targeted Thousand Impressions
CPV = Cost Per visit
CRM = Customer Relationship Management
CSR = Corporate Social Responsibility
CT = Click Through
CTA = Call to Action
CTR = Click-Through Rate
CTR = Click-Through Ratio
CYA = Cover Your Ass

DAGMAR = Defining Advertising Goals for Measured Advertising
DBA = Doing Business As
DD = Distracted Driver
DEC = Daily Effective Circulation
DFA = Designated for Assignment
DIFM = Do it for me
DINKY = Double Income No Kids Yet
DIY Goods = Goods produced for the "Do-It-Yourself" market
DMA = Designated Market Area
DMA MPS = Designated Market Area Mail Preference Service
DMA TPS = Designated Market Area Telephone Preference Service
DMO = Destination Marketing Organization
DMP = Digital Music Player
DMU = Decision Making Unit
DOMA = Defense of Marriage Act
DOT = Department of Transportation
DPI = Disposable Personal Income
DPI = Dots Per Inch
DRA = Direct Response Advertising
DRM = Digital Rights Management
DRTV = Direct Response Television
DSL = Digital Subscriber Line
DSS = Decision Support System
DTC = Direct to Consumer
DVR = Digital Video Recorder
DWD = Driving While Distracted

EA = Environmental Assessment
EAS = Emergency Alert System
ECR = Efficient Consumer Response
EEC = European Economic Community
EFTP = Electronic File Transport Protocol
EFTPOS = Electronic Funds Transfer at Point of Sale
ENP = Expected Net Profit
EOQ = Economic Order Quantity
EPG = Electronic Programming Guide
EPK = Electronic Press Kit
EPOS = Electronic Point of Sale System
EPS = Encapsulated Post Script
ESP = Envelopes and Stubby Pencil
ET = Electronic Transcription
ETA = Estimated Time of Arrival

FAA = Federal Aviation Administration
FAB = Features, Advantages and Benefits (Analysis)
FABS = Features And Benefits Selling
FAQ = Frequently Asked Questions
FAST Marketing = Focused Advertising Sampling Technique
FCC = Federal Communication Commission
FDA = Food and Drug Administration
FEMA = Federal Emergency Management Agency
FERPA = Family Educational Rights and Privacy Act
FFs = Freight Forwarders
FIDO = Forget it, drive on
FIS = Free In Store
FISA = Foreign Intelligence Surveillance Act
FLSA = Fair Labor Standards Act
FMCG = Fast Moving Consumer Goods
FOB = Free On Board
FOC = Front-Of-Counter
FOIA = Freedom of Information Act
FPS = Fax Preference Service
FSBO = For Sale By Owner
FSI = Free-Standing Insert
FTC = Federal Trade Commission
FTP = (Electronic) File Transport Protocol
FUD = Fear, Uncertainty and Doubt

GASP = Graphic Arts Service Provider
GFK = Growth for Knowledge
GIF = Graphics Interchange Format
GIS = Geographic Information System
GLAM = Greying, Leisured, Affluent, Middle-aged
GLB = Gramm-Leach-Bliley Act
GMO = Genetically Modified Organisms (food)
GMT = Greenwich Mean Time
GNP = Gross National Product
GOTV = Get Out The Vote
GPF = Global Pet Finder (GPS device)
GPS = Global Positioning System
GRPS = Gross Rating Points
GSM = Global System for Mobile
GSR = Galvonic Skin Response
GTD = Getting Things Done

GUPPIE = Grossly Under-Performing Person

HARO = Help a reporter out
HDTV = High-Definition Television
HHI = Household Income
HIF = Health Interference Foods (unhealthy food)
HIPAA = Health Insurance Portability and Accountability Act
HTML = Hyper-Text Markup Language
HTTP = Hyper-Text Transfer Protocol

IAB = Interactive Advertising Bureau
IABC = International Association of Business Communicators
ICE = In Case of Emergency Contacts (If in cellphone, should not be password protected)
ID = Station identification during a commercial break in a television or radio program
IED = Improvised Explosive Device
IEI = Industrial Employment Income
IFPR = Identify, Fragment (Segment), Profile, Rank
IM = Instant Message
IMC = Integrated Marketing Communication
IMU = Interactive Marketing Unit
IP = Intellectual property
IP = Internet Protocol
IPA = International Priority Airmail
IPA = Internet Protocol Address
IPO = Initial Public Offering
IPR = Intellectual Property Rights
IPS = Institute of Professional Sales
IPTV = Internet Protocol TV
IRC = Internet Relay Chat
ISAL = International Surface Airlift
ISBN = International Standard Book Number
ISDN = Integrated Services Digital Network
ISP = Internet Service Provider
ISPR = Identify, (fragment) Segment, Profile, Rank (audiences)
ITI = Information Technology Industry Council
ITS = In-service Training Sessions
iTV = Interactive Television
IVR = Interactive Voice Response
IVR = Telemarketing Interactive Voice Response

JIC = Joint Information Center
JIT = Just-In-Time Inventory System
JPEG = Joint Photographic Experts Group

KC = Key Communicator
KIPP = Knowledge Is Power Program
KIPS = Key Influence People
KISS Principle = Acronym for "Keep It Simple and Straightforward"
KMPs = Key Message Points
KOLs = Knowledge Leaders (or Knowledge of those in Leadership roles)
KSA = Knowledges, Skills and Abilities

LAN = Local Area Network
LCC = Low Cost Carrier
LCD = Liquid Crystal Display
LEED = Leadership in Energy and Environmental Design
LGBT = Lesbian, Gay, Bisexual, Transgender
Libor = London Interbank Offered Rate
LLC = Limited Liability Company

MAC Plus (P & T) = Message, Audience, Channel, Purpose, Timing
MAN = Does the prospect have the Money to pay? Does the prospect have the Authority to buy? Does the prospect have a Need for the product?
MAPs = Message Action Points
Marcom = Marketing Communication
MBO = Management By Objectives
MBWA = Management By Walking Around
MERS = Middle East Respiratory Syndrome
MIME = Multi-Purpose Internet Mail Extensions
MIP = Mobile Internet Provider
MIS = Marketing Information System
MLM = Multilevel Marketing
MLS = Multiple Listing Service
MOB = Mother of the bride
MOG = Mother of the groom
MOOC = Massive Open Online Course
MOR = Middle of the Road
MOS = Man On the Street
MOU = Memo of Understanding
MPS = Mailing Preference Service
MRC = Media Rating Council
MRI = Media Research and Intelligence

MRI = Media Research Institute
MRI = Magnetic Resonance Imaging

MRO Supplies = Maintenance, Repair and Operating Supplies
MSA = Metropolitan Statistical Area
MSM = Mainstream Media
MSRP = Manufacturer's suggested retail price
MVP = Most Valuable Player

NAB = National Association of Broadcasters
NAD = National Advertising Division of the Council of Better Business Bureaus
NAI = Network Advertising Initiative
NAM = National Account Marketing
NARB = National Advertising Review Board of the Council of Better Business Bureaus
NBC = National Broadcasting Company
NFC = Near Field Communication
NGO = Not a government organization
NILKIE = No Income, Lots of Kids
NIMBY = Not In My Backyard
NPD = New Product Development
NQT = New Qualitative Technologies
NSPRA = National School Public Relations Association
NYLON – New York to London commuter – usually for business purposes.

OCC = Office of the Comptroller of the Currency
OINK = One Income, No Kids
OCR = Optical Character Recognition
OL = Opinion Leader
OOH = Out Of Home (advertising)
OOP = Out of Pocket (expenses)
OPA = Online Privacy Alliance
OPA = Online Publishers'Association
OPAL = Older People with Active Lifestyles
Op-Ed = Opposite Editorial Page
OPIS = Oil Price Information Service
OPMA = Open Public Meetings Act
OPRA = Open Public Records Act
OTS = Opportunity to See
OYR = Operation Yellow Ribbon

P2P = Peer to Peer Marketing
P3P = Platform for Privacy Preferences Project
PAC = Political Action Committee
PAD = Public Affairs Director
PAN = Pay, Authority, Need
PBOC = People's Bank of China
PBR = Payment By Results
PCO = Public Communication Officer (Foreign term for PAD)
PCPs = Program Coordination Implanting (meeting)
PCS = Population Control Strategy
PDA = Personal Digital Assistant
PDF (File) = Portable Document Format
PDM = Physical Distribution Management
PDM = Product-Differentiated Marketing
PDMA = Public Display of Male affection
PDT = Potentially Dangerous Taxpayer
PDVR = Portable Digital Video Recorder
PED = Performance Enhancing Drug
PEEST = Political, Economic, Environmental, Socio-cultural and Technological
PERT = Program Evaluation and Review Technique
PEST Analysis = Political, Economic, and Social Trends
PESTLE = Political, Economic, Socio-cultural, Technological, Legal and Environmental
PET Scan = Position Emission Tomography
PHR = Personal Health Record
PIC = Picture
PII = Personally Identifiable Information
PILOT = Payment in Lieu of Taxes
PIMS = Profit Impact of Marketing Strategies
PIN = Personal Identification Number
PIP = Personal Improvement Plan
PIT = Pursuit Intervention Technique
PLI = Privacy Leadership Initiative
PLU = Price Look Up
PMP = Personal Media Player
PMS = Pantone Matching System
PODS = Portable On Demand Storage
POP = Point Of Purchase
POSLSQ = Persons of Opposite Sex Living in Same Quarters – It is sometimes written as POSSLQ – Persons of Opposite Sex Sharing Living Quarters

POSSLQ = Persons of Opposite Sex Sharing Living Quarters - It is sometimes written as POSLSQ – Persons of Opposite Sex Living in Same Quarters
POTUS = President of the United States
POX = Police
PPC = Pay Per Click
PPM = Portable People Meter
PR = Public Relations
PR-Pie = Purpose, Research, Implementation, Communication (Information), Evaluation
PRO = Patent Reported Outcome
PROC = People's Republic of China
PROGS = Progressive Proofs
PRSA = Public Relations Society of America
PRSSA = Public Relations Student Society of America
PS = Postscript
PSA = Prostate-specific Antigen (protein) Test
PSA = Public Service Announcement
PSL = Personal Seat License
PSP = PlayStation Portable®
Pub = Short for publication
PUT = Persons (People) Using Television
PVR = Personal Video Recorder
PVT = Persons Viewing Television

Q&A = Question and Answer
Qangos = Quasi-autonomous Non-government Agencies
QC = Quality Circles
QR(code) = Quick Response (code)
Q-TIP = Quit Taking It Personally

R&B = Rhythm and Blues
R&D = Research and Development
RACE = Research, Action, Communication, Evaluation
RAPPIES = Retired Affluent Professionals
RDC = Regional Distribution Center
RET = Right Emotional Tone (for the situation)
RMD = Required Minimum Distribution
RFI = Request for Information
RFQ = Request for Qualifications
RFP = Request for Proposal
RGM = Repertory Grid Method
RINO = Republican in name only

RMD = Required Minimum Distribution
ROAM = Return on Assets Managed
ROC = Return on Capital
ROCE = Return on Capital Employed
ROI = Return on Investment
RON = Run of Network
ROP = Run of Paper
ROS = Run of Schedule
ROSR = Radio On Scene Report
ROS = Run of Site
RPM = Resale Price Maintenance
RPM = Revolutions per minute
RSS = Really Simple Syndication
RTC = Residential Training Courses

SAR = Summary Annual Report
SAU = Standard Advertising Unit
SAUS = Standard Advertising Unit System
SBU = Strategic Business Unit
SCOTUS = Supreme Court of the United States
SDSL = Symmetrical Digital Subscriber Line
SEM = Search Engine Marketing
SEO = Search Engine Optimizing
SFX = Sound Effects
SGML = Standard Generalized Markup Language
SIC = Spelling (content) Is Correct
SIC = Standard Industrial Classification
SINBAD = Single Income, No Boyfriend and Absolutely Desperate
SIQ = Sick In Quarters (U.S.Military)
SITCOM = Single Income, Two Kids, Outrageous Mortgage
SITCOM = Situation comedy
SIU = Sets In Use
SKU = Stock-Keeping Unit
SLAP = Skills Level Analysis Process
SLEPT= Socio-cultural, Legal, Economic, Political and Technological
SMART system = Social media and traditional media measurement – Specific-Measurable-Attainable-Realistic-Timely or Tangible
SME = Small to Medium Enterprise
SMP = Simple Management Protocol
SMPT = Simple Mail Transfer Protocol
SMS = Short Message Service
SMT = Satellite Media Tour

SOMPS = Statements of Marketing Practice
SOSTT = Situation, Objective, Strategy, Tactics and Targets
SOT = Sound On Tape
SOV = Share-of-Voice
SPSS® = Statistical Package for the Social Sciences
SRO = Standing Room Only
SRDS® = Standard Rate and Data Service
SRM = Supplier Relationship Management
STEM = Science, Technology, Engineering and Mathematics
SUPPIES = Senior Urban Professionals
SWAG = Stuff We All Get
SWOP = Specifications for Web Offset Publications
SWOT = Strengths, Weaknesses, Opportunities, Threats

TA = Teaching Assistant
TARP = Troubled Asset Relief (Recovery) Program
TARPS = Target Audience Rating Points
TCP/IP = Transfer Control Protocol/Internet Protocol
TIA = Total Information Awareness
tiff = Tagged Image File Format
TIFs = Technology Involved Females
TINKIE = Two Incomes, Nanny and Kids
TIP = To Insure Promptness
TIP = Triumph In the Pursuit (of knowledge)
TO = Turn Over (technique)
TOSR = Television On Scene Report
TPC = Trade Practices Commission
TPS = Telephone Preference Service
TSA = Total Survey Area
TSA = Transportation Security Administration
TSR = Telephone Service Representative

UAB = Universal Accreditation Board
UMTS = Universal Mobile Telecommunications System
UPC = Universal Product Code
URL = Uniform Resource Locator
USB = Universal Serial Bus
USP USP = Unique Selling Proposition

VALS = Values and Lifestyle System
VAT = Value Added Tax
VNR = Video News Release

VMS = Vertical Marketing System
V/O = Voice Over
VoD = Video On Demand
VoIP = Voice over Internet Protocol
VOPAN = Voice-pitch Analysis
VPN = Virtual Private Network
VRU = Voice Response Unit

WAA = Wireless Advertising Association
WAN = Wide Area Network
WAP = Wireless Application Protocol
WAPs = Web Access Phones
WAS = Wrongfully Attributed Statement
WASP = Wireless Applications Service Provider
WATS = Wide Area Telephone Service
Wi-Fi® = Brand for wireless technology
WOM = Word of Mouth Advertising or Marketing
WOOPIES = Well-off Older People
WOW = Wireless On Wheels
WX = Weather

XML = eXtensible Markup Language

YAPPIE = Young Affluent Parent
YOLO = You Only Live Once
YUPPIE = Young Urban Professional

ZBA – Zoning Board of Appeals
ZUPPIE = Zestful Upscale Person in their Prime

1 Tips to Succeed: Leaders make the best teachers

We've all heard this one: If you give a man a fish, he has no reason to learn how to fish, but if you teach him how to fish, he won't have to go hungry.

The point? Leaders ought to be the best teachers. For example, if an employee comes to you and gives you a problem, should you:

A. Simply offer the answer, or

B. Ask questions to determine if the employee can arrive at the solution him or herself?

The answer is a resounding "B." Helping an employee to solve a problem on their own, when time and circumstances allow, is, by far, the best choice.

Forget the Golden Rule. Instead, follow The Platinum Rule: "Do unto others as they would have done unto themselves." In other words, if you really want to motivate people, ask them what will help them do a better job.

Robert Rosner, California Job Journal
Newstrack Executive Information Service
www.news-track.com • 800-334-5771

2 Techniques to Succeed: Phone etiquette

Part of doing business means doing business over the phone. Because the phone is such an important instrument in our daily business, below are some helpful hints, and proven phone techniques, that will help to make your phone conversations more effective.

Create a Good First Impression
- Try to answer the phone on the second ring. Answering a phone too fast can catch the caller off guard and waiting too long can make the caller angry.
- Answer with a friendly greeting. (Example – "Good Afternoon, IMT Customer Service, Sherrie speaking, how may I help you").
- Smile – it shows, even through the phone lines.
- Ask the caller for their name, even if their name is not necessary for the call. This shows you have taken an interest in them. Make sure that if you ask for their name, that you use it.
- Speak clearly and slowly. Never talk with anything in your mouth. This includes gum.
- Lower your voice if you normally speak loud.
- Keep the phone two-finger widths away from your mouth.

Putting Callers on Hold
When putting a caller on hold, always ask permission. If they ask why, provide them with the answer.

Examples:

"Would you mind holding while I get your file?"

"Can you hold briefly while I see if Mr. Jones is available?"

When taking a caller off of hold, always thank them for holding.

Transferring a Caller
1. If the caller needs to speak to another person or department, please transfer the caller directly to the desired person's extension, not to the operator. This will save the caller having to explain his/her requests another time, and it will cut the number of times the caller needs to be transferred.
2. When transferring a caller, tell them who you are transferring them to, and announce the caller to the person you are transferring them to.

Taking Phone Messages
When taking a phone message for someone, always be sure to include the following information:

- Caller's name and company name if applicable.
- Time and date of call.
- What the call is regarding.
- If the caller wants a return phone call, and if so,
- Obtain a phone number that is best for the return.

Last Impressions
- Before hanging up, be sure that you have answered all the caller's questions.
- Always end with a pleasantry: "Have a nice day" or "It was nice speaking with you."
- Let the caller hang up first. This shows the caller that you weren't in a hurry to get off the phone with them.

Azusa Pacific University – Azusa, Calif. Read more at www.apu.edu/imt/telecom/etiquette.php

3 Techniques to Succeed: Be interview ready

Looking for a new job can be stressful, but once you get an interview, landing the job could come down to a few minor details.

- Lack of preparation – this runs the gamut from not knowing anything about the organization or the job you're interviewing for, to arriving late and not dressing appropriately for the interview. Research the firm on the Web, learn all you can about what it does. Also, get directions ahead of time and arrive at least 15 minutes early.
- Being unprepared for difficult questions – you need to prepare for any type of question, from "Tell me what you know about our firm" to "Describe your most difficult work scenario and how you handled it."

Think about potential questions and prepare yourself to have a response.

- Not having questions prepared for the interviewer – a good interview should be a conversation between the interviewer and the applicant.

A few questions you can ask include: Why is this position open? Where are you in your hiring process? Tell me about your experience here at XYZ company?

Dawn Anthony - Director with OfficeTeam Division of Robert Half International
800-804-8367

4 Techniques to Succeed: Resolving client reluctance

Here is a five-step process to help resolve client conflict:

- Anticipate objections. When preparing presentations or proposals, keep in mind any issues the client might raise – anything they may have said or might say now. Have a planned response.
- Listen carefully. Show your value as a problem-solver to the client by listening closely to their concerns. Never interrupt or get defensive – work with them.
- Understand the objection. If you are not 100 percent clear about the client's objection, ask questions. Always check your understanding by restating the problem in your own words.
- Answer questions fully and honestly. Issues aren't resolved by being evasive, by manipulating the client or by misrepresenting your intensions. Always preface answers by showing you under-

stand that the concern is legitimate from the client's viewpoint. After responding, confirm that you've dealt with the objection and that the client has no other questions.
- Be flexible. Try to resolve an objection by staying flexible in your proposals. Partner with your client to reach agreement.

The more skilled you are in resolving objections, the more satisfied your clients will be.

www.dalecarnegie.com

Tips to Succeed: Know your audiences

"Keep your friends close and your enemies closer."

Advice from many successful CEOs and CCOs

Tips to Succeed: Be a team player

When interviewing for a position, it is always important to talk about the success you've achieved with the help of others. This discussion will inevitably lead to how you've also helped others achieve their goals. Companies like to hire people they can count on to work well with others. You are trying to fit into an already existing puzzle. You need to prove that you are willing to help others succeed and are willing to take advice and assistance from your new co-workers.

Steven Malloy - Career Counselor - University of Colorado

Tips to Succeed: Know where you are headed!

"It's okay to hit the ground running, just make sure you are going in the right direction."

Tips to Succeed: Online resources can improve writing

Writing well is more than just knowing the basics. A well-written letter, proposal or brochure could make or break a sale.

If you are not the best writer, the Internet offers many resources for helping create well-crafted materials.

These websites can help you with business or personal writing.

- www.onelook.com – An online resource where you can search almost 1,000 dictionaries.
- www.bartleby.com/100 – A listing of familiar quotations so you can find just the right phrase for the "write" occasion.
- www.c2.com/cgi/wiki?ChicagoManualOfStyle – The online home of the "Chicago Manual of Style" answers frequently asked questions about style.
- thesaurus.com – The online version of Roget's New Millennium Thesaurus helps you locate the right word for the idea you're trying to express.

Andrea C.Carrero - Word Technologies Inc., Cherry Hill, N.J. - 856-428-0925

Tips to Succeed: A user-friendly website

So many people flock to the Web that if your website is not user-friendly you may be sending potential clients elsewhere.

Here are some hints to assure your website is right for business:

- Can visitors find information easily?
- Is the navigation clear and consistent throughout the site?
- Can visitors easily find your contact information?
- Do the pages load quickly on a standard modem connection? Many users still have dial-up service.
- Are the most important elements of your site visible without scrolling up and down or side to side on computer monitors set to the 600 X 800 resolution size?
- Does the site look good and work with Netscape® and Internet Explorer® browsers?
- Can the visitor identify what your business does or what products you sell?

Research is clear, frustrated visitors leave difficult to navigate sites and may not return.

10 Tips to Succeed: Economical business trips

Business travel can cost a whole lot – or – a lot less. With a little planning, you can keep costs down.

Given today's technology – email, phones, websites – you may think the best way to save money on business travel is to just stay home. Wrong! Nothing beats the power of a face-to-face meeting for closing a deal or maintaining an ongoing client relationship.

It pays to be aware of costs and alternatives before booking a hotel, rental car or airline ticket.

In my years as a frequent traveler, here are a few money-saving business travel tips I've picked up:

- Use alternate airports
- Check low-cost airlines
- Shop prices on the Internet, but also call hotels directly
- Check the airlines' own websites in addition to the major Internet travel sites
- Try moderately-priced, business-oriented motels
- NEVER pick up the hotel phone before you know the charges
- When staying in a sprawling urban area, rent a car
- Use your frequent flier miles for expensive business trips rather than inexpensive leisure travel

Travel is an important and necessary part of business life. Don't avoid it, but don't spend more than you have to either.

Rhonda Abrams - www.rhondaworks.com/

11 Tips To Succeed: Five C's of Credit – Essential to obtaining a business loan

Looking for a loan? Be ready to show the bank you have the five C's of credit.

Character – This includes personal finances, how you're viewed in the industry, what's on your credit report. If there are discrepancies in your credit report, be up front and explain. Do not try to hide them.

Capacity – How much debt can your business handle? What will be the debt to income ratio? Make sure the loan will help your business, not break your business.

Capital – This is your businesses' cash flow.

Conditions – This would explain what the loan is going to be used for. This includes start-up costs, equipment and inventory. This also includes external effects on your business, such as market trends, government regulations or the weather.

Collateral – This is a second form of guarantee to the bank which includes the business property, inventory and personal assets such as your home.

Heather Mihal - Assistant Vice President - Hudson United Bank

12 Tips To Succeed: Mind your Manners for a good first impression

It takes only three to five seconds to make a first impression, but it can take a whole career to undo it. Here's what you should keep in mind during those first fateful moments to make a positive impression at an interview, conference, party or any other time you meet new faces.

The tardiness taboo

The most important guideline is the most fundamental: Don't be late. Ever.

Figure out how long it takes to get to your meeting point and allow extra time. It's better to arrive early than risk tardiness. For interviews and other important events, do a practice run in advance to clock the drive and make sure you know the route.

If you arrive more than 10 minutes ahead of schedule, take a short walk before going inside. Arriving too early can rattle the person you're meeting.

Appearances

It's an unfortunate fact of human nature that before you even say hello, people form an opinion of you based on how you look.

In business settings, look sharp by dressing slightly more formally than the people you're meeting with. Avoid distracting accents, like excessive jewelry or a goofy tie.

Your clothes should not draw attention to you. And don't leave a bad impression by forgetting the rear view.

Check the back of your clothes in the mirror for rips and stains. Make sure you're tucked in where you should be. Also examine the back of your shoes for mud splashes or worn-down heels.

Presenting yourself

At events where you have a chance to make new contacts, take a proactive approach. Peter Post (Emily's grandson) says, "Go in with an attitude that says you're going to participate, you're going to be willing to go up and introduce yourself to people and start conversations."

It takes guts to approach strangers, but if you do it with charm, those you meet will be impressed by your sociability.

Post recommends four actions to ensure a positive first impression:

- Stand up to get on eye level with the person.
- Look them in the eye.
- Give a firm handshake, but don't "bone crush" them. Keep your shoulders and feet oriented toward the person.
- Repeat the person's name and say you're pleased to meet them. Fine-tune and rehearse your self-introduction, a 10-second or less sound-bite (elevator speech) that includes your first and last name and a snippet of background information to kindle conversation. Example: Hello, I'm Denise Kersten, a careers columnist for USATODAY.com.

Making connections

Introducing others will make you seem gracious and well connected, but be sure to follow the proper protocol.

In social situations the order in which you introduce two people is based on gender and age (women and older people first).

In business settings the order is determined by rank.

Introduce the lower-ranking person to the higher-ranking person, then reverse the order, so you say each person's name two times. Try to add an interesting tidbit to start the conversation. If you were introducing Mrs. Smith, a vice president of the company, to Mr. Jones, a junior associate, for example, you might say:

If you are unsure who the more important person is, default to the gender and age guideline.

Don't panic if you forget a name. Most people will be happy to remind you and appreciate the introduction.

Chit chat

Conversation is more like a tennis match than a golf game. Hitting the ball too many times in a row is a serious faux pas. Instead, try to establish a back-and-forth volley.

Asking questions about the other person's background and mentioning that interesting item you read in the newspaper are tried-and-true chat starters or icebreakers. Stay away from politically charged or sensitive topics with people you've just met.

Also avoid alienating individuals with different professional backgrounds.

Stay away from industry language and acronyms. It may make you feel plugged in, but it can turn-off uninitiated listeners.

If you succeed at establishing rapport with a new contact, you may ask for their business card and offer yours. But only do so in the context of building a mutually-beneficial relationship, or you may come across as pushy.

The recovery

We all make etiquette slip-ups from time to time. Even Peter Post admits to the occasional oversight. But you can minimize the damage with a sincere apology.

"Acknowledge your mistake. Don't try to put it off on somebody else. Accept it as your mistake. Then correct it," Post says.

For the less serious offenses a simple "excuse me" goes a long way.

Denise Kersten - USATODAY.com
Dana May Casperson - Author of Power Etiquette: What You Don't Know Can Kill Your Career

13 Tips to Succeed:
Ad placement matters on the Web

According to Google, ads placed in particular areas of a (home) page will get noticed. The hottest spot for advertisers is in the middle of a page. Ads above the fold are also good. The fold is jargon for how much of a Web page a person sees without having to scroll down. But if a person must scroll to read an entire article, all hope is not lost. Advertisements at the end of articles perform well. That's because people want to do something else after reading an article.

Gannett News Service

14 Techniques to Succeed: Make the most of your ads

Give your proposed ad to several different people and ask them what product you are selling. Would it entice them to find out more, or even purchase your product?

Hand someone your flier and ask them to find your contact information. See how long it takes. If it takes them longer than five seconds, you need to make it bigger, or make the flier less busy. Hand someone your flier and have them look at it for five seconds. Then hide the flier and ask them what the flier said. If they had no idea, then your ad or flier is poorly written or too cluttered. Does the ad or flier excite the reader to call or buy? This can be done with a special offer, a discount, or something for FREE.

Fred Hueston and Lyna Farkas – Hosts of the radio show "Growing Your Business" – www.growingyourbusiness.net

15 Tips to Succeed: Six tips for keeping PR pitches out of newsroom recycle bins

The whole attachment business when emailing reporters is a huge deal — don't send unsolicited attachments. Attachments could shut email down because the system gets clogged.

These tips might help ensure that your email pitches don't get tossed — and help you boost your pickup rate among the media you target:

1. Hook journalists with brevity and timeliness. The best emails are the ones that are brief and that have great subject lines. That means the subject line conveys "just the facts." Like a newspaper headline, it needs to deliver details like "when and where" without going on. The point is to keep it straightforward — e.g., "Teens to Rally at 3:00 p.m. at Capitol Hill." That's good because it [gives] just the 5 W's.

Good subject lines also stress the time frame that we're dealing with. For example, "Labor Day Fashion" works because it has a timely element so the reporter knows he/she has to look at it quickly. Also, it implies you know lead times and deadlines.

2. Carefully consider using humor in subject lines. Another way to keep from [being deleted] is to try something funny. Many time, if your pitch has a fun subject line, curiosity will be piqued. "Teach Your Dog to Meditate" is an example of a catchy subject line that worked (in a pitch) for a book on behavioral tips for animals. But this type of approach is not going to work for everyone.

3. Include surprising numbers or factoids to grab attention. Using numbers, statistics and facts is another good way to make sure an email stands out. For example, the National Housing Conference sent me an email pitch, "U.S. Housing Prices Rise 20% Nationwide." It got the reporter's attention.

4. Work email pitches in tandem with phone calls. Emails can make a phone call not a cold call and vice versa. A great thing to do is to call in advance and say you're going to send me an email later. Include something like "Maria, per our phone call" in the subject line so the reporter knows it's not a blanket pitch or cold call.

5. Be prepared to answer questions via email or phone.
A lot of PR people aren't that prepared to answer questioned when following up on emails or phone pitches. That's not good. When good reporters have a PR person on the phone, they'll ask questions right then while pulling up the email pitch so they can see if they are interested right at that moment. If you don't have answers, it's a waste of time.

6. Stay flexible — play off your target's comments for greater buy-in. Equally important: Flexibility is key because it may be that the story you're pitching isn't the one that's going to get published. Maybe a different story will come out — one that still highlights your client, but in a different way than you expected. In other words, reporters can feel it when a PR person is reading from a script. They don't want to get off the scripted pitch — and so they don't give the reporter a chance to get into it. Don't be one of those PR "people."

Here is some advice: "Listen to the reporter's reaction. At least, consider where we may be coming from on an idea. Listen and then consider sharing (the reporter's) ideas with the client. Be open to expanding upon the ideas you pitched. For example, I might grab onto a phrase you say in passing that seems to have real news value — and then ask you to pursue that in more detail. If you allow for it and practice (active listening), then these pitches can become (collaborative)."

Maria Stainer - Assistant Managing Editor - The Washington Times

16 Techniques to Succeed: Budgeting – beyond the basics

1. Budgets are a necessary evil.
They're the only practical way to get a grip on your spending so you can make sure your money is being used the way you want it to be used.

2. Creating a budget generally requires three steps.
- Identify how you spend money now.
- Evaluate your current spending and set goals that take into account your financial objectives.
- Track your spending to make sure it stays within those guidelines.

3. Use software to save grief
- Quicken®
- Microsoft Money®

4. Don't drive yourself nuts.
Once you determine which categories of spending can and should be cut (or expanded), concentrate on those categories and worry less about other aspects of your spending.

5. Watch out for cash leakage.
If withdrawals from the ATM machine evaporate from your pocket without apparent explanation, it's time to keep better records.

6. Spending beyond your limits is dangerous.
But if you do, you've got plenty of company – but it's definitely a sign you need to make some serious spending cuts.

7. Beware of luxuries dressed up as necessities.
If your income doesn't cover your costs, then some of your spending is probably for luxuries – even if you've been considering them to be filling a real need.

8. Tithe yourself.
Aim to spend no more than 90 percent of your income. That way, you'll have the other 10 percent left to save for your big-picture items.

9. Don't count on windfalls.
When projecting the amount of money you can live on, don't include dollars that you can't be sure you'll receive, such as year-end bonuses, tax refunds or investment gains.

10. Beware of spending creep.
As your annual income climbs from raises, promotions and smart investing, don't start spending for luxuries until you're sure that you're staying ahead of inflation.

www.money.cnn.com/pf/101/lessons/2/

17 Technique to Succeed: Business dining: Dos and don'ts

Some tips to help make your business dinner successful:
- Have fun, but remain professional.
- Dress appropriately.
- Pick the right restaurant for your affair, making sure the atmosphere fits the tone of your business outing. If you are looking to have a quiet business dinner, and don't want to be disturbed by other diners, look for a place with private rooms or a very quiet environment.
- Go to a restaurant with which you are familiar. It's not the best idea to go somewhere that you have never been before.
- Make reservations in advance – not the day of a business dinner. You're usually safe on the same day during the week, but if you have a larger party you may be out of luck.
- Limit the alcohol.
- Order food you like. Don't order because of someone else.
- Make sure you have enough credit on your credit card if you are paying the bill.
- Always take care of your server.

Jim Haney - General Manager - Palm Restaurant - Atlantic City NJ
Courier-Post – Monday, April 4, 2005

18 Technique to Succeed: Business angels – bearing cash for business

Business angels are private funders of start-up or growing businesses. They fill the role venture capitalists filled 20 years ago. Now venture capitalists generally will only fund companies that can grow huge, investing a minimum of a few million dollars. That leaves a big gap in funding for early-stage companies, the type needing $200,000, not $20 million. Angels fill that gap.

In 2004, angels actually invested more money in new companies than venture capitalists – a whopping $22.5 billion in angel funds, compared with $18 billion in venture capital. According to the Center for Venture Research at the University of New Hampshire, 48,000 companies received funding from 225,000 active angel investors.

The primary distinction between angels and venture capitalists is that angels invest their own money. They don't have to justify their investments to others, so they invest in a broader variety of businesses. They can have more patience in getting a return on their money, and they can invest in ideas that are just plain interesting, exciting or fun. Most are successful entrepreneurs themselves, so they understand and appreciate what business people are going through.

Why would a private foundation spend money to organize groups of private investors?

To find out or to find your own angel, check the directory on the Angel Capital Association website, www.angelcapitalassociation.org. For assistance in forming an angel group in your community, contact the Kauffman Foundation, www.kauffman.org.

Courier-Post - Tuesday, May 3, 2005

19 Techniques to Succeed: When you think branding – think:

- Positioning – Where your company or product stands in the marketplace compared to the competition. It might be better to be different than to be better. To be a leader in the marketplace, you have to deliver.

- Promise – States expectationscontract – a simple strategic statement. Promise less, deliver more.

- Pipeline – Delivery systems, interaction – employees, advertising, public relations, communication, suppliers, vendors – from conception to customer service.

- Presentation – Name, logo, slogan, office space, employees, image (if the company is high-tech, it must be using the latest in technology).

- Personality – Emotional values, connecting with the customer–the characteristics of the firm or organization. Much like image–how your audiences perceive you, your products and/or company.

- Propositions – Rational values, claims, results, testimonials, deliverables.

Atlantic City (N.J.) Public Relations Council

20 Techniques to Succeed: The basics of budgeting–for business or personal

Crafting a budget is a must, especially if it is part of a business plan. But it is also important on a personal level. Here are some steps and categories that should be included:

- List all anticipated expenses starting with fixed expenses.
- Review previous years and estimate accordingly.
- Track your spending for a month. That means everything from rent to such incidentals as a pack of gum (include cash, check and credit card purchases).
- Divide by 12 to get a monthly average of your expenses.
- See where you may have gone over and cut accordingly.
- Some categories or line items would include:
    - RentCar
    - Gas
    - Loans
    - Home phone
    - Cell phone
    - Utilities
    - Food
    - Dry cleaning
    - Newspapers
    - Personal items
    - Entertainment
    - Insurance
    - Savings/401K

21 Techniques to Succeed: Establishing a consistent image – building a brand

Brand (v.) = A mental mark of ownership; to impress upon one's memory
- Reinforces the focus of the strategic plan
- Valuable asset (brand equity)
- Personal (brand loyalty and brand insistence)
- Experience (brand familiarity)
- Brand power

Atlantic City (N.J.) Public Relations Council
The Public Relations Practitioner's Playbook for (all) Strategic Communicators
(AuthorHouse - 2013) - M. Larry Litwin, APR, Fellow PRSA

22. Techniques to Succeed: Healthier business travel by car

- Instead of buying roadside meals, pack and take along healthy, travel friendly foods available for take out at many super markets. They would include whole-grain crackers, fruit, vegetables (baby carrots, plum tomatoes) and lean sandwiches.
- To avoid overeating, plan designated eating times and don't skip meals. Stop at a rest area to sit and eat your meals even if you have brought your own food.
- Curb boredom snacking by listening to audio books and making frequent stops to stretch.
- Drink bottled water or sugar-free beverages. Coffee and tea drinkers should add their own creamer and sweetener instead of purchasing such high-calorie specialty drinks as lattes and blender drinks.
- At restaurants, order salads and grilled chicken rather than burgers, French fries and fried chicken. Ask for low-fat dressings.

Nikki and David Goldbeck - Healthy Highways - Ceres Press-2004

23. Techniques to Succeed: Helpful budgeting guidelines

1. Know the cost of what you propose to buy.
2. Communicate the budget in terms of what it costs to achieve specific results.
3. Use the power of your computer to manage the program.

24. Tips to Succeed: Belt and suspenders

Always have a back up. For example, radio reporters having a second tape recorder or a photographer having a second camera with them in case the first fails. Many times, television anchors and/or newsmakers wear two lapel microphones plugged into two different amplifiers – one serving as a back up.

25. Tips to Succeed: The benefits of hiring a public relations or advertising agency

The agency-client partnership is the dominant organizational arrangement in public relations and advertising.

Full service or niche agencies:
- Offer objective advice.
- Draw on the collective experience and training of its staff.
- Provide people and management skills to accomplish advertising objectives.
- Provide supportive environment for professional advertising people.

In-house agencies:
- Handle most, if not all, of the functions of an outside agency.
- Provide more control for the advertiser over the costs and time schedule.
- Available for quick response and turn-around.
- Receive standard agency discounts
- May have a greater awareness of the company, products and services.

William Wells - John Burnett - Sandra Moriarty - Advertising Principles and Practice - (Prentice Hall)

26. Techniques to Succeed: A lasting behavioral change

One of PR's most effective approaches is to accomplish change by having members of the public persuade themselves after considering the issues and hearing the arguments (strategic messages).

27 Technique to Succeed: Annual Reports – Reading ease

Many company annual reports are difficult to read – and now we know why.

A study by suggests that annual reports of firms with lower earnings are harder to read – on purpose.

A study of more than 50,000 annual reports used two measures of readability:

- The Fog Index, which indicates the number of years of formal education a reader of average intelligence would need to read and understand a text.
- The Flesch-Kincaid Index, which rates text on a U.S. grade-school level.

The average Fog Index for all annual reports was a deplorable 19.4 (a score of 12-14 is ideal and higher than 18 is unreadable). In the same way, the annual report readability score on the Kincaid Index was 15.2 – about twice as high as the optimal score of 7 to 8.

Feng Li - Assistant professor of accounting - University of Michigan

28 Techniques to Succeed: Bad with names?

Listen. Make sure you hear a name clearly and can pronounce it correctly. Never proceed past an initial introduction unless you are certain you can pronounce their name correctly. If necessary, ask the person to repeat his or her name. If the name is an unusual one, ask the person how to spell it. Uncertainty over a name will become an instant distraction.

Repeat their name. If you did not hear their name clearly, simply ask them to repeat his or her name to you. After hearing the name correctly, use it in a sentence a few times – especially early in a meeting. You can also repeat the person's name to yourself several times to get it fixed in your mind. Not only will this help you retain their name, it will also inspire confidence and reassure the other person that you're interested and paying attention to the conversation.

Relate their name to physical characteristics. Get a distinct impression of the person. Note physical characteristics. Listen to the person's voice. Try to "visualize" the personality. Start noting characteristics that formulate the first impression. Make an association based on any unique physical characteristics. "Visualize" their personality and form a mental picture based on sight, sound and the impression you get from them.

Attach their name with something or somebody famous. Associate the person's name with a word picture that's colorful, action-oriented and possibly even exaggerated. Any image that instantly triggers the recall of a person's name will be of valuable assistance. You can also think of a famous person too.

Anita Zinsmeister - President - Dale Carnegie Training of Central and Southern N.J. - Dale Carnegie Training - ww.southjersey.dalecarnegie.com

29 Tips to Succeed: Be a better manager

Reward good work: Appreciate employees for a job well done to encourage continued good work. Make sure your compliments are spontaneous to avoid predictability. More specific comments mean more than a generic "good job."

Make everyday heroes: For those who've consistently performed well, make sure to spread the word throughout the company about their good work. Make them examples for other employees.

Avoid negativity: Don't indulge in office gossip or negative conversations. It's hard to create a positive environment if you're bashing others.

Find solutions, not problems: Rather than blaming employees for mistakes or problems, motivate them to seek out solutions.

Dr. Noelle Nelson - Author - The Power of Appreciation in Business

30 Tips to Succeed: Know your etiquette in business settings

Dining out with your boss or a client is your chance to make a good impression.

• Can I drink soda or beer from the bottle?

No. Use a glass.

• What if I am served something that I don't know how to eat?

Watch your host and do what he or she does. You may not be right, but you won't be wrong. And when you do have a choice of foods, don't order anything that you don't know how to eat.

- Is it OK to kiss colleagues in business social situations?

The handshake is the proper business greeting in most business and business social situations. Yet there can be situations where kissing may be OK, depending upon:

A. Your relationship with the person. If people know each other well, they may kiss at business social events.

B. The type of company you work for. Large, formal, or conservative companies usually have less kissing than smaller, creative or informal types of companies.

C. The type of business functions you attend. Company picnics may be more relaxed and informal than business dinners at a fancy restaurant.

D. When in doubt, shake hands.

Barbara Pachter - Author - When The Little Things Count...And They Always Count

31 Tips to Succeed: Boost a small firm's image

Small companies have the same goals as larger companies: more sales, greater productivity, higher profit, enhanced image and widespread recognition. Small businesses, however, have the disadvantage when it comes to image. Below are some ways to increase the image and success of your small business.

Maximize person-to-person communications. Clients will feel more important when they talk to a real person rather than an answering service. Your prospect's image of you becomes very different when a live person answers your phone.

Get an 800 number. A toll-free number communicates success. Callers like your willingness to pay for them to reach you.

Get a website. Even if it starts out very basic, get a website set up and list the address on your business cards and letterhead.

Kill your larger competition by responding to a client automatically.

Be personable with your prospects and clients.

Do not use regular stamps. Established businesses use postage machines.

Get out of the house. Conduct business in an environment that allows you to collaborate, socialize and exchange ideas and business opportunities. Even solo entrepreneurs must get out there and be with other business people.

Roger Kahn - President - Intelligent Office - New York, N.Y.

32 Techniques to Succeed: The communication audit

1. **What is a communication audit?**
   It is a complete analysis of an organization's communication program – a picture of its goal, objectives, strategies, tactics and evaluations.

2. **What is the scope of an audit?**
   The scope of an audit may be as broad and as deep as the size and complexity of the organization's demands. The audit can measure the effectiveness of communication programs throughout an entire organization, in a single division or department, or within a specific employee group.

3. **What does the communication audit provide?**
   It provides meaningful information to members of management concerned with efficiency, credibility, and economy of their communications policies, practices, and programs. It also provides valuable data for developing or restructuring communications functions, guidelines, and budgets, as well as recommendations for action tailored to an organization's particular situation as uncovered by an analysis of the collected data.

4. **When should an audit be conducted?**
   Generally, an extensive audit should be conducted every five to seven years. In the interim, reliable feedback techniques should be obtained periodically through the organization's routine communication function.

5. **What subjects are covered?**
   Typically an audit covers such areas as:

- Communication philosophy
- Objectives and goals
- Existing communication programs
- Existing vehicles and their uses
- Personal communications
- Meetings
- Attitudes toward existing communications
- Needs and expectations

Joseph A. Kopec - Kopec Associates Inc., Chicago, Illinois Read more at www.prsa.org/_Resources/resources/commaudit.asp?ident=rsrc3

33 Tips to Succeed: Cell phone etiquette

The cell phone etiquette guide: **Lights off, phone off!**
No one should take a call at a theater or in the movies.

Off means off!
Respect the rules and when asked by an establishment or airline to refrain from using a cell phone, do so.

Don't cross the personal space boundary!
Everyone should be mindful of how close they are to others when using a cell phone in a public place.

Stop noise pollution!
Remember to keep conversations private and not shout into the phone.

Heads up!
Act responsibly when walking or driving while on a cell phone. Many states now have laws for cell phone use in or on motor vehicles.

www.letstalk.com/promo/unclecell/unclecell2.htm

34 Tips to Succeed: Credit Card Act protects you

Have you ever purchased a product only to find it is damaged or poorly made and the merchant refuses to replace it or give you a refund? If you paid with a credit card, you may be in luck.

The Fair Credit Billing Act gives consumers the right to withhold payment on poor-quality or damaged merchandise purchased with a credit card.

What you need to do:

- First, try to resolve the problem with the merchant. Try to take the merchandise back.
- Put your complaint in writing and send via certified mail to the merchant. Keep two copies.
- Contact the credit card company and alert them to the disputed purchase amount.

- Send a letter to the credit card company explaining the disputed purchase.
  - Enclose a copy of your complaint letter to the merchant and any other documentation you may have. Send your letter by certified mail, return receipt requested, to the address for "billing inquiries" and not the one for payments.
- Follow up.

The caveats? The sale must be for more than $50 and have taken place in your home state or within 100 miles of your home address. While few issuers enforce the criteria, they are all free to do so.

Also, you need to act within 60 days after a disputed charge was billed.

If the card company sides with the merchant, you'll have to pay for the disputed item, plus any finance charges. If they side with you, you're not out a dime.

www.bankrate.com

35 Tips to Succeed:
Credit cards – Read those notices

Most people just throw them away. But those annoying mailers you receive about "important changes" to your credit card are actually valuable. You don't want to be surprised when your interest rate suddenly rises.

When you get such a notice, read it carefully, looking for:

- New or increased penalties for paying off your balance.
- Cutbacks in rebate programs, etc.
- Shorter waiting period before payments are late.
- Higher late charges.
- Penalty interest rate if you're late making payments.

www.checklists.com

36 Tips to Succeed: Understanding your credit report

A credit report is basically divided into four sections:

- Identifying information. Simply, this is information used to identify you. Besides your name and Social Security number, the report may include your current and previous addresses, date of birth, telephone number, driver's license number, employer and spouse's name.

- Credit history. Each account will include the name of the creditor and the account number, which may be scrambled for security purposes. Each entry will include account history, payment detail, balance and limit detail, and how well you've paid the account.

- Public records. This section, ideally, should be blank. It lists bankruptcies, judgments and tax liens, which all can damage your credit faster than anything else.

- Inquiries. A list of everyone who asked to see your credit report. Most inquiries are ignored by FICO scoring models and do not damage a credit score.

www.crediteducation.org

37 Tips to Succeed: 'Credit Killers' – 5 common mistakes that can ruin a credit score

- Staying out of debt: Having no credit history is nearly as bad as having a poor credit history, because creditors have no way to judge how the person will handle a loan.

- Rate shopping: Too many inquiries can damage a credit score. Generally, six or more inquiries within six months will scare a lender. Transferring balances on credit cards can negatively affect a score for the same reason.

- Assuming there's a grace period: If a payment is even one day overdue, it's late, and even one late payment can lower a credit score.

- Closing old accounts: It seems smart to close unused accounts, but it can actually shorten a person's credit history by lowering the credit score.

- Cosigning on a loan: Cosigning has many risks and little reward, because the primary borrower's mistakes will end up on both signers' credit reports. Just say no every time.

Centers for Financial Education, a division of Consumer Credit Counseling Services of New Jersey www.crediteducation.org

38. Techniques to Succeed: Convince vs. persuade

A person is convinced by evidence or argument made to the intellect (head). A person is persuaded by appeals made to the will, moral sense, or emotions (heart).

Convincing is long term – persuading is (for now) short term.

When you convince someone, you actually get them to believe something else.

When you persuade someone, you get them to act without convincing them.

39. Techniques To Succeed: Increase business by cold calling

A "cold call" is a sales call – on the phone or in person – when the person you're calling has not approached you or expressed interest in your products or services.

"Cold calls" can be effective, especially if potential leads are found through effective, unbiased research. If a business is stagnant, or is developing a new product or service line, cold calls can be a relatively inexpensive way to attract new customers.

What's the secret of cold call success?

- Change your perspective. "Cold calls" can help someone rather than be a "bother."
- "Qualify" your leads. Narrow your target list.
- Listen: Find out what your prospect wants and needs.
- Develop a great pitch. Be clear about what you are offering and the benefits to the customer.
- Take people literally. If a prospect says, "I'm not interested right now," believe they mean right NOW. Perhaps they'll be interested another time.
- Don't be obnoxious: Take "No" for an answer. If someone is not interested, why waste your time or theirs?
- Mind your manners: If you walk in on someone and they're on the phone, wait until they are free. If you're phoning, and the person says "Now's not a good time," ask when a good time would be to call

back, and get off the phone.
- Give yourself a quota. Set a minimum – but realistic – number of calls you have to make before you can call it quits for the day. Stick to it.
- Stay in practice. Cold calling is difficult, and it's easy to forget how to do it well.

Don't take rejection personally and don't get discouraged.
Remember, you've got to kiss a lot of frogs before you find a prince.

Rhonda Abrams - www.rhondaworks.com/

Tips to Succeed:
Cover letters: Get to the point

Whether pitching an account or applying for a job, an effective cover letter is a must.

- Immediate attention is given to pitches and resumes with good cover letters
- First paragraph must be a grabber (reader will spend, on average, 15-30 seconds on first glance)
- Say what you mean
- Mean what you say
- Keep it short – but specific
- Keep it conversational
- Ask for what you want
- If applying for job
  - The job posting or vacancy reference number, if one is given in the advertisement
  - Your precise areas of relevance and expertise (bullet points are fine)
  - Your full contact information – including telephone numbers
    Never forget this rule:
    If you wouldn't say it in normal speech, don't write it.

Maury Z. Levy - www.levywarren.com
David Carter - www.job-hunting-tips.com

41 Techniques to Succeed: Knowing how to correspond

Whether you have just met someone, or have known the person for some time, it is important to follow-up meetings with written correspondence.

A. Write a follow-up letter/thank-you note within 48 hours.
1. Whether a handwritten note or formal letter always follow guidelines for writing effective business letters.
    1. Women should be addressed as "Ms." no matter what their marital status.
    2. Do not forget to sign your letter.
    3. Always proof for typos and misspellings.
2. Letters usually contain the following elements:
    1. Opener – the opener should be friendly and tells the reader why you are writing.
    2. Justification – the second paragraph reinforces or justifies what you are looking for and why you should get it.
    3. Closing – close the letter by seeking the person to act on your behalf or request.

Email etiquette has some specific guidelines.
1. Email is appropriate to use, but never use all caps and watch for typos.
2. Always include a subject line in your message.
3. Make the subject line meaningful.
4. Use correct grammar and spelling.
5. Always use a signature if you can; make sure it identifies who you are and includes alternate means of contacting you (phone and fax are useful).
6. Use active words instead of passive.
7. Do not ask to recall a message.
8. Use proper structure and layout
9. Avoid long sentences.
10. Be concise and to the point.

More and more, proper business etiquette is viewed as an important part of making a good impression. These visible signals are essential to your professional success.

The Career Center - Florida State University
www.career.fsu.edu/ccis/guides/etiquette.html

42 Techniques to Succeed: In front of the camera

Unless you are an expert in front of the camera, DO NOT look directly into the camera. Look at the interviewer or if the interviewer is remote, pick a spot that is slightly off-camera.

If there is a TV monitor within view, ask that it be removed or placed out of view. If that cannot be done, DO NOT look at the monitor at all.

If you must look into the lens of the camera, pretend that the person who you most want to convince is behind that lens. If that makes you uncomfortable, then pretend that your mother, best friend, daughter or son, or anyone else you feel comfortable with is behind that lens.

43 Techniques to Succeed: Dollar Bill Test

The Dollar Bill Test is simple: take a dollar bill and turn it on a page of copy. To pass the Dollar Bill Test, it must touch at least one copybreaker. If it does, your publication passes. If not, you fail.

Rowan (N.J.) University Professor Claudia Cuddy has her own list of copybreakers to assure publications pass the Dollar Bill Test:
- Heads
- Subheads
- Pull quotes (Blurbs)
- Rules
- Initial (or drop) caps
- Shaded (screened) boxes
- Pictures
- Art (line art)
- Bullet lists

Tips to Succeed: Communicating with older people

Communicating with older people often requires extra time and patience because of physical, psychological and social changes.

Some suggestions:
- Reduce background noises.
- Talk about familiar subjects.
- Keep your sentences short.
- Give the person a chance to reminisce.
- Allow extra time for a response.

Tips to Succeed: When a crisis strikes– communicate early and often

- Contact the media before they contact you
- Communicate internally – then externally
- Put the public first
- Take responsibility
- Be honest
- Never say "No comment"
- Designate a single spokesperson
- Set up a central information center (staging area)
- Provide a constant flow of information
- Be familiar with media needs and deadlines
- Be accessible
- Monitor news coverage and telephone inquiries
- Communicate with key publics
- Be accessible

46 Tips to Succeed: When a crisis strikes – learn from the best

- Don't duck the issue
- Take responsibility
- Offer to make good on broken promises
- Cover all the bases
- Measure results

Delahaye Medialink Worldwide

47 Tips to Succeed: Bill Jones' 10 Commandments of Crisis Communication

1. Perception is reality. If your audience thinks it is, it is.
2. Response is control. The community wants access to information, and no crisis is unmanageable if you give clear, cool facts.
3. Information is power.
4. Credibility is survival.
5. Body language is crucial. If you behave like you have something to hide, people will think that you do.
6. Calmness is essential. Unflappability is your best asset. Always act knowledgeable and calm.
7. Give a confession. The public and the media want a confession; so don't be afraid to admit mistakes.
8. Tell the franchise what happened. It is in the best interest of the community to keep them informed.
9. Preparation is 99% of success.
10. Out of every crisis comes the chance to "build a better mousetrap." From every crisis there are major lessons to be learned.
11. Pray like hell that you never have to handle numbers 1 through 10!

J. William Jones - Former School Information Services Director
Philadelphia School District

48 Tips to Succeed: David Ogilvy's Advertising Tenets

- "Never write an advertisement you wouldn't want your own family to read."
- "The most important decision is how to position your product."
- If nobody reads or looks at the ads, "it doesn't do much good to have the right positioning."
- "Big ideas are usually simple ideas."
- Every word in the copy must "count."

David Ogilvy - Founder - Ogilvy and Mather

49 Tips to Succeed: Credit Report vs. Consumer Report

Credit Report – Summarizes historical financial information collected to determine an individual's or an entity's credit worthiness – the means and willingness to repay an indebtedness.

Consumer Report – Information on a consumer's character, general reputation, personal characteristics, or mode of living obtained through personal interviews with neighbors, friends, or associates of the consumer reported on or with others with whom he is acquainted or who may have knowledge concerning any such items of information. The information does not, necessarily, include specific factual information on a consumer's credit record.

50 Techniques to Succeed: Cracked Egg Persuasion Model

8. Mass Sentiment

1. Mass Sentiment

7. Social Action Based On

5. Time Between Debate and Decision

2. Incident Issue

3. Publics Pro/Con

51 Technique to Succeed: Stretching your cash

Here are some tips for stretching the cash from your first real job.
- Create a budget. Know what's coming in and what's going out.
- Match your company's 401(k) contribution.
- Pay down your credit card debt.
- Create an emergency fund to cover at least three months of living expenses. One idea: Start with the cash gifts from graduation.
- Automatically deposit a portion of your paycheck into a savings account.
- Repay your student loans on time.
- Be thrifty. Make your lunch. Watch for sales. Monitoring your cell phone bill.

Courier-Post - Camden, N.J. - July 7, 2005

52 Tips to Succeed: Get yourself ready for a career move

The average American stays at a job for only four years.

Here are important steps to take while you're not job hunting to further your career.

- Develop your career plan and goals.
- Make a list of 40 to 60 contacts you would like to keep in touch with or meet. Some of these people can help you in years to come.
- Attend meetings of professional organizations to boost net working. Accept leadership roles within these organizations.
- Build your reputation by public speaking and writing for publications.
- Take courses or teach them — continue learning.
- Review your resume and try to add new accomplishments every six months.
- Every year, assess where you are in your career and set new goals in writing.
- Do an annual checkup with a career coach and revise your longterm plan. Using the coach as a sounding board can help you achieve perspective in your career.

The Five O'Clock Club – A career coaching network – New York, N.Y.

53 Tips to Succeed: Cell phone guidelines

Cell phone use at work can be annoying to co-workers and inappropriate. Here are guidelines every professional with a cell phone needs to know:

- Do not use inappropriate songs as your ring, such as TV theme songs or current pop songs.
- Avoid making sensitive or confidential business calls or mention the names of clients in trains, restaurants or any public setting.
- Don't use your cell phone to send messages or surf the Web during meetings.
- Don't wear more than one wireless device on your body.
- Avoid walking around work while talking on your cell phone. You need to be meeting and greeting people.
- Do not answer your cell phone when you're having a conversation.

Barbara Pachter - Pachter & Associates Business Communications Training - Cherry Hill, N.J.

54

Techniques to Succeed:
Businesses can learn through osmosis

Jonathan Tisch, chairman and CEO of Loews Hotels, believes the lessons he has learned in the luxury hotel business can be translated to other industries.

The most basic: Turn customers into guests.

At the core of all thriving businesses is a meaningful, long-lasting customer connection.

In the hotel business, for example, he says, "Over the years, I've learned a lot about the art of welcome. Chocolates on the pillow aren't enough."

"It's something all successful hoteliers must master... a skill that virtually every organizational leader must learn, since nowadays, we're all in the business of attracting and keeping customers."

The major stresses facing many kinds of business that are making it harder to retain customers:

- Shrinking brand loyalty.
- Increased price sensitivity.
- More competition.
- Increasing customer knowledge, skepticism and power.

In the spirit of thinking we can all learn from each other. A variety of consumer-driven businesses seem to be getting it right.

The aim is to illustrate how a bank, for instance, might be able to learn good practices from a retailer.

Don't be afraid to learn from seemingly unrelated businesses. These mini-profiles include Commerce Bank, Cherry Hill, N.J.; clothing retailer Urban Outfitters; In-N-Out Burger, Irvine, Calif.; and Duke University Medical Center.

From each vignette, Tisch pulls a series of tips or lessons, called "Your Big Aha's."

Some of the tips are obvious, but worth noting. They include:
- Don't be afraid to stand for something.
- When you find a formula that works, stick with it.
- Adopt the outsider's view of their company.
- Visit your organization's retail outlets, sales offices, or service departments in an unfamiliar town without identifying yourself.
- Call the customer hotline with a complaint, concern or question.
- Visit the website, and try ordering a product or asking a question. Tisch salutes retailer Urban Outfitters for harnessing "the power of welcome to attract customers."

> Jonathan M. Tisch - Chairman and CEO of Loews Hotels and Co-Author (with Karl Weber) - Chocolates on the Pillow Aren't Enough: Reinventing the Customer Experience

55

Techniques to Succeed:
One expert's 'New 4 P's of Marketing'

According to Lior Arussy, president of Strativity Group, Parsippany, N.J. and London, the traditional four P's are being replaced.

The original four P's are Product, Placement, Price and Promotion, but any new product that hits the market today faces significant competition. Arussy suggests that companies who still practice the traditional four P's are usually at-par with their competitors–holding but gaining little ground.

HERE ARE ARUSSY'S FOUR P'S OF MARKETING:
Premium price – If the customers perceive your product as superior, differentiated and worth their business, this will affect your ability to charge a higher or "premium" price for your product. Companies that cannot command price are losing ground and heading towards cost cutting, value depreciation and reduced margins.

Preference of company (or product) – It involves public support and a willingness to refer friends and peers. Thus, customers lend personal credibility to and actually assist the company in selling it. This is measured by how often and how many referrals you receive.

Portion of overall customer budget – When a customer gives more of their budget to your product and/or service than they do to your competitors, it's a sign of commitment.

Permanence of relationship longevity – Based on a personal relationship. It is the ultimate measure of marketing success. The longer a customer stays with a vendor, the deeper and more invested a relationship becomes.

Newstrack Executive Information Service
www.news-track.com - 800-334-5771

56 Tips to Succeed: Getting a handle on debt

According to the Federal Reserve, outstanding consumer credit is at $2.09 trillion, a record high.

Here are a few tips to improve your personal debt.

- Concentrate on paying off the debt with the smallest balance first.
- Move, then, to repaying debts with the highest interest rate. This will allow you to save a significant amount of money in frivolous interest charges over time.
- Be persistent, and responsible. If you find that you are unable to meet your basic financial obligations, contact your creditors immediately to advise them of your situation.

Most will offer an individual short-term solution, but be careful to consider the benefits of a long-term payoff strategy.

www.crediteducation.org

57 Tips to Succeed: Business dining etiquette

You're having dinner with a prospective client. Do you know which fork to use?

OK, so you might not lose a potential deal because you grabbed the wrong utensil to eat your salad, but bad table manners can affect your overall professionalism.

Business etiquette is more than dining. It's also about professional presence and image. Manners and etiquette are not usually taught in school, but necessary to give workers extra "polish." Many of the things are little, but when you put them together they create an impression of you in the workplace, which can work for or against you.

Here are some sample dining etiquette tips:

- No grooming at the table – Don't reapply your lipstick, comb your hair or use your napkin as a tissue.
- Don't lick your utensils or fingers.
- Know your distance – in the United States, average distance between two people in business is about three feet or arm's length. Don't stand too close.

- Never tell ethnic, sexist, religious or racial jokes.
- When dining out, don't launch into a business conversation immediately. Make small talk first. It might be wise to follow the lead of others – unless you are the host.

Barbara Pachter - Pachter & Associates - Author -
When Little Things Count - 856-751-6141
Courier-Post - April 29, 2005

58 Tips to Succeed: Help your employees get the most from their doctor visits

Most people use doctor appointments to confirm that they're sick, but many would benefit if they took them as an opportunity to ensure they're actually well.

Here is a blueprint for getting the most out of any doctor visit:

- Provide family history: Raise your family's health issues with your doctor as they can provide important red flags for preventative treatment.

- Do your homework: Keep a log of your health, including the frequency, duration and intensity of symptoms, and bring it to your visit.

- Define success for drug prescriptions: When prescribed medication ask the following:
  1. Is it OK to drive after I've taken it?
  2. What are the side effects?
  3. How will I know if it's working or not working?
  4. At what point will we re-evaluate its effectiveness and determine whether or not to stay on it?
- Ask questions: Solicit your doctor's opinion of your overall fitness. Most physicians don't offer lifestyle advice such as "lose weight, exercise more," unless the patient has an active medical condition or asks.

Dr. Alan Muney - Pediatrician - Former Chief Medical Officer - Oxford
Health Plans LLC - www.oxhp.com/

59 Techniques to Succeed: Address the mess: A clean desk clears the working mind and the working area

Still looking for last Wednesday's lunch? Before the health department breaks down the door to your office, you might want to think about cleaning your desk.

After all, if, as they say, cleanliness is next to godliness, how does that translate at work? A sloppy desk can stifle your creativity and thinking, make a bad impression on your co-workers, and even make you sick.

To help tackle the mess, we've put together a four-step method that will make cleaning your cube no sweat.

Step 1: Garbage time
First, tackle the mounds of paper littering your desktop. File what you want and toss what's obsolete. Then empty overflowing wastebaskets and recycle those old newspapers.

Step 2: Farewell, germs
Scientists say desktops typically contain more bacteria than a toilet seat. Buy some wipes labeled "disinfecting" or "sanitizing" and clean everything you touch, including your mouse, phone and desk surface.

Step 3: Desk re-org
Place only the bare necessities on your desktop and put away things you only use once or twice a week. Try to reserve at least one drawer for personal items like breath mints and contact solution.

Step 4: Personal touch
Try making a few enhancements to your workspace. Bring in some tasteful pictures of your friends and family or put up a colorful calendar. Bringing some of your personality to work can inspire creativity and demonstrate your commitment to the boss.

Philadelphia Inquirer - May 15, 2005 - www.philly.com/careerbuilder

60 Tips to Succeed: How to safeguard your debit card – from 'phishing' & 'skimming'

Don't respond to unsolicited emails seeking account numbers and passwords: Emails can be disguised as customer-service messages from banks to trick victims into giving up personal financial information. Debit cards are a prime target for these "phishing" scams.

In a typical "phishing" scam, the email will ask you to type your account number and your password or PIN into an official-looking website. With that information, crooks can embed your account number in a phony debit card. Armed with your PIN, they can use the card to withdraw money from your account.

Legitimate financial institutions don't email requests for personal information.

- Be on the lookout for "card skimmers" when using automated teller machines: In these schemes, criminals place scanners over ATM card slots to lift account information from debit cards. They use hidden cameras or old-fashioned shoulder surfing to get PINs. Avoid suspicious ATMs and shield your transactions from prying eyes. If the ATM eats your card, contact your bank immediately.

- Don't keep your PIN anywhere near your debit card: If someone steals your wallet or purse, he has the keys to the kingdom.

- Practice vigilance: Set up online accounts with your financial institutions and monitor them regularly. You'll be able to see fraudulent charges early on, rather than waiting 30 days for your bank statement.

USA Today - May 20, 2005 Jordana
Beebe - spokeswoman for the Privacy Rights Clearinghouse

61 Techniques to Succeed: Karl Rove's 3 D's

When asked a question you would rather not answer:

    Deny

    Deflect

    Delay

Karl Rove - Adviser to President George W. Bush

62 Techniques to Succeed: Drip-Drip-Drip

The steady output of information from the time it is decided an event is going to take place.

As the event draws closer, the release of information intensifies. The heaviest barrage of information is released shortly before the actual event or launch.

Nike uses this technique "to build anticipation and demand."

M. Larry Litwin, APR, Fellow PRSA - The Public Relations Practitioner's Playbook for(all) Strategic Communicators (AuthorHouse – 2013)

63 Techniques to Succeed: Call it 'reverse psychology'

Philadelphia advertising executive Steve Schulman takes a reverse approach to educating communicators about the importance and effectiveness of advertising. He offers 10 easy steps on why **NOT** to advertise:

1. DON'T ADVERTISE. Just pretend everybody knows what you have to offer.
2. DON'T ADVERTISE. Tell yourself you just don't have the time to spend thinking about promoting your business.
3. DON'T ADVERTISE. Just assume everyone knows what you sell.
4. DON'T ADVERTISE. Convince yourself that you've been in business so long customers automatically come to you.
5. DON'T ADVERTISE. Forget that you have competition trying to attract your customers away from you.
6. DON'T ADVERTISE. Forget that there are new potential customers who would do business with you if they were urged to do so.
7. DON'T ADVERTISE. Tell yourself that it costs too much to advertise and that you don't get enough out of it.
8. DON'T ADVERTISE. Overlook the fact that advertising is an investment - not an expense.
9. DON'T ADVERTISE. Be sure not to provide an adequate advertising budget for your business.
10. DON'T ADVERTISE. Forget that you have to keep reminding your establishment (customers/clients) that you appreciate their business.

64. Techniques to Succeed: The Double (Triple) Bottom Line Public Relations Theory*

Public relations has evolved from products (newsletters, brochures, etc.) to counseling, strategizing and training. Two-way communication is imperative.

First Bottom Line:
- An organization's successful efforts to please its publics before and during doing business with it.
- Who knows what's in the public interest better than the public relations professional?
- Who knows if a public is satisfied with an organization's image, management and motive toward the public better than the public relations professional?
- Once this essential relationship is established, the company can do business with its publics.

Second Bottom Line:
- The actual acceptance of the products or services by the public.
- The sale from the fruit of the relationship in the first bottom line leads to profits.

Who better to strategize the Double Bottom Line Theory – reputation leading to profits – than the public relations practitioner or relationship manager? In fact, Bank of America has an executive staff position – vice president for relationship marketing – responsible for achieving the first bottom line.

* See "Triple Bottom Line Theory" in *The Public Relations Practitioner's Playbook for (all) Strategic Communicators* – Page 17

Patrick Jackson - Jackson, Jackson & Wagner - Exeter, N.H.

65. Technique to Succeed: Be alert for workplace problems

Supervisors and employees should be aware of the people around them, and be able to identify those who are at risk for workplace violence. Here are some behavior indicators that may be present in at-risk employees:
- Attendance problems
- Decreased productivity
- Inconsistent work patterns

- Lingering depression
- Poor on-the-job relationships
- Inability to concentrate
- Fascination with weapons
- Chronic excuses or blaming
- Evidence of substance abuse

FirstCALL - An Employee Assistance Program - www.courierpostonline.com - July 12, 2005

Tips to Succeed: Choosing the correct coach

Business coaches are becoming a common part of executive development and are assisting in career transition in companies reducing ranks.

Here are tips for choosing an executive coach:

- Most executive coaches work by phone. Schedule a half-hour get-acquainted session with potential coaches to learn about their backgrounds and experience. Discuss your goals, the process the coach follows and their costs.
- Look for chemistry. Is this a person who you will be comfortable working with on a regular basis? Will you be able to listen to both positive and negative feedback from the coach?
- Check some references.
- Be prepared to commit to a minimum of three months — this is the amount of time it normally takes for a solid coaching relationship to develop.
- Check the coach's flexibility. Sometimes it is critical for the coach to come to your location to meet, to observe you and others in group settings.

Courier-Post - Camden, N.J. - Nov. 21, 2005

Tips to Succeed: College seniors preparing to jump into the job market

- Prepare a 2-3 minute response that best highlights your achievements and skills, especially moments during an internship or school assignment that pertain to the job. (Recruiters will often ask the question, "Tell me about yourself.")
- Show enthusiasm for the job.
- When talking to the recruiter, use language common to the field.
- Dress appropriately. "Dressing inappropriately is the biggest nono," she said. "Make the change from collegiate appearance to professional. If you look like a professional, the recruiter will have an easier time seeing you fit in at the company."

Lizziel Sullivan-Williams – Director of Career and Academic Planning - Rowan University – Glassboro, N.J

Tips to Succeed: Improve your credit score

- Sign up for automatic bill payment. A late bill can make your credit score drop by as much as 100 points.
- Watch the timing of your spending, especially if you plan to apply for a loan. The lower the balance, the better the credit rating.
- Limit credit-card applications. Each time a lender inquires to view a credit report, it gets noted and can reduce the score.
- Think twice before canceling cards. Consumers gain points if they are tapping only a small percentage of the total credit available to them.
- Make sure credit limits are posted.

Consumer Reports

69 Tips to Succeed: Store-brand goods rival national names

Store-brand products have the same quality as brand name products.

Comparison tests were conducted on 65 grocery products in six categories – peaches, yogurt, plastic bags, facial tissues, paper towels and french fries.

Consider this when buying:

- A national-brand manufacturer might make several formulations of the same product to appeal to consumers with different needs — and snatch valuable shelf space from competitors.
- Most store brands come in several tiers to dispel the notion that store brands are strictly for penny pinchers.

Consumer Reports

70 Tips to Succeed: Renew your workplace enthusiasm

Many professionals, whether in business, sports or just in life, lose their zest and enthusiasm. At times, energy is elevated, enabling you to maintain enthusiasm for years. Other times, you can be lackadaisical about work – and that can continue for weeks – or even months.

Dale Carnegie Training and others offer these tips to help you overcome that lack of enthusiasm – especially if you own a small business or manage a larger one:

- Connect with other managers to gain new perspectives. For example, join a local chamber of commerce or get involved in a trade association.
- Assess your business life. Have you deviated too far from the areas of your job that you love? Have you lost sight of your goals? Have you forgotten what makes you happy?
- Discover your legacy. Ask yourself whether you've lost site of where you are going. Reassess your vision and the company's mission and then rewrite them so they reflect your new mindset. (Remember, the mission and vision statements are not the same.)
- Set concrete short-term goals. Sometimes we just have to get through a "funk." Set specific goals for each day, each week and each month – some people even set goals for each hour.

Ensure that you are on the right path – you will rediscover your enthusiasm along the way.

www.dalecarnegie.com

71 Tips to Succeed: PR practitioners don't make excuses

Don't make excuses – make it happen.

Losers make excuses. Winners make it happen!

72 Techniques to Succeed: Getting on the air

The National Association of Broadcasters (NAB) suggests that if your appeal is to be effective, you should have the answer to some key questions before contacting local stations: (Some refer to it as the MAC Triad - message, audience, channel.)

- What is your message? [Message] Are you sure of the basic idea you want to communicate?
- Who should receive your message? [Audience] Is it of general interest to a large segment of the audience? Can it be tailored to reach a specific audience?
- How can you best put your message across? [Channel] Does it have enough general interest for a special program? Would a PSA serve just as well?

Your answers to these questions should help you determine in advance whether your pitch will achieve the desired result – coverage.

National Association of Broadcasters Washington, D.C.

73 Techniques to Succeed: For those who commit industrial or corporate espionage

Sometimes illegal. Almost always unethical. None the less, many use it in this competitive environment.

1. Gather the information – use a camera
2. Transmit the information – use email or fax
3. Destroy the information after getting out of it what you want–use a shredder

74 Tips to Succeed: Shaping your life

"Define yourselves not by what you do, but by what you believe in, not by how much money you make, but by how you live your life, not by how many hours you work, but by how well you love and are loved. That is the most important charge."

Dr. Donald Farish - President - Rowan (N.J.) University
Commencement - May 13, 2005

75 Techniques to Succeed: Reducing stress at work

Stress has a tendency to build up or snowball. The best way to reduce stress is to handle it when it's small and take advantage of relaxing moments.

- The way to reduce stress early on is by breaking the momentum of the snowball rolling down the hill by taking breaks.

- Allow yourself to relax, refuel and regroup throughout the day. Do not do too much, feel guilty for relaxing, or think about your "to do" list.

- Force yourself to take several mental breaks throughout the day. Even if they are only five minutes each, they will make a huge difference in your stress level. Anytime you do something other than relax during your 5 minutes, start the time over.

- Do something that feels relaxing, like listening to music, going for a brief walk, talking with a friend or co-worker. Try different activities to see what helps you feel less stressed and more focused on your work afterward.

Larina Kase - Doctor of Psychology, career coach and former counselor at the University of Pennsylvania - www.extremecommunicator.com

76 Tips to Succeed: Work etiquette

- Be timely. Arrive to work and meetings on time. Complete work assignments on time.
- Be polite, pleasant and courteous.
- Learn office politics – use effective listening skills to discover appropriate office behavior. Pay attention to the way things are done.
- Understand the unwritten rules of business.
  - The Boss is the Boss – right or wrong, the boss always has the last word.
  - Keep the boss informed. Good or bad, you don't want the boss to hear information mentioned from an inappropriate source.
  - Never go over the boss' head, without telling him/her first. – Make your boss look good. Promotion and opportunities will arise when you help to reach the organization's goals.
  - Appear as professional as possible. Being well groomed and clean is essential. Dress for your next job/promotion.
  - Adopt a can-do attitude. Those who accept challenges and display creativity are valuable.
  - Be flexible. By remaining flexible and implementing change you gain a reputation as a cooperative employee.
  - Give credit to everyone who made a contribution to a project or event.
  - Don't differentiate people by position or standing in a company.

The Career Center - Florida State University

77 Techniques to Succeed: How to improve your customer relations

- If nothing else, improve customer service.
- Offer value: a solid balance of quality, price and selection.
- Make it easy to get there and get around.
- Welcome the children.
- Don't add entertainment unless the shopping experience is already a good one.
- Give back to the community.
- Provide a positive and memorable experience.
- Acknowledge that mom's influence stretches far and wide and make sure she knows you know.

Nora Lee - Author - The Mom Factor www.momfactor.com/

78 Techniques to Succeed: Customer satisfaction– Make it an experience

"Customers want to bank with you not because you give them a better rate but because you give them a better retail experience."

Vernon Hill - CEO - Republic Bank
Cherry Hill, N.J.

79 Technique to Succeed: Achieving goals takes planning

To maximize productivity, either in the office or at home:

- Carefully plan your day to achieve your goals. Look at your goals and estimate how long it will take to accomplish each one. Plan for some "buffer" time to allow for an unexpected interruption. This will help in setting up your schedule correctly.
- Start your day by planning out exactly what it is you want to accomplish. Be realistic, not overly ambitious. Remain aware of time and schedules and watch out for pitfalls or time traps. Another key is sorting your list by projects and then the steps that need to be worked on.
- Develop a plan that will enable you to achieve that day's goals. This can include a calendar book, a personal digital assistant or just a piece of paper. This will allow you stay on track with you goals for that day and keep your goals achievable.
- Remember to stick to your plan. A certain amount of flexibility and dexterity will always be necessary, but avoid tangents that will distract and cause a shift in focus. Keep to your plan and remember that unforeseen circumstances will no doubt arise. The key is to adapt your plan to achieve the goals without rendering it unrecognizable.

Dale Carnegie Training of Central and Southern New Jersey

80 Technique to Succeed: Retaining talented employees

Looking for ways to keep employees on board? The following tips can help to retain talented employees:

- Provide a competitive compensation and benefits package to show employees you place a fair value on their work.
- Promote activities that build rapport among staff members.
- Lend a hand and be willing to make concessions when employees encounter personal difficulties.
- Acknowledge staff contributions during a meeting or with a personal note.
- Give them a break. Consider closing early on Friday.

Tracey Fuller - Executive director of The Creative Group, a national staffing firm - www.creativegroup.com

81 Tips to Succeed: From the late Frank Perdue – 'Not all chickens are alike' – or fronting your brand

By establishing Perdue® as the brand of chickens that was different from all others, Frank Perdue's Perdue Farms Inc. increased sales from $56 million in 1970 to $1.2 billion in 1991. At one point in time, telephone surveys showed that 97 percent of people asked to name a brand of chicken came up with Perdue. By putting a brand name on an inseparable product like chickens (Chiquita® did it with bananas and Morton's® did with salt) it set the product apart and made Perdue a household name.

Ed McCabe, a copywriter at Scali, McCabe & Stoves believed that chickens could be "hawked" but that the spots had to be funny. Frank Perdue was skeptical that a man with a deadpan expression and a funny-sounding voice, a balding, big-nosed man who looked a bit like a chicken himself, could make his brand into a household name. He not only did that, but he started a trend that continues today – having a CEO or some other company "face" or "voice" front a product or service.

Philadelphia Inquirer, April 2, 2005

82 Tips to Succeed: If you think you'll be fired

The writing is on the wall: You're getting fired.

Maybe you've done your darnedest to keep it from happening, but there's no denying it – the pink slip is coming.

You're mad. You're devastated. You're depressed. You think of just quitting. Maybe you should snoop in computer files to see what is being said about you.

Here are some important rules of an "imminent termination," including:

- **Documenting performance:** It's always a good idea to keep personal hard copies of memos, email or reports showing the work you did for a company. When facing termination, however, it may be against the employer's rules for you to take home anything pertaining to your employment, and that includes your work records. Showing great care in this area – taking anything that you do not have the authority to have "could jeopardize your ability to recover full damages at trial" should you decide to sue your former employer.

In case you are not allowed to take anything home, make a log of key documents relating to your employment, especially those showing a good performance. Make sure you note date, parties, subject, content and location.

Do not make illegal tape recordings, which will be thrown out of court anyway. Do not go near the boss's written or computer files – any such action is grounds for instant termination.

- **Keeping an events diary:** As soon as you feel your job is threatened, begin keeping a written chronological account of your time at a company, with lots of detail. At the top of the page, write "to my attorney," which will make it privileged information. Write down when you were hired, how you performed, when things started to sour, why you think it happened and significant dates that led to the problems.
- **Listing witnesses:** These are people you believe could help your case. Get full names, addresses and telephone numbers.
- **Starting a job search:** Don't wait until you have the pink slip in hand. Start making contacts and sending out resumes.
- **Doing your job:** Don't slack off or sulk. Perform to the best of your ability, and don't give the boss any more reasons to let you go.
- **Schmoozing:** Now is the time to get along as best you can with those around you. You want to leave the company with a good reputation. Don't leave co-workers holding the bag.
- **Never quitting:** Those who quit not only lose income, but put unemployment benefits or future legal action in jeopardy.

Anita Bruzzese - Gannett News Service - April 4, 2005
From: Richard C. Busse, Esq. - Portland, Ore. - Fired, Laid-off or Forced Out (Sphinx)

83

Tips to Succeed:
The right way to get a favor

Many people, when they need a favor, frantically call long forgotten contacts and ask for, or even demand, help. Asking for favors, if done wrong, can strain or even break a relationship. Effective networking is the proactive solution.

If you think ahead and network well, asking for a favor can be an easy, natural thing to do. Sometimes you may find that you don't even need to ask! Here are a few easy ways to maintain your relationships so that favors come easily:

1. Get organized
   - Keep track of your contacts whichever way works best for you. You can use computer databases, Pads or even index cards
   - Keep track of birthdays, anniversaries and other miscellaneous information
   - Know your contacts' needs, such as information, jobs and other contacts

2. Keep in touch
   - Review your contact list regularly and make a follow up plan
   - Send notes and cards on occasions such as birthdays and holidays
   - Regularly call and set up lunch meetings or dinner appointments

3. Nurture mutually beneficial relationships
   - Send any helpful information to your contacts
   - Connect your contacts with others who can help them
   - Use your skills to help others

If you care for your network of friends, colleagues and acquaintances, it will be your best resource. Whether the favor you need is information, a job referral, technical help or even more clients, the best solution is a strong network. Most importantly, always remember to say thank you with an email, a hand-written note or a gift.

March 2005
420 E. 51st Street • Suite 12D • New York, NY 10022
email: info@mybusinessrelationships.com

84. Tips to Succeed: View your failures as a learning experience – or – turning a stumbling block into a stepping stone

"What's the key to being a successful entrepreneur?" Change how you think about failure.

Failure is the "F word" of business – It's not polite to mention it. After all, failure is what happens to other people, right? But what happens when we ourselves fail? We either try to quickly forget the experience, or we wallow in self-doubt and recrimination.

If you're in business, sooner or later, you're going to have failures. But sometimes, these "failures" can turn out to be fortunate. They force you to re-examine your goals, decisions, methods. Then, you can choose to take a different – better – path.

Here's how the best entrepreneurs deal with failure:

- Redefine it. Experienced entrepreneurs make a failure a learning experience.
- Analyze it. If – when – you fail, take a close look at the causes. After each and every setback, big or small, take a clear cold look at what happened.
- Depersonalize it. Stop kicking yourself; everybody fails. While you must analyze your mistakes, you won't learn anything if you're too busy beating up on yourself.
- Change it. Remind yourself of what you learned and actively try to change your behavior. Be patient and forgiving because change takes time.
- Get over it. Move on. Don't dwell on your successes or on your failures. You've got a life to live, and each day is precious. So, like the old song says, "Pick yourself up, brush yourself off, and start all over again."

Rhonda Abrams - www.rhondaworks.com/

85 Tips to Succeed:
Family businesses need to have rules, too

Here are some tips for working with family members:

- Write a business plan describing your mission, documenting assets and defining roles. It should contain:
  - Goal
  - Objectives
  - Strategies
  - Tactics
- Agree upon succession.
- Establish exit options for family members wanting to leave the business.
- When hiring your child, be clear about expectations, give feedback, expect mistakes and allow time for learning and growth.
- Encourage different points of view and make an effort to discuss and understand them.
- Remember the shared family bond and the shared commitment to success.
- Don't use sarcasm or belittle family members.
- Institute "rules of behavior" for meetings.
- When a solution has not been agreed upon within an established time, table that item for later discussion. If that fails, seek outside help and advice.
- Leave work at the office.

Family Business Institute www.
Entrepreneur.com
Family Business magazine

86 Tips to Succeed: Terminology of mutual funds

Mutual funds, like stocks and bonds, have a language all their own. Here are some terms public relations practitioners might find in reports from mutual fund companies:

- **Prospectus.** The official document that describes a mutual fund to investors. It contains information required by the Securities and Exchange Commission, such as investment objectives and policies, risks, services and fees.

- **Redeem.** To cash in mutual fund shares by selling them back to the fund. The investor receives the current share price, called net asset value, minus any deferred sales charge or redemption fee.

- **Round trip.** Redemption out of a fund, followed by a purchase back into the same fund. Some funds limit the number of round trips an investor can make during a 12-month period.

Gannett News Servicewww.content.gannettonline.com

87 Techniques to Succeed: Try a charette design

Charettes began as an intense effort to solve any architectural problem within a limited time. However, there is no rule stating public relations counselors can't use them. In fact, charettes strongly resemble focus panels and in many cases – town meetings. From a creative standpoint, a charette can be divided into three portions:

> **1. LISTEN.** Listen to what the financial backers, realtors, owners, and other specialists have to suggest. Work together with them to come to an understanding about the project, what their goals and limitations are, and how these might fit with your ideas.

> **2. ENVISION.** Imagine together all of these various considerations to come up with a realistic and creative proposal which will be interesting while at the same time financially, environmentally, and otherwise feasible.

> **3. DRAW FAST!** The ability to work with creative team who can bring ideas to a tangible design sketch quickly, allows for instant communication ... a picture is worth a thousand words!

How a charette facilitates the process – much like focus panels, which are a tactic of a public relations plan. There are two main advantages to working in the context of a charette.

1. A charette operates in a highly collaborative atmosphere. Instead of an architect (or PR practitioner) taking ideas and plans and going away to develop them on his or her own (oneway), a charette allows for the participation of everyone involved with the project, resulting in a highly charged and creative atmosphere. The inclusion of many points of view results in wellrounded and realistic proposals, with everyone satisfied that they were able to contribute.

2. Charettes are fast, and relatively inexpensive.

    In the initial stages of a project, the venture is necessarily highly speculative. It is important to keep costs at bay, while also moving forward quickly to take advantage of changing situations and often critical deadlines.

www.masterplanning.com/masterplanning/charette.html
www.doverkohl.com/writings_images/charrettes_for_NU_in_FL.htm

88 Tips to Succeed: You are hired for a reason

Your public relations approach should contain your fingerprint.

CBS Sunday Morning

89 Tips to Succeed: Workplace relationships

A leader, whether in or outside of the office, must be able to understand the different types of personalities on his or her team.

Here are some tips to help strengthen professional and personal relationships:

- Don't criticize, condemn or complain. Avoid being negative and offer only honest and sincere appreciation when warranted.
- Always show you're happy to see someone. A pleasant or warm greeting, especially after some length of time, is a particularly effective approach.
- Be a good listener. Encourage others to talk more about themselves, reaffirming your sincere interest. When you do speak, always try to talk in terms of the other person's interests. This is an excellent way to redirect a conversation should you want to move on to a different subject.
- Never forget that people are always impressed when you remember their name. Nothing can strengthen a relationship like showing you are interested enough in a person to recollect his or her name. It adds an effective personal dimension to any relationship. And saying the person's name when you meet them is exactly what they want to hear.
- Make the other person feel important. Use a sincere and honest manner to establish a sense of worth and importance. Remember that everyone has some quality or skill that makes him or her important. When you recognize this in others, point it out in a proactive manner – like catching them doing something good.

Dale Carnegie Training of Central and Southern New Jersey

90 Tips to Succeed: Dressing for work

TIPS FOR MEN

If you're looking for a classic suit:

Gray, blue or black suit with a white dress shirt.

Do not experiment with the color of the shirt; you can add color through the tie.

Ties can have a simple pattern with basic colors like blue, gold or red.

Do not wear pastels or try the monochromatic shirt and tie look if you're meeting someone, like a hiring manager or a client, for the first time.

Stay away from tan-colored suits or bold pin stripes.

TIPS FOR WOMEN

Women have more options when dressing for work than men. Pay attention to four key items: fit, accessories, color and style.

Fit – Do your clothes fit properly? It doesn't matter how expensive an item is – if it is too tight or too big, it isn't going to look good on you.

Accessories – Are your accessories too big, too bold or too bright? Your accessories should be good-quality items that add to your outfit without overpowering it.

Color – Are you wearing clothing that is noticed because of its color? Darker colors convey more authority than lighter ones. Bright colors can "shout," and you should decide whether you want to shout or not.

Style – Are your clothes very stylish or part of the latest fashion trend? If so, they will be noticed. This may be appropriate for your social life but less so for work.

Neil Rosenthal - Owner - Executive Clothiers Barbara
Pachter - Pachter & Associates - Cherry Hill, N.J

91 Tips to Succeed: Dress up to move up

A woman who wants to climb the ladder of success might have to do it in tasteful, mid-height pumps.

A man intent on getting ahead might invest in a few new ties—and keep them straightened.

In fact, a recent survey (Office Team, a subsidiary of Robert Half International) reports 93 percent of managers said an employee's work dress influences his or her odds of winning a promotion; 33 percent said wardrobe plays a "significant" role in moving up.

KEY QUESTIONS

- Would my manager wear this?
- Could my outfit be a distraction for others?
- Does my attire make me feel self-assured and confident?
- Are my clothes clean, pressed and in good condition?
- Is my outfit comfortable and well-fitting?

It's not about wearing expensive clothes, it's about being appropriate It is suggested professionals maintain business attire, suits with trousers or skirts for women and suits and ties for men.

Our business casual should be sweater sets and dress slacks. It's important for workers starting out at a company to know the corporate culture regarding dress.

In building a career wardrobe, stock your closet with the basics:

- A navy blazer is a good staple for a man or a woman.
- A black suit is versatile because you can throw on different shirts to change the look.
- Keep clothes clean and pressed, with hair neatly groomed.
- Women to use a light hand in applying makeup and to avoid flashy jewelry.

Another suggestion: before you go for that promotion, visualize yourself in the job.

Ask yourself, "would my manager wear this?" If there are two candidates with equal skill sets, the person who presents himself more professionally has the edge.

www.courierpostonline.com

92 Techniques to Succeed: Sculpt email to make it stand out

It pays to spend a little time thinking about an email before you send it. Paying more attention to what you write can make your messages more effective and guard against workplace catastrophes.

There are numerous ways to make emails stronger and more likely to be read faster.

- To get your message recognized, read and acted upon, strengthen the subject, sculpt the body.
- The way to get fewer emails is to send fewer emails.
- Cut down on your use of the "cc" and "reply to all" functions, as well as group distribution lists, he said.
- A better email starts with a better subject line. Instead of writing "Meeting," be more specific, like "Sales team meeting from April 3rd."
- If you're confirming a meeting, write back in the subject line, "Confirmed." And when you're sending information the recipient requested, use the word "Delivery" before describing what you're sending.

Like the title of this book, have an ABC structure:

A stands for "action summary." In the first line should be the "summary point." It should leave no room for guesswork. An example might be: "Action: Please submit business plan by 5 p.m. on April 3rd." It's important to list a deadline or time element, he said.

B stands for "background." This second part should be a series of bullet points, with information the recipient needs to know. This avoids a "wall of words" that no one will want to read, or an email that, conversely, doesn't provide enough detail.

And C stands for "close." This final portion should speak to the next steps that need to be taken, or perhaps a personal message to lighten the email. Finish it with an auto signature with contact information, such as:

M. Larry Litwin, APR, Fellow PRSA
"Loyalty, Judgment, Trust, Ethics, Integrity" = PR Counselor/Strategic Adviser/Synergist/Ethicist
856-767-7730 (office)
www.larrylitwin.com

> Mike Song - Co-author - The Hamster Revolution: How to Manage Your Email Before it Manages You

93 | Tips to Succeed: Fashion choices for workplace

When temperatures climb, workers wrestle with finding the middle ground between cool summer clothing and appropriate work attire. Here is a summer fashion refresher for women:

- Show respect with how you dress at the office. Social skills are 75 percent of what determines a person's success in business. Those skills include knowing how to dress.
- Business casual should be a mix of both. Pressed khakis and a crisp shirt are a better choice than a T-shirt and jeans.
- Beachwear such as flip-flops, tank tops, short skirts and shorts are not appropriate for the office.
- Women should choose sandals with straps over the flip-flops. Shoes should be closed-toed and beware of backless shoes that make an annoying clap-clap-clap sound when you walk.
- Do not wear sleeveless shirts, but if you have to wear one, pick a nice-looking sleeveless shell that can be worn under a jacket in case you need to look formal, fast.
- Other shirts that should be banned on most professionals: Shirts with spaghetti straps and anything that shows cleavage or bare midriffs.
- Your skirt should not be more than a dollar bill's width above your knee.

Leah Ingram - Author - The Everything Etiquette Book: A Modern Day Guide to Good Manners and Gannett News Service

94 | Tips to Succeed: Advice from Google®

"Anything you don't develop is a garden left unattended."

Google founders

95 Tips to Succeed: Chicken soup for the investor

Relationships between investors and the ever-changing financial markets can be complex.

These principles have withstood the test of time.

- People don't invest to become rich. They invest so they don't become poor. Individuals invest in stocks to keep up with the rate of inflation. Bonds and cash will not allow you to keep up.

- Don't constantly look up your account balance. You wouldn't pull up your plants every day to check on the roots, would you?

- Most people underestimate how long they will live after retiring and how much money they will need. Living longer has had a major impact on retirement planning. You don't want to run out of money before running out of time.

- Your investment decisions should be based on careful analysis of your time horizon, risk tolerance, expected return and asset allocation preference. If a salesman starts fishing around and talks about investments before addressing these issues with you, don't take the bait.

- It is never too late to start saving and planning for retirement. The key is to get started and have a plan.

Joseph M. Johnson - Vice President
Main Street Financial Group - Pitman, N.J. - 856- 218-0080

96
Tips to Succeed:
Doing business with government

The U.S. Government is the world's largest customer, and it routinely does business with small businesses. There is a procedure to follow when doing business with the "feds."

- Educate yourself extremely well on the process.
- Make sure you meet the basic requirements for doing business with the government, such as accepting electronic funds transfer and credit cards.
- Determine your NAICS code (North American Industry Classification System – www.census.gov/epcd/www/naics.html) and make sure you qualify as a small business.
- Determine who in the government purchases your products or services.
- Determine if there are any special programs for which you may qualify.
- Obtain a DUNS (Data Universal Numbering System) number for free from Dun & Bradstreet.
- Register with the Small Business Administration (SBA) and the agency with which you wish to do business.
- Subscribe to the Commerce Business Daily, which lists notices of proposed government procurement actions, contract awards, sales of government property and other procurement information.
- Respond to the bids effectively and get awarded contracts!
- For more information, get in touch with the local Small Business Administration office. Go to www.sba.gov.

Scott Allen - www.about.com

97 Techniques to Succeed: Stress and anxiety

It's important to understand the difference between stress and anxiety because the strategies to deal with each are actually the opposite of one another.

STRESS
- Stress is the feeling of being overburdened and overwhelmed. This is having a desk full of papers in front of you, 100 unread emails in your inbox and a tight deadline quickly approaching.
- Stress makes you feel pressures with physical symptoms such as muscle tension, headaches and backaches.
- The way to deal with stress is to decrease it. You want to find ways to relax in and outside of work.
- Improving your time management or assertiveness skills can help you decrease the burden of your workload.

ANXIETY
- Anxiety is an internal, fear-based response to difficult situations.
- It is the trembling, heart-palpating, short-of-breath feeling you get when you are singled out in front of everyone or the adrenaline rush before doing a major presentation.
- The way to deal with anxiety is to increase it. It sounds crazy, but the way to get over a fear is to confront it over and over. For instance, if you're afraid of public speaking, find as many opportunities to do it so that over time it will become easier and your confidence will grow.

Larina Kase - Doctor of Psychology, career coach and former counselor at the University of Pennsylvania - www.extremecommunicator.com

98 Techniques to Succeed: Beware of office gossip – it will come back to 'getcha'

If you want to be trusted, never gossip. When you talk negatively about others – especially in business – to people you just met, or even to people you have known for some time, but don't know well, you may have been seen as a gossiper. And, many times, it is not what you say, but how you say it.

Be nice to people on your way up because you never know who you will meet on the way down. Never treat anyone poorly. You never know when someone will become your boss.

The dos and don'ts of office gossip:

- If you must gossip make sure your indiscretion won't get either you or your colleague into trouble with the boss.
- An incredible 70 per cent of workers are shocked that their secrets are common knowledge in the office. Don't be. If you gossip about your workmates the chances are they will gossip about you.
- If you are uncomfortable with a situation at work go straight to one of your superiors.
- If you're bored, find something other than gossiping to fill your time.

Keith Ferrazzi and Tahl Raz - Authors - Never Eat Alone: And Other Secrets to Success, One at a Time (Currency - 2005) http://www.ivillage.co.uk/print/0,,164246,00.html

99 Tips to Succeed: Know the branches of government

They are known as the "three powers." In a Democratic society, power is in principle divided between the three branches of government:

- **Legislative** – makes the laws
  (e.g. the US Congress)
- **Executive** – Makes executive decisions on a day-to-day basis (e.g. the US President)
- **Judiciary** – Interpret the laws (e.g. the US Supreme Court).

The powers/branches are designed to counterbalance one another. This system of "checks and balances" works to ensure that none of the three powers becomes too strong. Thus, for example, the President can send troops to war, but the Congress can refuse to vote the budget to sustain the war. Congress can pass a law, but the Supreme Court can rule it unconstitutional.

100 Techniques to Succeed: Gunning Fog Index

The Gunning Fog Index, developed by Robert Gunning in Technique of Clear Writing is the easiest of the readability indexes to use, most popular and considered the most effective. Here is how it works:

STEPS IN APPLYING GUNNING

1. Select a sample
2. Count 100 words (continue counting until you finish a sentence)
3. Determine the average number of words per sentence
4. Divide the number of sentences into the number of words.
   (Remember, an average sentence should not exceed 17 words.)
5. Determine the percentage of hard words
   a. Count all words containing three or more syllables.
   Do NOT count:
   - proper nouns
   - verbs made into three syllables such as excited, persuasive or devoted
   - words of three or more syllables that are combinations of easy words such as butterfly, lawmaker, bumblebee.
6. Add the two factors (Steps 4 and 5) and multiply by 0.4

The result is the minimum grade level at which the writing is easily read.

> M. Larry Litwin, APR, Fellow PRSA The Public Relations Practitioner's Playbook for (all) Strategic Communicators (AuthorHouse – 2013)

101 Tips to Succeed: De-clutter your space

Does your office contain two filing systems: the desk and the floor? Here are some tips for de-cluttering a messy work space:

- Keep only the items on your desk that relate to your current projects.
- Clean out your files, but before you go through the expense of buying more file cabinets and folders, purge all unnecessary paperwork and materials.
- Don't waste time searching for papers. Keep all paperwork that pertains to a certain project together in one large folder.
- Don't overstuff file cabinets. Leave enough room so you're not using all your energy to get a piece of paper in and out.
- Add shelving for reference books and manuals. Add space extenders in desk drawers. Use stacking bins.

www.courierpostonline.com - Oct. 17, 2005

102 Tips to Succeed: Demand attention in cover letter

- **Make yourself stand out**. Get the competitive edge by writing a cover letter that focuses on your unique and exceptional qualities.
- **Target the right person.** Sending your letter to the proper person can make all the difference.
- **Stay simple**. Keep your cover letter brief. Never send a letter that is more than a page in length; half a page is ideal. Be sure to use clear, professional language while steering away from buzzwords, acronyms, jargon, or anything overly personal.
- **Make it shine**. The overall visual impression of your cover letter can be just as important as what's written upon it.
- **Be an attention getter**. Don't waste your first paragraph by writing a dull introduction.

www.allbusiness.com

103 Techniques to Succeed: Bookkeeping – Don't get overwhelmed

Small-business owners can be overwhelmed by all the different tasks they perform. If you are a small-business owner and you can't perform these duties, it might be time to outsource:

- Maintain accounting records after working 10- to 15-hour days.
- Set up, select and computerize an accounting system.
- Deal with filing and processing payroll.
- Reconcile bank accounts and actively monitor cash balances.
- Possess the expertise to code expenses, assets and other income to provide a CPA with information to prepare tax returns at year's end.
- Prepare financial information to monitor trends, profitability, cash balances and accounts receivable.
- Hire and train a bookkeeper to run the financial aspects of the business.

www.osyb.com - Outsource Your Books

104 Tips to Succeed: Make your email effective

Use the technology of email to your professional advantage. Emails must give the right impression.

- **Get to the point fast**. Make sure the important information is within the first couple sentences.
- **Make your subject line like the headline of a newspaper article**. The subject line should give the reader a reason to open the message.
- **Avoid constantly checking your email and responding right away**. This can take your focus off work. Instead, turn off your computer's "you've got mail" signal and give one succinct reply to several messages from the same person.
- **Keep email professional, even if you're writing to a work buddy**. Keep in mind that every email you send is subject to forwarding.
- **Use active instead of passive language**. It sets a professional image and gets the point across quickly. Active language is energetic and clear while passive language weakens your writing.

Janis Fisher Chan - Author - Email: A Write It Well Guide

105 Techniques to Succeed: Burnout busters

To prevent burnout:

- Start your day with powerful high-energy music. Whether it's rock or country or jazz or pop, listen to music that "pumps you up" and makes you feel great about yourself.
- Set aside blocks of time to complete various tasks. During those blocks of time, do not allow yourself to be interrupted for other things. (For example, the hour from 2 to 3 p.m. might be set aside for reading and responding to emails.)
- Make "Fix it, then forget it" your mistake mantra. Do not allow mistakes to ruin you. Do everything you can to fix a problem with a client or associate in order to make them happy. After that, do not dwell on what went wrong.
- Get an accountability partner to help you stay focused. Ask someone other than your spouse or romantic partner to fill this role. Make sure it's someone you trust and feel comfortable with to just be yourself. You should meet with this person at least once a week to talk about your goals, progress, setbacks, and thoughts on your personal and professional life.
- Use "comic memos" to ease anxiety at work. The comic memo technique involves attaching a funny cartoon to routine, boring paperwork that has to be distributed at the office.

The Staver Group - 914 Atlantic Avenue - Suite 1E - Fernandina Beach, FL 32034

106 Techniques to Succeed: Home entertaining for business

Entertaining successfully at home can add to your personal image – if done well.

Some techniques for business entertaining at home:

- Make the invitation specific
  - Dress code
  - Time the party starts and ends
  - Whether spouses or dates are invited
  - If a meal will be served
- Check dietary requirements ahead of time and plan simple, easy food to eat
- Prepare your spouse or partner.
  - Try to share something about each person so that they can make conversation with all of your guests
- Make sure children are well-behaved or have a baby sitter available.
- Be cautious with alcoholic beverages.
- As the host, make sure you mingle with everyone.
  - Help others mingle, also.
  - If everyone doesn't know everyone, make the introduction.
- Don't just talk about business.
  - This is an opportunity to get to know others outside of the business environment. (Just don't get too personal.)
- Offer a brief speech or toast to welcome your guests

Barbara Pachter - Business Coach When The Little Things Count -
And They Always Count - (Marlowe & Company)
856-751-6141

107 Tips to Succeed: Update HR (Talent-Acquisition) policies to avoid lawsuits

In August 2003, two Caucasian plaintiffs sued Ricoh Electronics Inc., headquartered in West Caldwell, alleging they had been passed over for promotion based on their race or national origin. They claimed the firm had a practice of promoting Japanese and other Asians ahead of Caucasians.

In March 2005, a jury unanimously found that the company did not discriminate on the basis of race or national origin.

Employers should consider these practices to minimize their exposure to a similar claim:

- Maintain good human resources policies, including harassment and discrimination policies, and communicate those policies to all employees.
- Ensure that management and employees adhere to the company's policies.
- Maintain and enforce policies for handling a complaint of harassment or discrimination.
- Provide training for all management on harassment and discrimination awareness and on what to do if management receives a complaint.
- Conduct regular employee performance reviews to document employee performance; and provide clear written feedback to employees.

(**Talent-acquisition strategist** – A human resource (director) practitioner. One who is responsible for placement, recruiting, compensation and team building.)
Dan Callahan - Partner with law firm Callahan & Blaine (represented Ricoh®)
714-241-4444

108 Techniques to Succeed: The proper business handshake

There are five basic types of handshakes most of us have experienced – none is correct.

Try this for success:

PROPER HANDSHAKING

The protocol for handshaking is simple to learn: Walk up to the person you want to meet. Look into their eyes, smile and extend you hand. Offer a warm, firm, palm-to-palm handshake.

When you proffer your hand to a stranger or a distant acquaintance, simultaneously say, "My name is......(use both first and last names). This way you eliminate the awkward moment of the forgotten name. The person being greeted is often relieved at being reminded, and will usually respond with their full name, which will in turn relieve you.

Both men and women should rise to shake hands. Rising is a compliment – it shows energy and eagerness to connect.

Initiating a proper handshake will make an incredibly positive impression. You will be perceived as a person who is knowledgeable, possesses excellent social skills and has leadership capabilities.

An excellent handshake shows your charm and self-confidence. It becomes an integral part of your style.

DON'T BE ONE OF THESE:

- **Knuckle Cruncher**
  This type of person is earnest but nervous. While meaning to convey warmth through a tight grip of your hand, the person only causes you pain. The impression created is definitely that of a person who lacks sensitivity.

- **Dead Fish Handshaker**
  This type of person, who places a limp, lifeless hand in yours, is sending a negative message. While the knuckle cruncher hurts you, at least there is a desire to express a real feeling. You are left with the impression of this person having a lackluster personality.

- **Pumper**
  This handshake is overly eager but also insecure. This person doesn't know when to quit, almost as if stalling because of not knowing what to do next. They keep on vigorously pumping your hand up and down – and with it your entire arm. You may not feel pain but you certainly feel foolish.

- **Sanitary Handshaker**
This person will barely put three or four fingers in your hand-and then withdraw them quickly, almost as if afraid of catching a dread disease. They appear timid and sheepish.

- **Condolence Handshaker**
This is the person who comes across as too familiar, clasping your right arm or hand, and perhaps attempting to hug you. This behavior may be appreciated at a funeral, but it comes across as condescending and inappropriate.

The Canadian Progress Club - Bob Lockhart - National President Elect
www.progressclub.ca/Whats_New/Progression/2005_03/04Features_01.htm

109 Tips to Succeed: Impress the boss – know the difference between home in and hone

Home in – Direct onto a point or target. For example: The firm homed in on the public relations plan's goal.

Hone – To sharpen or perfect. For example: A speaker honed her delivery by practicing. Hone your skills before asking for a raise.

110

Tips to Succeed:
Look for errors in handbooks

Even small firms – with just one employee – should have an employee handbook. But often employers forget to include key elements in their manuals.

Employers should review their manuals to make certain these five top errors are avoided and the issues have been addressed:

- Lack of acknowledgment. Employers forget to have the employee sign an acknowledgment page stating they have received the manual and are responsible for reading it. The paper should be filed in the employee's personnel file.

- Employers are still using the term "probationary" for their introductory period of employment, which is usually 90 days. Probationary implies that at the end of the 90 days they will become a permanent employee. This in turn implies an employment contract.

- Employers might have a harassment policy, but often they don't spell out clearly and plainly how to and whom to see to file a complaint. Too many policies are too vague.

- Employers often use the term "salaried" instead of defining employment categories as regular full time with exempt and nonexempt categories, and regular part time.

- Forgetting to update. Most employers don't update their handbooks often enough. Manuals should be reviewed regularly and updated every two to three years or as necessary to reflect law and employment regulation changes.

Christine Mazza Schaefer - President of CEM HR Strategies,Inc. Woodbury,N.J.856-845-0060

111 Tips to Succeed: Avoiding holiday office party overload

How to get in, get out, and stay in line

According to a recent survey of nearly 3,000 adults conducted by New York based market research firm Harris Interactive, the average American will attend 2.7 office parties during a holiday season and spend 2 hours and 36 minutes at each. Now that you know you'll be spending at least a few wonderful evenings this December wearing funny hats, eating crazy cracker creations and avoiding those darned mistletoed doorposts, how can you make the most of this season's merry making?

Here are a few tips on how to tackle office parties:

1. **Appropriate Dress is Essential** – If in doubt, leave it out. Save your party clothes for personal gatherings.

2. **Limit Libations** – Keep any type of a drink other than eggnog to a minimum. Holiday party '"disasters" follow you back into the office for the whole year.

3. **Ho, Ho, Ho, It's Almost Review Time** – Make sure you say hello to your boss, his or her boss and other co-workers that you haven't seen recently.

4. **Bring Your "Ball and Chain"** – If your work allows it, bring your spouse. He or she can be helpful when conversing with co-workers you really don't know, can help you remember others and help keep the conversation flowing.

Look at the holiday office party as an opportunity to see and be seen. Make the most of it, enjoy your co-workers, indulge in a piece of fruitcake and have your exit strategy when you've made all of your holiday connections. Remember, you will see them at work again very soon!

www.selfmarketing.com

112 Tips to Succeed: Hosting a business dinner

When you host a business dinner, remember one crucial point: You are in charge.

Doing business over dinner is a good way to introduce yourself to clients, build relationships and seal the deal. Get it right, and it's duck soup. Get it wrong, and you're dead in the water.

HELPFUL HINT NO. 1: Be sure the date works for you. This seems obvious, but if you have to postpone or cancel, you'll look disorganized and will have wasted your clients' time.

- Always call ahead and make it clear to the maitre d' that you will be hosting an important business dinner. Stress that everything must be perfect and that you'll pay the bill. Make arrangements with the restaurant to pay the bill prior to the dinner.
- Be sure to call your clients the day before to confirm the dinner. If there's a mix up on their end, be gracious and reschedule.
- When preparing for the event, dress in appropriate business attire, and kick it up a notch. This underscores your seriousness about the clients and their business. It's better to be a little overdressed than woefully under-dressed.
- On the day of the meal, get to the restaurant ahead of time so you'll have a chance to attend to any last-minute details. A tip in advance never hurts.

HELPFUL HINT NO. 2: Don't forget seating strategy. Work out the seating before your guests arrive.

- Make sure the guests have the best seats – those with a view of the water or skyline, for example. You don't want your guests facing the wall, kitchen or restrooms. If the table isn't suitable, don't be bashful about asking for a better one.
- This is a business dinner, and you don't want to shout across the table. If you have one client, sit next to each other. If you have two clients, seat one across from you and the other to your side.

HELPFUL HINT NO. 3: Limit the amount of alcohol you and your guests consume at dinner.

- The meal is about business. It might be wise to stick with wine.
- If you must excuse yourself, do so only between courses.

- As the host, you determine when to discuss business. Dinner is a social occasion, so wait until the main course has been completed before getting down to details. At lunch, wait until you've ordered so you won't be interrupted. At breakfast, get to the point quickly.

Scott Reeves - www.forbes.com

113 Technique to Succeed: Customer Service – Practice the 'Customer Delight Principle'

Turning regular customers into loyal customers assures repeat business. Determine what they need, want and expect – and give them more. It's achievable through relationship marketing – learning as much as you can demographically, psychographically and geodemographically.

Smiling at clientele, promptly responding to requests or complaints, and honoring warranties isn't enough to make the rigorous customer service grade any longer. Many experts would argue that standard amenities don't represent customer service at all because they are expected as a matter of course.

- Ask for customers' email addresses and send them special offers.
- Empower your employees to handle customer disputes.
- Meet daily with employees to discuss customer issues and invite input from your staff on how each should be handled.
- Keep an eye on the competition.

Do as Nordstrom's does:
Start with the Basics
1. Make customer service a core value.
2. Hire the right people.
3. Empower your employees.
4. Solicit and use feedback.
5. Target your customers.

Get Your Creativity Flowing
Once the basics are in place, you and your employee team can unleash your collective creativity to develop ways to further enhance customer service.

Here are some ways to get that process moving.

1. Order pizza and have a freewheeling brainstorming session. Create an atmosphere that encourages everyone to share their "wild and crazy" ideas. Be open to any suggestions – reject nothing at this stage.
2. Make it fun.
3. Bring in professional trainers to conduct a seminar on a particular aspect of customer service.
4. Give everyone on your staff a copy of a popular customer service book and hold a round-table discussion to see if any of the suggestions might be applicable to your business.
5. Start a rewards program for the best customer service idea, making it something significant and enticing that employees will strive to achieve.

Examples of Innovative Ideas
1. **Give your customers something unexpected** – a special treat.
2. **Extend the warrant on your product.** This communicates both a quality statement and a commitment to customer satisfaction.
3. **Add value through information.** Provide your customers with new ways to use your products or increase their efficiency. This can include newsletters, special seminars or face-to-face consultations.
4. **Use the Internet.** Improve the frequency of your customer communications via email. Brief notes with tips on product usage, coupons and special offers – even just a seasonal greeting – can keep your firm top of mind. One caveat: always give your customers an easy way to be deleted from your email list if they so desire.
5. **Celebrate with your customers.** Sending birthday cards and congratulatory notes on new babies and job promotions may seem "old hat," but in today's depersonalized world, it's appreciated once again. Add a coupon for a special gift or discount on the customer's next visit. (Hello, Sports Fans! – Cherry Hill, N.J. found great success from this relationship marketing technique.)
6. **Expand your services or product line.** In today's harried environment people prize convenience and time savings. Ask your clientele how you can serve them better – subsequently extending your product and service offerings to provide additional benefits for your customers and additional profits for you.
7. **Employ mass customization.** Offer your clients options that result in products that are "tailor-made" to their needs. As Burger King has said for years, "Have it you way!"

The ultimate key is to put yourself in the position of your customers. Give them what they want—and a little bit more. They will be delighted and, in turn, will delight you with a prosperous and rewarding business.

Bill Kalmar - Former Malcolm Baldrige National Quality Award examiner (judged firms for annual U.S. Commerce Department awards) - Lake Orion, Mich. Gannett News Service

114 Tips to Succeed: The elevator 'speech'

The "elevator pitch" is a short description about your company that you can convey in the time it takes to ride an elevator. And not an elevator in a skyscraper, either. Your elevator pitch must be clear and concise and show that you understand the core aspects of your business.

Because it must be short, you have to decide what facets of your company to leave out. Often, these can be the things you're most excited about – a new technology, a great location, outstanding customer service, etc.

But if they're not central to the core or success of your business, they don't belong in an elevator pitch.

You should touch – very briefly – on the products or services you sell, what market you serve, and your competitive advantage.

You must be brief and clear. Unless you're in a highly technical field, your neighbor or grandmother should be able to understand your business well enough to describe it to someone else. After all, you want grandma marketing for you too, don't you? People you meet need to quickly understand the nature of your business if you want them to send business your way.

Make sure your employees, investors, even vendors know your company's elevator pitch. Have your employees practice your company's elevator pitch so they're able to network for you as well.

It's often a good idea to use an analogy, especially if you're in a new or difficult-to-grasp field. "We're the Google for car buyers" is a good shorthand way to say that you're trying to create a search engine for people wanting to purchase an automobile.

Think in these terms (sort of like a mission statement):

- This is who we are;
- What we think about ourselves;
- What we want to do;
- Why we deserve your support

You'll find you use your elevator pitch often – in emails to prospective customers and investors, to introduce yourself at organizational meetings or when running into an old friend at a ballgame. Who knows? You may even use it if you meet a potential customer in an elevator.

So go out and find a three-story building with an elevator, ride up and down and practice your pitch. That way, you'll be prepared the next time some one asks you, "What do you do?"

Rhonda Abrams - Gannett News Service
M. Larry Litwin, APR, Fellow PRSA - Author - *The Public Relations Practitioner's Playbook for (all) Strategic Communicators* (AuthorHouse – 2013)

115 Techniques to Succeed: Internet security: Password creation takes homework and creativity

Develop different strong passwords for every system or program you log into.

If an attacker does guess it, he would have access to all of your accounts. You should use these techniques to develop unique passwords for each of your accounts:

- Don't use passwords that are based on personal information that can be easily accessed or guessed.
- Don't use words that can be found in any dictionary of any language.
- Develop a mnemonic for remembering complex passwords.
- Use both lowercase and capital letters.
- Use a combination of letters, numbers and special characters.
- Use different passwords on different systems.

U.S. Department of Homeland Security

116 Techniques to Succeed: Perfecting business letters

The ability to write a perfect business letter is an important skill. Here are some ways to improve your letter writing:

- Map out your thinking and go to others for suggestions.
- Make a bold statement in the beginning of the letter to grab the reader's attention.
- Write simply.
- Be specific.
- Accentuate the positive things your company has done.
- Edit your work.
- End with a catchy statement.

Gannett News Service

117 Tips to Succeed: Product placement

A growing number of advertisers are using technology that makes their products appear in places they weren't before.

It's called digital product integration, and it's the new frontier for paid product placements – embedded advertising.

Advertisers such as Chevrolet® and Dannon® yogurt are among the marketers using technology to digitally insert their products into scenes of popular prime-time TV episodes after the episode has been filmed.

In general, product placements – in which products are strategically placed in TV shows, movies, video games, songs and books – are booming as advertisers try to grab the attention of consumers who have video recording devices to dodge the traditional 30-second commercial.

www.courierpostonline.com
M. Larry Litwin, APR, Fellow PRSA - Author - *The Public Relations Practitioner's Playbook for (all) Strategic Communicators* (AuthorHouse – 2013)

118 Tips to Succeed: Just what does APR stand for?

When it comes to communication professions, it has nothing to do with interest rates.

APR is Accreditation in Public Relations, a designation for public relations professionals who are selected based on broad knowledge, strategic perspective and sound professional judgment.

The APR program is administered by the Universal Accreditation Board, which was created in 1998. It is a consortium of 10 professional communication organizations.

www.praccreditation.org

119 Tips to Succeed: Be proactive to keep identity secure

- Centralize your banking – Keep credit cards, mortgages, bank accounts, all in one place.
- Ask your bank or credit organization about its policy for selling customer information.
- Request your information not be sold to brokers.
- Reconcile bank statements, credit card statements and other accounts monthly.
- Check your credit report at least once a year.
- If you think you've been a victim of fraud, ask about a fraud alert.

Websites worth checking:

✓ The Identity Theft Resource Center: www.idtheftcenter.org

✓ Federal Trade Commission's identity theft unit:
  www.consumer.gov/idtheft or (877) 438-4338. Its TTY line is (866) 653-4261.

✓ Equifax: www.equifax.com or (800) 525-6285

✓ Experian: www.experian.com or (888) 397-3742

✓ TransUnion: www.transunion.com or (800) 680-7289

Jim Walsh - Co-author - Identity Theft: How to Protect Your Name, Your Credit and Your Vital Information ... and What to Do When Someone Hijacks Any of These

120 Techniques to Succeed: Audience Segmentation (ISPR)/ Audience Fragmentation (IFPR)

- Identify
- Segment/Fragment (demographically, psychographically, geodemographically, behavioristically, benefits)
- Profile
- Rank
  – Audience Power Structure
    - Elite (Key Communicators)

- Pluralistic or Diffused
- Amorphous/Latent

Audiences are I(S)FPRd as matters of understanding and economics. Public relations practitioners and their clients may have limited resources. Audiences must be I(S)FPRd to help determine which are most important and how much time and money will be allocated trying to reach them to either change, maintain or reinforce behavior. All four steps (IFPR) are imperative to a successful PR plan.

121 Techniques to Succeed: Keeping sane when stressed by client or co-worker

It doesn't matter what you do, you're likely to have at least one difficult co-worker or customer. Staying sane during chaos doesn't have to be difficult.

- Draw in as few people as possible. Try to address the situation with the individual without bringing in other people like supervisors. You never know how the situation can be turned around to make you look like the problem. Show yourself and the other person that you have the confidence and competence to handle it yourself.

- Don't make it personal. Realize that the reason the person is being difficult might have nothing to do with you. Try to empathize with them and recognize that they need to learn how to manage stress.

- Take control. Ask yourself what you have control over in the situation. It may be that you can control how you choose to respond or that you choose not to discuss the situation at that moment.

- Turn the situation into a challenge or a game. Try to make the best of difficult interpersonal situations by seeing the humor in them or by creating opportunities to learn. For instance, an irate customer lets you practice your poise and assertive communication skills.

- Take a look at yourself. We may be fostering annoying behavior by others based on how we respond to it. Try out a different response and see what happens.

Larina Kase - Doctor of Psychology, career coach and former counselor at the University of Pennsylvania - www.extremecommunicator.com

122 Tips to Succeed: Tips to make investing work

Investing is a way to make money – but before you invest:
- Pay off consumer loans
- Keep no more than a percentage approximately equal to your age in fixed-income investments
- Don't invest in anything you don't understand
- Don't invest in anything quickly
- Don't hold onto an investment for sentimental reasons
- Get professional advice

www.checklist.com

123 Tips to Succeed: Looking for a job: These tips should help

In addition to Handout No. 30 on www.larrylitwin.com, these tips should come in handy – especially for women:

THE DAY BEFORE THE INTERVIEW
- Make your travel plans for getting to the interview; know exactly where you are going and to whom you will be speaking.
- Buy your ticket of fare for transportation, fill your car with gas, or re-confirm other transportation plans.
- Make sure that you have several clean copies of your resume to take with you.
- Decide what you will wear and check that it is clean, pressed, no missing buttons, etc.
- Check that you have at least two pairs of new or as-good-as-new hosiery – sheer, off black or nude; no opaque or white!
- Confirm child care plans and any other plans which leave you depending on someone else. Have a back-up in mind in case you need it.
- Try to learn two or three facts about the company and/or its products, so you will sound well-informed at the interview (visit their website).

THE NIGHT BEFORE THE INTERVIEW
- Check the weather forecast! Will you need an umbrella? Should you wear a coat?
- Decide what you will be taking in your handbag and set it aside. Be sure to include a pen and paper as well as an extra pair of hosiery.
- Plan how you will wear your hair and make-up. (You shouldn't try anything new in the morning.) Make-up should be appropriate for daytime, not Saturday night. No glimmer or shimmer and keep eye makeup to a minimum or wear none at all.
- Check your nails! They should be conservative in length and color; no chipped polish.
- Do as much of your morning preparation for both yourself and your family as you can.
- Do something to relax: take a warm bath, exercise, etc.
- Have a light dinner (no alcohol) and get to bed early.

THE DAY OF THE INTERVIEW
- Remember to take directions to the interview, the name of the person you are meeting, your resume and other relevant items with you.
- Give yourself plenty of time to get there, get comfortable and find the restroom.
- If you feel nervous, try breathing in to the count of 10 and then exhale to the count of 10. Try to increase the count.

Don't leave anything to chance. Remember: you can't be too prepared!

www.larrylitwin.com www.appearance.com/interview_tips/

124

Tips to Succeed: The phone: Friend or foe?

Here are 10 Steps to assure the phone is your company's friend:

1. **Preparation** – You can actually prepare to take a phone call. Taking certain preparation steps will help you listen better and concentrate more fully on what the customer is saying.

2. **A Strong Start** – If a phone call gets off to an awkward start, it can go downhill quickly from there.

3. **Building Rapport** – Whether the caller's a high-powered businessman or a soft-spoken elderly person, there are appropriate and effective ways to build rapport.

4. **Effective On-Hold Techniques** – There's a right way and as wrong way to put a caller on hold. For example, when's the last time a receptionist politely asked you if you were able to hold?

5. **Effective Call-Transferring** – Be polite. Alert the caller they are being transferred. Offer a direct number should the caller be disconnected.

6. **Speaking Clearly** – Anyone who wants to succeed in business today should be able to enunciate and speak clearly.

7. **Proper Tone of Voice** – Tone of voice is the nonverbal component of your telephone personality. Learn how to treat each phone call as a separate "performance".

8. **Positive Speech** – Your use of language can make or break a call. There are certain words and phrases that can quickly turn off a caller; conversely, there are words and phrases that are music to a caller's ears.

9. **Effective Listening** – Don't just hear the caller, listen to what is being said. That will help you form a response.

10. **Practice the Golden Rule** – Wouldn't it be a better world if we all treated each other the way we wish to be treated? When you're on the telephone with a client, you should treat the caller with the same dignity and respect you extend to the owner of your company.

www.thephonecoach.com/products-TPC-G10.htm#TenSteps

125 Techniques to Succeed: Just what is integrated marketing communication – synergy?

Like many practitioners, you may spend much of your life trying to get friends and relatives to understand what you do for a living. Try this example:

- You see a gorgeous girl at a party. You go up to her and say, "I'm fantastic in bed." That's **Direct Marketing**.
- You're at a party with a bunch of friends and see a gorgeous girl. One of your friends goes up to her and pointing at you says, "He's fantastic in bed." That's **Advertising**.
- You see a gorgeous girl at a party. You go up to her and get her telephone number. The next day you call and say, "Hi, I'm fantastic in bed." That's **Telemarketing**.
- You're at a party and see a gorgeous girl. You get up and straighten your tie, you walk up to her and pour her a drink. You open the door for her, pick up her bag after she drops it, offer her a ride, and then say, "By the way, I'm fantastic in bed." That's **Public Relations**.
- You're at a party and see a gorgeous girl. She walks up to you and says, "I hear you're fantastic in bed." That's **Brand Recognition**.

126 Techniques to Succeed: Why information campaigns fail

- The voter is generally uninformed.
- There are large groups in the population who admit to having little or no interest in public issues.
- People tend to expose themselves to material that is compatible with their attitudes and beliefs and to avoid exposure to issues, candidates and products that do not match their beliefs (selective perception).
- Selective perception and interpretation of content follows exposure: individuals perceive, absorb and remember content differently.
- Changes in attitudes (even following exposure to a message), are difficult to achieve. It may be a mistake to take too much time or spend too many resources in an effort to lead to a more favorable behavior. (Concentration should be placed on getting out the vote of those in agreement with your candidate or issue.)

127 Techniques to Succeed: The on-camera interview

DO
- Use first names
- Speak to the interviewer and not to the camera
- Stand up for your rights
- Deliver your message early
- Be prepared from the time you leave your office/home
- Couch your position as necessary (avoid specifics)
- Speak only the truth; be ready with facts
- Be aware of and sensitive to time
- Know what the interviewer wants
- Be big enough to learn from your mistakes
- Thank the interviewer and crew for their time

DON'T
- Let the topic/subject drift
- Assume anything
- Be afraid to take a compliment (but keep your guard up)
- Consider the interviewer a friend…or an enemy
- Gossip, criticize or speculate
- Use YES and NO answers
- Put the interviewer on defensive without good cause
- Forget the importance of body language
- Speak too fast or too slow
- Go into any situation without preparation
- Be too hard on yourself
- Never say "NO COMMENT"
- Ask for a copy of the final interview

128 Tips to Succeed: Calming those interview butterflies

Many prospective employees get "the butterflies" before a job interview. Here are tips to stay calm and present yourself in the best way:

- Get a good night's sleep and maintain your usual morning routine – If you never eat breakfast, for example, don't eat a hearty morning meal on interview day.
- Try remembering some of your happiest memories or a proud moment before arriving for the interview.
- Come prepared with a briefcase containing resumes, pen and paper for recording your interviewer's name and the date and time for a possible future interview, an application and references and examples of your work such as writing samples.

Federal Citizen Information Center - Pueblo, Colo.

129 Tips to Succeed: Prepare for interview with questions

Before going to a job interview, it is important to practice describing yourself. As a starting point, respond out loud to the following questions:

- Tell me about a time you worked as part of a team?
- Why should I select you over other applicants?
- What are your greatest strengths and weaknesses?
- Tell me more about the project you described on your resume.
- Describe a work or school-related problem and how you solved it.
- What are your short-term goals?
- Why do you want to work in this occupation and for this company?

U.S. Department of Labor

130 Tips to Succeed: Slash your phone bills

- Switch to Internet phoning. Voice over Internet Protocol, or VoIP, transmits phone calls via a highspeed Internet connection. VoIP providers include phone and cable-TV companies and some, such as Packet8 and Vonage, that specialize in the service.
- Use your cell phone for everything. Drop your landline and use wireless at home and on the go.
- Trade down to a cheaper cell plan. Some providers have less-costly plans than the ones they tend to push, but you might have to ask or poke around their websites.
- Take a local/long-distance bundle.
- Buy a phone card for long-distance. A prepaid long-distance card can cut costs if you don't make many long-distance landline calls.

Consumer Reports

131 Tips to Succeed: New rules: Have right goals and strategy for job hunt

The average job seeker commits two drastic sins: having the wrong goal and having no strategy. Now do you know why you're not getting anywhere?

To change from a getting-nowhere-fast direction to one where you're making headway, here are your new rules.

NEW RULE NO.1: CHANGE YOUR GOAL FROM GETTING A JOB TO GETTING INTERVIEWS.

When your goal is to "get a job," you're fixated on selling yourself. If you do get interviews, you go in thinking, "I gotta get this job" and "What do they want to hear?" You sound desperate. Remember, a job interview is a conversation, not a sales call.

Once you do get the interview, you should have the same objective as the interviewer: to explore whether this is a good fit while making a positive impression. If you've done that well, you're more apt to get to what you want – an offer.

NEW RULE NO.2: CREATE A STRATEGY.

Plopping yourself in front of your computer and sending your resume to job sites is not a strategy. It's one activity that's part of an overall strategy. To create a strategy, look at your objective.

Then work your strategy:

- Focus on what it is you want to do.
- Conduct a search of the companies that make those products or provide the service (public relations, advertising or manufacturing).
- Figure out the best way to approach them. Going through your list, write down names of people you might know at each company. Write down those you know who might steer you to a decision maker. Research hiring managers.
- With your goal being to get an interview, "practice" what you want to say in a phone call, letter or email to entice them.
- Check out the companies' websites for posted positions, apply online and follow up by mail.
- Talk to other people you know who could suggest companies you didn't know about or are starting up or know of other openings that fit your criteria.
- Through website and elsewhere, learn as much as you can about the company you are interviewing with so that you are thoroughly familiar with it and can answer and ask questions.

Your strategy may shift. But two things stay the same. You need to get the right person's attention then develop a plan and work it.

Andrea Kay - Gannett - April 8, 2005

132 Tips to Succeed: Getting a job after graduation

- **Be nice to nerds**: The friendships you develop in college can be some of the richest relationships you ever have. They might also be your ticket to the top and your way to help your friends. You never know, that computer whiz you were nice to in freshman English might need a right-hand person when he takes over a multimillion-dollar media corporation.

- **Make noise**: Look for opportunities to let people know who you are and what you offer. Tell people that you're graduating and create a way for them to ask you what you want to-do with your life. And remember to always say and send a thank-you.

- **Keep on talking**: Start conversations at sporting events, while you're eating out or even at the park where you're enjoying the spring weather. Find a positive way to follow up so that you collect their contact information and stay in touch. You just might run into someone who needs you on their team.

- **Call your hero**: Find successful people in your field of interest and take them to lunch. Let them know your aspirations and ask for advice.

- **Turn obstacles into opportunities**: Challenges are inevitable in searching for a career. Keep a positive perspective and figure out how to improve and convince the next person you meet to make you CEO of their company.

Andrea Nierenberg - Author Nonstop
Networking: How to Improve Your Life, Luck and Career
www.mybusinessrelationships.com/

133 Tips to Succeed:
Call it – 'An applicant statement'

Polish your resume by including a summary paragraph stating what you bring to the table, qualifications, experience and examples of a job well done. It should be succinct and contain buzzwords human resource managers look for – containing many of the same key message points you would include in an elevator speech.

Here is an example:

Applicant Statement: My supervisors describe me as "mature beyond her years, articulate, well tailored and polished, loyal, has a passion for the profession, outstanding writer, and a skilled organizer and strategic thinker. "It is my dream to bring those qualities, passion and dedication to ELLE's readers – just as I do the residents of Cherry Hill. My zest for knowledge and new challenges is contagious and should appeal to ELLE magazine's staff and target audience.

Nina Ebert - President - A Word's Worth - Plumsted, N.J.
M. Larry Litwin, APR, Fellow PRSA - Author - The Public Relations Practitioner's Playbook for (all) Strategic Communicators (AuthorHouse - 2013)

134 Tips to Succeed:
Choosing good restaurants

- Take a look inside.
- Study the menu.
- Keep it affordable.
- Ask someone leaving who just ate there.

135 Techniques to Succeed: Send positive vibes to your co-workers

The ability to work well with others is a skill that will make for a stronger team atmosphere in your workplace. Teammates who get along are much more effective in accomplishing their daily goals and tasks. Follow Dale Carnegie Training's steps to become the type of person everyone wants to be around.

- Do not criticize, condemn or complain: People enjoy others who are upbeat.
- Show appreciation: Everyone needs to be recognized.
- Arouse those around you: Establish a mutual goal.
- Become interested in others: Genuinely care about their desires.
- Smile: A smile draws people to it.
- Use proper names: It is the badge of individuality.
- Listen: Focus on what is being communicated.
- Talk about what others like: Turn the spotlight on them.
- Make people feel important: We all want to be special.

www.southjersey.dalecarnegie.com

136 Techniques to Succeed: Prebusiness plan for the small business

Thinking about starting or expanding your own small business?

- Start at the beginning. Establish a company goal, objectives, strategies and tactics.
- Determine your company's name: Make sure the name you want isn't taken.
- Decide your location: Can you work at home? Do you need office or manufacturing space? Local Realtors have listings for commercial space to lease or buy.
- List the equipment you will need: Make a list of everything – from office paper and computers to company cars and machinery. You will get a feeling for start-up costs and be able to start thinking about how you are going to pay for it all.
- Calculate your compensation: Some business owners forgo a salary when getting started. Others pay themselves too much. Sit down with the other pieces of your pre-business plan and calculate a practical salary for yourself.

Andrew Glatz - Sun National Bank - www.sunnb.com

137 Techniques to Succeed: Meeting people

When meeting people both your nonverbal and verbal behavior help to define your social skills. Using effective handshakes, good eye contact, and making the proper introductions show proper etiquette.

A. Handshakes are vital in social situations.
1. Develop a comfortable handshake and keep it consistent.
2. Handshakes should not be too hard; or too soft.
3. Make a solid connection of the web skin between the thumb and forefinger.
4. The host or person with the most authority usually initiates the handshake.

B. Eye contact is another critical factor when meeting people.
1. Eye contact increases trust.
2. It shows confidence and good interpersonal skills.
3. Eye contact shows respect for the person and business situation.

Proper introductions help to establish rapport when meeting people.
1. Authority defines whose name is said first. Say the name of the most important person first and then the name of the person being introduced.
2. Introduce people in the following order:
   1. younger to older
   2. non-official to official
   3. junior executive to senior executive
   4. colleague to customer
3. Keep the introduction basic.
4. Remember names for future reference.
5. Provide some information about the people you are introducing to clarify your relationship with that person.
6. Always carry business cards.
7. Keep notes on people in order to follow-up both personally and professionally.

The Career Center - Florida State University

138. Tips to Succeed: PRSA's Code of Ethics

PRSA lists the following 10 principles of behavior for the practice of public relations:

1. Conduct in accord with the public interest.
2. Exemplify high standards of honesty and integrity.
3. Deal fairly with the public.
4. Adhere to highest standards of accuracy and truth.
5. Do not knowingly disseminate false or misleading information.
6. Do not engage in any practice that corrupts the channels of communicationor processes of government.
7. Identify publicly the name of the client or employer on whose behalf any public communication is made.
8. Do not make use of any individual or organization professing to be independent or unbiased but actually serving another or undisclosed interest.
9. Do not guarantee the achievement of specified results beyond member's control.
10. Do not represent conflicting or competing interests.

139

Tips to Succeed:
Make your customers your friends

Are you a friend to your customers? If not, you should be.

At least 50 percent of all the sales made in America on any given day are made on the basis of friendship.

If you and your company are looking for more sales, then you ought to be developing more friendships. Successful salespeople and relationship builders don't just give customers and clients free tickets to attend a sporting event, a concert or some other entertainment event. They attend with the client.

Why would any salesperson pass up the opportunity to spend time with a customer away from the work environment? This is when many friendships begin. By spending quality time with people, you get to know them, and if they're people who spend money with your company, the time spent is beyond price.

Some "place" to go with customers and potential clients:

- ball games
- theater
- concert
- gallery
- Chamber of Commerce event
- community-help project
- breakfast
- lunch
- dinner
- seminar given by your company
- I-Max theater with your customer and all your children.

While you and your sales people should all be well-versed in all the best selling techniques, sales is still about relationships, and friendships. You can only earn a commission using a sales technique, but you can earn a fortune building friendships and relationships.

Jeffrey Gitomer - Author - The Sales Bible and Customer Satisfaction is Worthless, Customer Loyalty is Priceless- www.salesman@gitomer.com
njbiz - Feb. 7, 2005
Newstrack Executive Information Service - www.news-track.com - 800-334-5771

140 Tips to Succeed: Are you a new leader?

New leaders think, act and are different. The new leader embodies four hallmarks that together deliver extraordinary impact:
- Steadfast passion
- Inclusive culture
- Global proaction
- Continuous exploration

The new leader has a learnable approach to drive business growth, build productive cultures and create exciting careers.

Roslyn Courtney - "The New Leader Beyond Hierarchy and Power"
www.rozcourtney.com

141 Tips to Succeed: Leadership

What is leadership?

It's a title

It's charisma

It's expertise

Dr. Philip Tumminia - Special Assistant to President for University Advancement
Rowan University - Glassboro, N.J.

142 Tips to Succeed: Often-made loan mistakes – beware

- Agreeing to co-sign. Some studies have found that of co-signed loans that go into default, as many as three out of four co-signers are asked to repay the loan.
- Not reading the fine print. When you obtain a line of credit or loan, you are entering into a legally binding agreement. Read everything to understand

why and how often interest rates could change and what will cause the account to default.
- Borrowing your way out of debt. The only real way to get out of debt is to pay it off. "Moving money" has as many risks as rewards and will never work unless you are committed to a lifestyle change.

www.crediteducation.org.

143 Tips to Succeed: Building relationships leads to leadership

Want to advance in the workplace? Here are some strong suggestions. They are characteristics of a strong and successful leader:

Strong leaders spend most of their day:
- consensus-building
- offering recognition and reward
- negotiating
- planning
- organizing
- collaborating
- helping others reach their potential
- stressing ethics
- giving feedback (both positive and negative)

Leaders show greater respect on the job for others by:
- Meeting with employees a level below for ideas and feedback.
- Using cross-training and job swapping to develop employee understanding for other workers' duties and perspectives.
- Moving front-line supervisors to other departments for an entire year to fully experience the challenges of that position.
- Putting fun and creative rewards into place to recognize outstanding employee effort and achievement.

The bottom line – do the right thing.

Anita Bruzzese - Author of Take This Job and Thrive
(Impact Publications) - Gannett News Service

144 Techniques to Succeed: Leadership development

There are five areas that define the success of an executive training program:
- Satisfaction (were the participants happy?)
- Learning (did knowledge increase?)
- Application (did on-the-job behavior change?)
- Business impact (were there changes in business outcomes?)
- Return on investment (did the company make more money resulting from the training than it spent on the training?)

Newstrack Executive Information Service www.news-track.com
800-334-5771

145 Techniques to Succeed: Communication and leadership

A coach's 10-point game plan:
- Have a concrete vision – in other words, be clear about your vision for the group's future.
- Be your own messenger – direct communication is important not just on major issues, but on the day-to-day matters, as well.
- Build a team ego – it is the difference between mediocrity and being something special.
- Act with integrity – don't cut corners or bend rules; it will only undermine your effort.
- Act decisively – you won't always be right, but you must be willing to put your ideas and yourself on the line.
- Be adaptable – you must change, and so must those around you or everyone gets behind.
- Be consistent – have a strategy for when things go wrong to get through it quickly without panic.
- Maintain focus – this is a discipline, so you must train yourself at it, learning from the tough times.
- Live for the future, not in the past – "short-term goals to manage the present, long-term goals for the future," he writes.
- Act selflessly – "leaders are judged by the successes of the people they lead."

Rick Pitino - Author - Lead to Succeed

146 Tips to Succeed: Pointers for Fridays before holidays

The Fridays before holidays are typically slow workdays. Here are some ways to get organized and separate yourself from your co-workers, according to, a manufacturer of organizational products.

- Deal with a document as soon as you receive it, instead of allowing it to get lost.
- Keep a document only when you need it for the long term.
- Save time by clearly labeling folders.
- Use a portable filing system if your desk is too cluttered.
- Use a to-do list to keep projects running on time.

Pendaflex® - The Pendaflex Adviser®

147 The plan is nothing–planning is everything

Some of the things your business plan needs to do:

- **Define your strategy**. Figure out what you're really selling, who wants it, why they want it and how your business provides something different from the competition.
- **Control your destiny**. Determine where you want to go and break that down into specific, concrete steps with dates, deadlines and budgets.
- **Plan your cash.** You've got to make a good, educated guess, then manage your planned cash flow vs. actual cash flow very carefully.
- **Allocate resources realistically**. This doesn't just have to do with cash, but also with knowhow and responsibility. Who's in charge?
- **Communicate your plan.** The business plan is the standard tool for communicating the main points of a business to a spouse, partner, boss, banker, investor, manager or other interested person.

Careerbuilder.com

148 Tips to Succeed: Keep holiday cards professional

- Holiday greeting cards should be more tailored and formal than cards for family and friends. Keep messages brief and secular unless you are certain of the recipient's religious faith.
- Sign each card personally – even if your name is preprinted on the card.
- An email greeting is a poor substitute for a real greeting card.
- Mailing holiday greeting cards first class will ensure they are delivered to a forwarding address or returned if the address cannot be located.
- Include your return address in the upper left-hand corner or on the back flap of the envelope.
- Use an office address when mailing holiday greeting cards to business associates.
- Take the extra step to verify how recipients' names are spelled.

Marc Wagenheim - Hallmark®

149 Techniques to Succeed: Litwin's 9 P's of Marketing

- Public Relations
- (Sales) Promotion
- Positioning (Place)
- Price
- Personal Selling
- Product (itself)
- Politics (in the workplace Brainstorming)
- Policy
- Packaging

Litwin's 9 P's of Marketing
M. Larry Litwin, APR, Fellow PRSA - The Public Relations Practitioner's Playbook for (all) Strategic Communicators (AuthorHouse – 2013)

166

150 Tips to Succeed:
Some reasons to earn an MBA degree

Here are some reasons Rowan (N.J.) University and other graduate students pursue an MBA:
- To improve management/leadership knowledge and skills.
- To increase opportunities for obtaining a new job or finding a better job.
- To increase earnings opportunities.
- To improve knowledge in areas of finance and accounting.
- To improve personal skills, quantitative, oral, writing, critical thinking.
- To increase job opportunities in current workplace.

Robert Lynch - Professor, College of Business - Rowan (N.J.) University
www.rowan.edu/mba

151 Tips to Succeed:
Think twice before challenging the media

Have your facts straight before arguing with the person who buys ink by the barrel and paper by the ton.

Many newspaper editors

152 Techniques to Succeed:
Key elements of a mission statement

- This is who we are
- What we think about ourselves
- What we want to do
- Why we deserve your support

Larry Litwin and Ralph Burgio © 1971; © 1999; © 2013
www.larrylitwin.com

153 Tips to Succeed: 14 ways public relations practitioners should deal with the media

1. Make the CEO responsible for media relations.
2. Face the facts.
3. Consider the public interest in every operating decision.
4. Be a source before you are a subject.
5. If you want your views represented, you have to talk.
6. Respond quickly.
7. Cage your lawyers.
8. Tell the truth – or nothing.
9. Don't expect to bat 1.000 (to be perfect).
10. Don't take it personally.
11. Control what you can.
12. Know with whom you are dealing.
13. Avoid TV unless you feel you can speak candidly.
14. Be human.

M. Larry Litwin, APR, Fellow PRSA - The Public Relations Practitioner's Playbook for (all) Strategic Communicators (AuthorHouse - 2013)

154 Techniques to Succeed: Top 10 list of media relations mistakes

BEST EVIDENCE

10. Lack of preparation/plan
9. Failure to identify audience
8. Reluctance to accept responsibility
7. Inability to show compassion
6. Failure to focus
5. Natural bias against reporters
4. Inability to shut mouth
3. Natural tendency to want to sound more intelligent than we really are
2. Fear & loathing
1. Panic

Best Evidence, Inc. Executive Communications Counsel
Crisis Communications Management Cherry Hill, N.J.
bestevidence911@aol.com

155 Tips to Succeed: Understanding reporters and editors

Generally, journalists strive for:
- Accuracy
- Balance
- Fairness
- Memorable (what will the reader get out of the story?)

When pitching a story, the public relations practitioner must answer two questions:
- What is news?
- What is the point (to the story)?

A goal of editors is to:
- Educate
- Inform
- Inspire
- Motivate (staff)

…to help the public make intelligent decisions.

Ev Landers - News Coach - Gannett

156 Techniques to Succeed: Media interviews: Dos and don'ts

Executives faced with a news media interview should seize the opportunity to deliver a positive message on behalf of their company.

Keep these tips in mind when preparing for news media interviews:

- Return calls promptly. Reporters are usually on deadline, and if they don't hear from you quickly, they will move on to someone else – possibly your competitor.

- Be candid. If a reporter thinks you're misleading them or trying to hide something, the story they write may not present you in the best light.

- Help them understand your business. Reporters are a proxy for your audience, the readers, and you need them to communicate your messages accurately.

- Be proactive – Cultivate relationships with reporters. Drop them a note commenting on a story that interested you; offer to be an expert or to refer them to other experts. Every story doesn't need to be about you or your company, but if reporters know you are a reliable, helpful source, they will call you again.

Steve Lubetkin - Lubetkin & Co. Communications, Public Relations and Technology Counsel, LLC - www.lubetkin.net

157

Techniques to Succeed: Ways to meet on the job

New on the job and not sure how to meet people? Just get out of your cubicle and start talking with new colleagues or managers to build your network.

Here's what to do:

- Start slowly by attending different functions at a company. Choose your seating. Don't sit down next to an empty chair. Try to sit next to someone new and introduce yourself — don't expect someone to come over to you.

- Are you shy? Try an ice-breaker like "did you hear what the speaker said?" to initiate a conversation.

- While waiting for a speaker, maximize the time and exchange numbers with the person sitting next to you.

- Use the elevator as talk time (known as 30-second elevator conversation or message).

- After leaving a meeting, use the time to chat up colleagues or meet someone new.

- Compliments are key – an easy way to make an introduction is to comment on an article of clothing or jewelry.

- Plan a lunch – follow up with new contacts by setting up one-onone meetings to foster the relationship.

Stacey Sweet-Belle - Chubb Insurance - wwww.chubb.com/

158 Tips to Succeed: A 5th 'P' of marketing

Jonathan Byrnes, a senior lecturer at MIT, has joined others in expanding the original four "P's" of marketing - product, place, price and promotion.

Dr. Byrnes' fifth "P" is profitability, which can be improved through:

- Control of internal knowledge
- Selectivity
- Coordination
- A shift from mass marketing to precision (more focused or niche) marketing

Jonathan Byrnes - Harvard Business School's Working Knowledge
Newstrack Executive Information Service www.news-track.com
800-334-5771

159 Tips to Succeed: Don't blame the reporter

Never hold a reporter responsible for an editorial stand his newspaper may have taken even if you believe the reporter had input in the action. Unfortunately, a paper has the right to take any stand it wishes and usually has an editorial board that establishes the opinion.

160 Tips to Succeed: The basics of conducting a scientific survey

HOW-TO-DO-IT
1. Decide what you want to learn from the survey.
2. Ask why you want to learn this.
3. Ask yourself whether you could get this information without doing a survey.

4. Decide whom your public or audience is going to be.
5. Determine the type of survey method you will use.
6. Establish confidence levels for your survey.
7. Develop a timeline from start to finish for your survey.
8. Decide how the information will be analyzed and disseminated to your publics or audience (especially those surveyed).

161 Tips to Succeed: iPod® (MP3)etiquette

Assuming your company allows iPods and similar digital devices:
- Let your colleagues know you're turning it on to work.
- If anyone in your workplace approaches you, always take out the earbuds from both ears, even if your iPod is off. Anyone you have a conversation with deserves respect.
- No singing, head popping or taking your iPod to meetings.
- Be aware of your iPod's volume.

Robin Craig - Scottsdale, Ariz.

162 Tips to Succeed: Be specific when giving presentations

If you're nervous about making the next big presentation, keep the following tips in mind:
- Don't wing it. Prepare an outline of what you want to say and practice it.
- Be specific and talk about the things you know best. Don't try to teach people everything you do.
- Use handouts, visuals or PowerPoint® slides to support your presentation.
- Remember you're the expert. Think about ways that help show that and are not threatening for you.

Ivan Misner - Business Networking International - Claremont, Calif.

163 Techniques to Succeed: Recovering from a crisis

Executives believe it takes companies slightly more than three years – 3.2 years – to recover from a crisis that damages their reputation.

The top 10 crisis turnaround strategies are:

1. Quickly disclose details of the scandal/misstep (69 percent)
2. Make progress/recovery visible (59 percent)
3. Analyze what went wrong (58 percent)
4. Improve governance structure (38 percent)
5. Make leaders accessible to media (34 percent)
6. Fire employees involved in the problem (32 percent)
7. Commit to high corporate citizenship standards (23 percent)
8. Carefully review ethics policies (19 percent)
9. Hire an outside auditor (18 percent)
10. Issue an apology from the CEO (18 percent)

Burson-Marsteller - New York, N.Y.

164 Techniques to Succeed: Wanted: A strategic adviser (communicator) with a deep understanding of the process

Strategic advisers must have credibility throughout the professions (see cover of this book) and the ability to deal deftly with challenges anytime, anywhere. The strategic adviser must be politically adept, a consensus builder, be unflappable and have – at least some – business experience.

165 Techniques to Succeed: The right way to get a favor – networking

Effective networking is the proactive solution. If you think ahead and network well, asking for a favor can be an easy, natural thing to do. Sometimes you may find that you don't even need to ask! Here are a few easy ways to maintain your relationships so that favors come easily:

1. Get organized
   - Keep track of your contacts whichever way works best for you. You can use computer databases, PDAs or even index cards.
   - Keep track of birthdays, anniversaries and other miscellaneous information.
   - Know your contacts' needs, such as information, jobs and other contacts.

2. Keep in touch
   - Review your contact list regularly and make a follow up plan.
   - Send notes and cards on occasions such as birthdays and holidays.
   - Regularly call and set up lunch meetings or dinner appointments.

3. Nurture mutually beneficial relationships
   - Send any helpful information to your contacts.
   - Connect your contacts with others who can help them.
   - Use your skills to help others.

If you care for your network of friends, colleagues and acquaintances, it will be your best resource. Whether the favor you need is information, a job referral, technical help or even more clients, the best solution is a strong network. Most importantly, always remember to say thank you with an Email, a hand-written note, or a gift.

Andrea Nierenberg - The Nierenberg Group 420 E. 51st Street Suite 12D New York, NY 10022
www.mybusinessrelationships.com/

166 Tips to Succeed: Hiring an accountant takes research

Choosing an accountant for any size business — even a small one would be a smart move, but it does have its challenges. These tops could help avoid mistakes:

- Determine what services you'll need (tax preparation, filing monthly local and state taxes, payroll).
- Ask with whom you will be working. Hiring a big firm doesn't necessarily mean you'll be working with the most experienced people.
- Inquire about fees. Hourly rates can range from $150 to $300 an hour for a larger firm, and between $75 and $100 an hour for a smaller one.
- Find a firm with your general philosophy and approach. They should be as aggressive as you are about tax strategies.
- Obtain recommendations and work with someone you trust.

Tony Lee - www.startupjournal.com

167 Techniques to Succeed: Meet the new boss with an open mind

Just when you feel you've got a good relationship going with the boss, she leaves. Now a new person is coming in, and you have no idea what to expect.

Will the new boss be as receptive to your ideas? Do you have to start all over, proving yourself? How will you let the new boss know of your past achievements without sounding like a braggart?

Many may look at a new boss as a curse when it actually may be a blessing. Remember, just as the new boss can't know of your past successes, he can't know of your failures. So in a way, it's like starting over with a new chance at impressing the boss with your abilities.

- One of the first lessons is not to assume anything about a new boss.
- Next, do your homework. Review your achievements, how you participated in various projects, the role you play both officially–and unofficially – on the job.
- If you're looking to get out from under work the old boss dumped on you, now will be the time to make the case that the work can be done more efficiently in another way.

Some other things to keep in mind when the new boss shows up:
- Listen and watch carefully: You should be able to get clues immediately as to what the boss likes and doesn't like.
- Don't gossip: It's going to be tempting to dissect with co-workers everything the new boss says and does. Don't! Give the new boss every benefit of the doubt, and don't offer an opinion that may come back to haunt you.
- Be helpful: You don't want to schmooze the new boss too much, because it looks false and may tick off co-workers.
- Ask questions: Don't assume you know how the new boss wants things done. Always ask when you're not sure, and especially don't say anything like "Well, Mary (the old boss) always liked it done this way."
- Be open to change: It's not always easy to accept change, but fighting it will only hurt you in the long run.

Anita Bruzzese - Gannett News Service

168 Techniques to Succeed: Organize better for networking

Organize your contacts to make the most of your efforts. Author Andrea Nierenberg, a nonstop networker, divides her list into three different categories: A, B and C, and follows up accordingly.

Here's how you can make it work for you.
The "C" list consists of "touch base" people – acquaintances whom you want in your network. However, you're not involved with them on a business or personal level. Keep in touch by sending:

- A quarterly newsletter with a short personal note.
- A card or note once or twice a year.
- A holiday card in December.

The "B" list consists of "associates" – people you're actively involved with, either professionally or personally and you would keep in touch by:

- Meeting them for a meal, tea or coffee at least two times a year.
- Sending at least six personal notes in a year.
- Giving them holiday and premium gifts.

The "A" list is for "close friends and associates" – people you keep in touch with often.

If you effectively follow up with everyone on your list, from your closest friends to the person you see only on rare occasions, your network will continue to thrive.

Andrea Nierenberg - Author - Nonstop Networking (Capital Books)
www.mybusinessrelationships.com

169
Techniques to Succeed: Networking at non-networking events

Nonstop networkers find places and times to network outside of scheduled meetings and business events. Whether in an elevator, at a sporting event or waiting in line, networkers are always looking for ways to connect with others. This kind of networking is a great way to meet contacts that could become good friends or associates.

However, networking inappropriately can be destructive to possible relationships. It is important to be considerate both of the person you are talking to and to those around you. Here are a few ways to avoid embarrassment for yourself and your potential contact:

- Recognize where you are and what you are there for.
- Be prepared to graciously suggest that you talk about business at a more appropriate time and place. You could say, "Perhaps this is not a good time to discuss business, so may I give you a call on (date) and we could discuss this further, (consider some options), (I could help you out)?"
- Ask permission before exchanging business cards, and do so discreetly.
- Remember that some establishments, such as private clubs, simply do not allow the conducting of business. Be aware of this and follow the prescribed behavior.

Successful networkers care about the person they are speaking with as well as those around them. Showing respect is one of the best ways to make and keep contacts. Network whenever and wherever you can, just do so with discretion, so that you will avoid embarrassment and build a strong, reliable network.

Andrea Nierenberg - author of Nonstop Networking (Capital Books)
www.mybusinessrelationships.com

170
**Tips to Succeed:
Talk and drive? How to survive**

The Harvard Center for Risk Analysis estimates that the use of cell phones while driving causes about 2,600 deaths and 330,000 injuries each year in the United States.

The safest approach is to never use the phone in a car, except in an emergency. But if you absolutely must talk and drive at the same time, here are some tips to improve the chances that you and your car will make it home in one piece.

- Preprogram frequently dialed numbers. Speed dialing and voice activated dialing help to keep you from taking your eyes off the road.
- Memorize your keypad. If you insist on dialing while you drive, learn how to operate your phone without looking at it.
- Use a hands-free device. Studies show that hands-free users react to trouble no quicker than do drivers with hand-held phones. But when you are forced to respond to trouble, two hands are definitely better than one.
- Avoid long, emotional or complex calls. They make you even more distracted.
- Use voice mail. More than 40 percent of cell phone-related accidents occur when drivers take an incoming call.
- Secure your phone. Loose phones can become projectiles in a crash.
- Be a wireless Samaritan. Cell phones are ideal for promptly reporting crimes, emergencies or drunken drivers.

AAA, the University of Delaware and the Cellular Telecommunications & Internet Association - www.udel.edu/

171

Techniques to Succeed: 20 ways to rate your website©

1. Is your content segmented for specific audiences?
2. Does the site encourage interaction between end-users and your company?
3. Does the website meet your visitors' expectations?
4. Is the site content focused, rather than design or technology focused?
5. Is the site easy to maintain?
6. Is the site search engine friendly?
7. Is your content timely, relevant, concise, consistent and honest?
8. Does your content reinforce your company's mission and business objectives?
9. Is the navigation intuitive?
10. Does your site contain dead links or dated content?
11. Does your site contain a site map and search capability?
12. Does the site reflect your organization's brand standards?
13. Is your site visually appealing?
14. Is the typography, spacing, headline treatment, graphics and copy consistent?
15. Do employees, customers, prospects, media and others view your site as a valued source of company news?
16. Is the site consistent with your offline PR, marketing and sales materials?
17. Is the URL short and easy to remember?
18. Does the site employ gratuitous use of Flash?
19. Is your site user-focused rather than company-centric?
20. Is contact information easy to find?

Bonus: Is the site jargon-laden and acronym heavy?

Rick Alcantara - Tara Communications LLC, Strategic Public Relations, Marketing and Internet - www.tarapr.com

172 Tips to Succeed: Practice organizational learning

Organizational learning requires:
- A clear understanding of recurring problems
- The willingness to allocate resources to address the root cause of those problems
- Cultural values that foster learning – which means encouraging workers to find, fix and report mistakes rather than heroically patching over recurring failures

Jeffrey Pfeffer - Professor of Organizational Behavior-Stanford University Graduate School of BusinessBusiness 2.0, January/February 2005 Newstrack Executive Information Service www.news-track.com - 800-334-5771

173 Tips to Succeed: On and off the record

When talking with reporters you are always on the record – even during informal or chance meetings. Avoid casual comments or "off the record" remarks unless you specify first that what you are about to say is not for publication or air. And be sure the reporter will accept "off the record" information before volunteering it. **Background** information is just that – for background only – not to be used and not to be attributed until such a time (if ever) that the newsmaker gives the go ahead.

M. Larry Litwin, APR, Fellow PRSA
The Public Relations Practitioner's Playbook for (all) Strategic Communicators (AuthorHouse - 2013)

174 Techniques to Succeed: Getting you out there!

How often do you tell your clients and your prospects what's going on in your company or organization? Probably not enough. Try a basic communication technique (not just "fancy" newsletters):

- Write a letter
- Write one every few months
- Don't make it a pitch piece
  - Be honest
  - Be straight forward
  - Be conversational
    - Something like: "It's been a while since I told you about what's happening here. We've been growing nicely. I just want to share some of those successes with you."
  - Tell them what you've been up to
    - Without breaking any confidences, talk about the successful work you've done for your clients and customers.
    - Offer a little behind-the-scenes strategy and talk about results the bottom lines – relationships and finances.

Be certain not to overstate the message. The truth works. And the truth will get you and your client and/or firm out there.

Maury Z. Levy - Levy Warren Marketing and Media
Jenkintown, Pa. - www.levywarren.com

175 Tips to Succeed: Encourage thinking outside of the box

Creativity and innovation are essential to healthy businesses, corporations, and their business and public relations plans. Encourage creativity in the workplace, by:

- Setting aside chunks of time to concentrate on creative projects
- Brainstorming (getting the most out of mind share)
- Envisioning multiple futures.
- Looking in other worlds and outside of your organization.
- Restructuring your problem or challenge.
- Making new associations.

Jo Anne White - Therapist and Temple University Professor
www.drjoannewhite.com

176 Tips to Succeed: Take stock when traveling

If you're preparing to travel here are thoughts on how to avoid lost luggage stress.

- Remember to keep valuables, such as prescriptions, electronics or jewelry, on you or in a carry-on bag.
- Have with you, in a carry-on, whatever you might need to get through a 24-hour period if your bags are lost.
- Make a list of what you pack so if your luggage is lost you can file a claim more effectively. Include a good description of the items.
- Wear clothing suitable for your trip.
- If traveling on business, dress appropriately in case the rest of your items are lost.
- Check to be certain that you have an ID tag on the outside and also put identification inside your bag.
- If you check luggage, confirm that the three-letter destination tags attached to your bags are actually for your location.

Diana Dratch - www.bankrate.com

177 Tips to Succeed: A personal Code of Ethics

Every strategic message must be Open, Honest, Thorough, Valid (relevant).

M. Larry Litwin, APR, Fellow PRSA
The Public Relations Practitioner's Playbook
for (all) Strategic Communicators (AuthorHouse –2013)

178 Tips to Succeed: Making the best impression on your audience

1. **Always be prepared** – Audiences quickly detect lack of preparation.
2. **Make others comfortable** – If you are comfortable, your audience will be, too. Comfort, on your part as the sender, exudes confidence.
3. **Be committed** – Commitment is crucial. Audiences can detect lack of commitment or sincerity.
4. **Be interesting** – An interested audience is more apt to receive your message as it was intended to be received.

Roger Ailes and John Kraushar - Authors - You Are The Message

179 Tips to Succeed: Take the time for workspace spring cleaning

Everyone thinks their stuff is important and other people's stuff is just clutter.

There are a few rules to take into consideration when doing an office overhaul. A checklist can serve as a handy guide for "cleaning up."

- Is this a duplicate? Does the information exist somewhere else?

- What is the worst that can happen if it is thrown away?

- Is it a legal document that needs to be retained? If it is, is there a better place for its safekeeping?

- Do I need to take some kind of action on this information?

- Is it out of date?

- Do I know exactly how the information can be used?

- Am I sure the person I plan to refer this to really wants it?

- Where will I keep this information? Do I have a place labeled for it, or does a new file need to be created? Does one already exist that would suffice?

- To retain it, are the supplies available? Would it be best suited for hanging files, manila envelopes or the "immediate action" box?

- Being careful: It's easy to get caught up in the cleaning frenzy and overdo it. Workers should be cautioned to avoid heavy loads, and lift with their knees, not their backs.

- Organizing the piles: Boxes should be labeled with "to be filed" or "discuss with ..." or "move to ..."

Anita Bruzzese - Author - *Take This Job and Thrive* (Impact Publications)

180 Tips to Succeed: Reaching the desired outcome

EDUCATION - Providing knowledge or training to employees or other targeted audiences.

KNOWLEDGE - What employees know about the organization or company for whom they work.

ATTITUDE - Beliefs, a state of mind or inner feelings acquired through education and observation.

BEHAVIOR - What employees say about their employer and how employees act. (Expression of attitude.)

OUTPUT - Is affected by education, knowledge and behavior.

OUTCOME - Determined by output. The firm or organization that achieves its desired outcome has been successful in educating and bringing about the desired behavioral changes.

Education > Knowledge > Attitude > Behavioral Change > Output=Desired Outcome

(When output = desired outcome, synergy has been achieved.)

Ed Ziegler - Director of Marketing Rowan (N.J.) University

181 Techniques to Succeed: Big 12 Dining Etiquette Rules

1. Always wear your nametag on your right.
2. Allow the host to point out where the guests should sit.
3. Follow the host's lead. Once the host begins to eat – you eat.
4. Once seated, immediately place the napkin in your lap.
5. Utensils: eat from the outside in – NEVER pick up dropped silverware.
6. Your bread is to the left, water is to the right.
7. Elbows should never rest on the table while eating.
8. Use the silverware to signal you're finished (the 4:00-10:00 position on a clock).
9. Take out food the same way it went in. (If you put a piece of food in your mouth with your fork and the food is unpleasant (tough or not tasty), you should remove the piece of food with your fork. Don't spit the food into a napkin or use your fingers to remove it.)
10. If you have to pick or clean your teeth – excuse yourself from the table.
11. Never order alcohol – even if the host does.
12. Whoever invited the guest will be paying unless discussed.

Elon University - Public Relations Student Society of America -
Professor Jessica Gisclair, Esq.- Adviser

182

Techniques to Succeed:
It's all about preparation

Here's how you can use the time before your next sales call to maximize your chances of advancing the sale by preparing thoroughly:

Learn about your prospect: Visiting your prospect's website is a good start. Try "Googling" the company name or product names to get information about their marketplace. Learn about challenges that might be facing your prospect's industry.

Ask intelligent questions: Use the info you gathered to help prepare intelligent questions. With your product and service in mind, prepare questions that uncover challenges you can help them solve. Be ready to ask follow-up questions.

Polish your presentation: Never prepare a canned, memorized presentation. Your prospect will see right through it and feel like the 100th person this week to hear that pitch from you. Instead, prepare talking points that are flexible enough to be interwoven into a sales discussion.

Use your sales tools: In the classic Batman television show, the one starring Adam West, it was impressive that the superhero always had exactly what he needed within easy reach on his utility belt. Before facing off with the dastardly Mr. Freeze, Batman made sure that he had ice-thawing Batspray on his hip. When you're selling, anticipate the tools you'll need in each upcoming encounter so that, like Batman, you can pull out the right tool at the right time. Have the right samples, literature and other resources readily available.

Handling objections: Sales managers tell you to anticipate the objections you might hear from customers. That's fine, but anticipating is not enough. You need a well-thought-out plan for responding effectively to the objections you anticipate. What are the five most popular objections you encounter? What are the five toughest objections you hear? Invest a couple of hours in developing great responses to those objections and watch your sales success rates rise.

There aren't too many volunteer salespeople around. By default, that makes the rest of us professional salespeople. As professionals we must be prepared to demonstrate the professional level of service and preparedness that will help us succeed. If you decide to "wing it" on your next sales call, a well-prepared competitor might be the one who writes the order with your prospect.

Al Uszynski - Sales Trainer - www.SalesBeat.com

183 Tips to Succeed: You are what you wear

When dressing for work, what you wear can dictate how others act toward you. Here are four key items to keep in mind:

Fit – Do your clothes fit properly? It doesn't matter how expensive an item is — if it is too tight or too big, it isn't going to look good on you.

Accessories – Are your accessories too big, too bold or too bright? Your accessories should be good-quality items that add to your outfit without overpowering it.

Color – Are you wearing clothing that is noticed because of its color? Darker colors convey more authority than lighter ones. Bright colors can "shout," and you should decide about whether you want to shout or not.

Style – Are your clothes very stylish or part of the latest fashion trend? If so, they will be noticed. This may be appropriate for your social life but less so for work.

Barbara Pachter - Pachter & Associates Business
Communications Training - Cherry Hill, N.J.

184 Tips to Succeed: Staying positive: Smile

We all know we should appreciate who we are and what we have. But sometimes it's so much easier for many of us to believe the negative things we hear and think about ourselves than it is to listen to, and believe, the best.

Here are some tips on what you can do to become more aware of the positive things in life right now, feel better and be more productive.

- Send yourself an email or call your voice mail and say something positive about yourself or note one thing you are happy about today. Make this a daily routine.
- Add an area to your things-to-do list where you can list at least one thing each day that makes you smile.
- Once an hour, stop, look around and find something or someone that you can say something positive about. The harder you have to look to find that silver lining, the better.
- Decide today that you will no longer compare yourself to others.
- Create a place where you can keep photos, positive letters, articles and other reminders of good things that you have accomplished and that are a part of your life.

Lee Silber - Organizational Expert and Author - www.creativelee.com

185 Tips to Succeed: ABCs of strategic public relations

- **Anticipate** = For every public relations action there is a reaction. Explore all possible reactions in advance. Successful practitioners are never surprised.

- **Be Prepared** = For that first call from the media. Don't go public until you are absolutely ready.

- **Communicate** = Clearly, Concisely, Calculatingly, Consistently and Completely (Specifically and Simply)

M. Larry Litwin, APR, Fellow PRSA - The Public Relations Practitioner's Playbook for (all) Strategic Communicators (AuthorHouse – 2013)

186 Tips to Succeed: Think first – then carry out CBAs of strategic public relations

- Conceive = Head
- Believe = Heart
- Achieve = Hands

Public relations practitioners conceive their plans through research and thought. A great majority have a strong belief, which helps them achieve it through hands on tactics (by doing or carrying out)…thus they achieve with their head, believe in the heart and achieve with their hands.

Anthony J. Fulginiti, APR, Fellow PRSA, Professor-Public Relations
Rowan (N.J.) University

187 Tips to Succeed: Know your audiences

AUDIENCE POWER STRUCTURE

Audiences within a community or organization can be segmented into elite, diffused and amorphous and illustrated by using a pyramid – elite is where the power is concentrated at the top (a few opinion leaders or key communicators who are actively involved); diffused or pluralistic is where the power is spread throughout (aware of issues, but not aware of effects on them) and amorphous or latent is where the power has yet to surface (probably not concerned or even aware of how issues affect them – e.g. a new condominium community).

M. Larry Litwin, APR, Fellow PRSA - The Public Relations Practitioner's Playbook for (all) Strategic Communicators (AuthorHouse – 2013)

188 Techniques to Succeed: Grunig's Four Models of Public Relations

James Grunig and Todd Hunt developed four models of public relations Each differs in the purpose and nature of communication.

Press Agentry/Publicity – one-way communication – uses persuasion and manipulation to influence audience to behave as the organization desires (One way with propaganda as its purpose.)

Public Information – one-way communication – use news releases and other one-way communication techniques to distribute organizational information. Public relations practitioner is often referred to as the "journalist in residence." (One way with dissemination of truthful information.)

Two-way asymmetrical – two way – Sometimes called "scientific persuasion" (short term rather than long term). Uses persuasion and manipulation to influence audience to behave as the organization desires – incorporates lots of feedback from target audiences and publics – used by an organization primarily interested in having its publics come around to its way of thinking rather changing the organization, its policies, or its views.

Two-way symmetrical – two way – Uses communication to negotiate with publics, resolve conflict, and promote mutual understanding and respect between the organization and its public(s). Research is used not only to gather information, but also to change the organization's behavior. Understanding, rather than persuasion, is the objective. (Every attempt is made for each side to understand the other's point of view. If your public agrees with you, then you must find a way to communicate with the public and motivate it to act.) Seems to be used more by non-profit organizations, government agencies and heavily regulated businesses (public utilities) rather than by competitive, profit driven companies.

James Grunig and Todd Hunt - University of Maryland - 1984

189. Tips to Succeed: Like artists, public relations practitioners should see the whole apple before painting it

Even before starting the formal research, PR practitioners should do as architects and artists do – develop their own blue print, look at situations with a painter's eye – view the scene from every angle and perspective. Gather as many "nuggets of knowledge" as possible – then research after determining why you are doing what you are doing (purpose), plan (goal and objectives), inform (strategies and tactics) and evaluate. That's why this public relations process is called PR-Pie. As the "nuggets of knowledge" take shape, you will move closer to the plan's goal and achieving *synergy*.

190. Techniques to Succeed: Turning the 'green' handshake into the 'confident' handshake

Delivering a proper handshake can make or break your first impression on a person. A handshake that's too limp or weak can convey weakness or lack of self-confidence. A handshake that's too strong or crushing can convey hostility. A well-executed handshake is one that conveys self-confidence, trust and a genuine interest in the other party. Several factors contributing to a good handshake, from start to finish. A handshake is generally common courtesy during most introductions, and when greeting a familiar person.

- **Eye contact**. Once your hands have met, you should make eye contact and maintain it throughout the handshake. If you're particularly coordinated, or gifted with great peripheral vision, make eye contact prior to the handshake, and maintain it for the duration.

- **Grip**. Grip with your whole hand, not just the fingertips or just the thumb. Make it firm, but not crushing. A good help for learning this would be asking a friend to help you practice your handshake grip. In most situations, you should only use one hand. Using both could convey hostility, or intent to overpower.

- **Position**. Your body should be approximately 12 to 20 inches away from the other party. Both parties' hands should be straight up-and-down, even with each other. The web of your hand (skin running between the forefinger and the thumb) should meet the web of theirs.

- **Shake.** Should be smooth, not limp or over-enthusiastic. Shake from the elbow, not the wrist or the shoulder.
- **Flow.** Before the handshake, establish eye contact. Break eye contact, if needed, to extend your hand to meet theirs. When the web of your hand meets the web of theirs, re-establish eye contact and engage your grip. Shake two or three times, for a duration of one to three seconds, breaking off cleanly and smoothly before the introduction is over.

To test your handshaking finesse, try shaking hands with a few close friends.

www.faqfarm.com/Q/How_does_one_give_a_proper_handshake

191 Techniques to Succeed: Newsome's Principles of Persuasion

Familiarity (audience, message, surrogates)
Identification (rewards/benefits)
Clarity (avoid jargon/passive verbs)
Action (ask for behavior/what you want) try! buy! sell! (relate).

Earl Newsome - Researcher

192 Techniques to Succeed: Recency-Primacy – try it; it works

There are a number of approaches. Here are just a couple:

The last statement made (the most recent information received) is most recalled or remembered. That's why having the last word is better. It leaves the most lasting impression.

There is also the primacy effect–the greater impact of what we first learn about someone (first impressions). Remember, we get just one chance to make a first impression.

193

Tips to Succeed: A picture is worth 1,000 words – scoring more coverage with newsworthy photo opps

Treat photographers like you would other journalists – and treat them equally.

- Don't try to micro manage the photo shoot.
- Incorporate newsworthy photo opps into your media relations efforts:

1. **Avoid logos and "CEO shots" in media photos.** Recognize that photographers want "real" photos. They want to capture natural moments with some "real emotion."

2. **Avoid photo opportunities that look staged.** Readers can tell when someone is smiling for the camera or when body language looks awkward. (Avoid the grip "n" grin shots.)

3. **Treat photographers like "back doors" to the front page.**
Try to accommodate the photojournalist. Think about these things – human drama, emotion and reader interest – and try to provide them using real people when photographers show up.

4. **Be a good host – facilitate and foresee photojournalists' needs.** Another common mistake organizations make is they don't have things like parking passes available for photographers. They'll have one for the reporter, but not the photographer. Photojournalists have to lug a lot of equipment and gear. It can be a [real headache] when there's nowhere to park and we're not given access.

5. **If you must shoot your own photos – then hire qualified photojournalists.** The problem with most PR-provided photos is that they have no life or emotion. "They are very static, and usually feature a lot of logs and people looking right into the camera. These people tend to be important figures, but the reader doesn't care about your CEO or CFO. They want to be drawn to someone like them."

Other problems with PR photos include a lack of compelling composition, an [absence of] technical excellence – including things like focus, balance and proper exposure – and an overall sense that they were taken by an "amateur."

Marie Poirier Marzi - Photojournalist - Washington, D.C. - www.mariemarzi.com/

194 Techniques to Succeed: Getting 'pinged'

Think war movies: A submarine is looking for an enemy ship. Sonar emitted by the hunter returns a "ping!" Everyone starts running around yelling, "Man the torpedoes!"

Hackers send out streams of small data packets to thousands of IP (email) addresses. When the packet bounces back to the hacker, he knows he has "pinged" a computer that is currently online.

The ping, though, is nothing more than a probe and cannot affect your PC.

The hacker's version of a torpedo – a program that can infiltrate your PC and open it to the hacker – is of no use if you have a firewall protecting the PC.

John J. Fried - Philadelphia Inquirer johnfriedfaq@phillynews.com

195 Techniques to Succeed: How pay-to-play works

1. The politicians in power need money to get re-elected

2. They solicit donations from professional firms that do work for the town (lawyers, engineers, etc.).

3. Professionals feel obliged to contribute large sums to re-election campaigns to get municipal contracts.

4. The money funds expensive campaigns, overwhelming all challengers.

5. Re-elected officials reward contributors with no-bid contracts.

6. The result: Overpriced contracts and higher taxes for residents. Lack of diversity in contractors.

196 Tips to Succeed: Punctuality – important in the U.S.

While being punctual is not important in other countries, it is in the United States. It has a number of definitions – but they all arrive at the same destination – and on time and or deadline–as should you when you have an appointment or other commitment.

Punctuality is exactness – arriving at or before the time of the appointment fully prepared for any eventuality.

197 Tips to Succeed: Public relations practitioners

- Analyze conditions
- Assess policies
- Inform
- Develop programs
- Make recommendations
- Persuade
- Get people to act

198 Techniques to Succeed: An effective public relations planning rule

Generally, a campaign will have only one goal. That goal may have several objectives associated with it. Each objective could have a number of strategies, although experts believe the strategies (messages) should be limited so that audiences remember them. However, the number of tactics that can be developed for a given strategy is almost infinite [certainly, there are many ways to deliver the message(s)]. A campaign is a premeditation to act.

199 Tips to Succeed: When it came to planning, the general knew

"It's not the plan; it's the planning."

Gen. Dwight D. Eisenhower

200 Techniques to Succeed: Plan before you publish

- Save time and misunderstanding by creating a design brief or thumbnail(s)
  - Clarify your objectives
  - Provide designers (if you use them) with key organization points

A number of other considerations fall under production:
- Choosing the right paper
  - Weight, texture and size affects look and feel
  - Paper can account for up to half the job's cost
  - Seek printer's advice
  - Ask how printer purchases, uses and charges for paper
  - Use printer's advice to limit waste and save money

- Choosing colors
  - Increases readership
  - Adds cost
  - Spot color is less expensive than process color because the color separation work is less tedious.

- Folding
  - Publications should be designed with folding and binding in mind
  - Think in terms of "signatures" (a folded sheet containing 4, 8, 12, 16 and so on, pages that are folded to form a part of a book or pamphlet. Also called a "section.")

- Choosing the proper binding
  - Plan binding before printing
    - Saddle stitch
    - Side wire
    - Spiral
    - Perfect (book)

  - Consider margins, staples, etc.

  - Ask whether it will be done in-house

201 Techniques to Succeed: Maslow's Theory of Motivation

Human needs arranged into five categories in ascending order:
- Physiological needs
- Safety needs
- Belongingness and love needs
- Esteem needs
- Self-actualization needs

Abraham Maslow - Human Psychologist -1954

202 Tips to Succeed: A dozen tips to produce top publications

1. Never lose sight of your audience
2. Know the purpose of your publication
3. Have your design enhance the message, not obscure it
4. Be judicious in use of color
5. Use photographs well
6. Don't print over designs unless you are certain it will enhance the product
7. Avoid using too many type faces in the same publication
8. Design your publication for different types of readers
9. Use informative headlines
10. Avoid large tinted or screened boxes
11. Avoid a layout that looks "busy"
12. Read your writing aloud and determine if it sounds conversational

203 Tips to Succeed: Planning ahead

When planning… !sdrawkcab kniht*

*Think backwards!

204 Techniques to Succeed: Fly with less 'turbulence'

KEY TRAVEL TIPS

- Fly early. The atmosphere needs time to heat up to produce the severe weather that tends to hit later in the day.
- Select nonstop flights. Consider connecting thru airports other than major hubs.
- Avoid flights that are chronically delayed.
- Confirm your reservation and flight status in advance.

Following these tips will help you reduce your wait time at the security checkpoint.

BEFORE THE AIRPORT

- Do not pack or take prohibited items to the airport.
- Place valuables such as jewelry, cash and laptop computers in **carry-on baggage only.** Tape your business card to the bottom of your laptop.
- Avoid wearing clothing, jewelry and accessories that contain metal. Metal items may set off the alarm on the metal detector.
- Avoid wearing shoes that contain metal or have thick soles or heels. Many types of footwear will require additional screening even if the metal detector does not alarm.
- Declare firearms and ammunition to your airline and place them in your checked baggage.
- Do not lock your baggage.
- Do not take lighters or prohibited matches to the airport.
- Do not pack wrapped gifts and do not take wrapped gifts to the checkpoint.

AT THE AIRPORT
Each adult traveler needs to keep available his/her airline boarding pass and government-issued photo ID until exiting the security checkpoint. Due to different airport configurations, at many airports you may be required to display these documents more than once.

- Place the following items in your carry-on baggage or in a plastic bag prior to entering the screening checkpoint:
  - Cell phones
  - Digital devices
  - Keys
  - Loose change
  - Money clips
  - Large amounts of jewelry
  - Metal hair decorations
  - Large belt buckles

- Take your laptop out of its bag and place it in a bin provided at the checkpoint.

Take off all outer coats, suit coats, jackets and blazers.

www.tsa.gov

205 Techniques to Succeed: The power of the personal note

The art of writing personal notes is sadly disappearing. A personal note is one of the best ways to connect and re-connect with others. There are several kinds of notes to let people know you're thinking of them.

1. Thank-You Notes are one of the least expensive and most effective networking tools. You can send them to acknowledge:
   - Compliments you receive
   - Gifts given to you
   - Referrals
   - Time and consideration

2. FYI Notes help you keep in touch at any time. You can send many things, such as clippings or articles. This lets them know that you:
   - Thought of them when you read it
   - Know what they are interested in
   - Care about their business

3. Congratulations notes are a perfect opportunity to let someone know you are cheering them on. You can give these out on many occasions:
   - Promotions
   - Awards or Honors
   - Anniversaries

4. Nice Talking to (or, Meeting) You Notes help a person to remember you fondly. You can send these out after several events:
   - Meetings
   - Chance encounters
   - Phone conversations

The post office reports that only four percent of mail is personal correspondence. This means that now, more than ever, a handwritten envelope will stand out among the piles of bills and advertisements. A note will get someone's attention, let them know you care about them, remind them of you, and, ultimately, strengthen your network to help you succeed.

Andrea Nierenberg - Author - Nonstop Networking (Capital Books)
www.mybusinessrelationships.com

206 Techniques to Succeed: Political Advertising

The purpose of political ads is to persuade people to vote for a candidate, or in some cases, an issue. While the Federal Trade Commission and Federal Communication Commission view political ads liberally when it comes to "truth in advertising" and "deceptive" practices, there are certain guidelines that must be followed:

- Political advertising does not have to adhere to truth in advertising as other types of ads do. They may use deception and misleading information.
- If a printed piece is mailed, the name and address of the candidate or representative must be on the ad.
- All printed pieces, brochures, fliers, and newspaper and magazine ads must indicate who is paying for them.
- Radio commercials must contain the candidate's voice and television commercials must show the candidate's face (even a still shot). They must also state who is paying for the commercial.
- Candidates for federal office must disclaim their radio and television ad – either at the beginning or end – stating their name and saying "I approve this message." On TV, they must be shown saying it.
- Generally, both print and electronic media charge the lowest rate on a rate card for a section or page in the newspaper or magazine, or "day part" in radio or TV. (Congress is considering legislation related to political pricing charged by TV stations.)
- As a safety precaution, most media outlets require that payment is made at the time ads are placed.

M. Larry Litwin, APR, Fellow PRSA - The Public Relations Practitioner's Playbook for (all) Strategic Communicators (AuthorHouse – 2013)

207 Techniques to Succeed: Pricing Strategies

Customary or Traditional – A single, well-known price for a long period of time. Movie theaters and candy manufacturers employ this pricing strategy in the hope that the customer will become less sensitive to price. It's the price that consumers expect to pay for a certain product.

Odd – Strategy of having prices that end in an odd number, as in $5.95, $19.99; sometimes referred to as odd-even pricing.

Line – All products sell for same price. For example, Southwest Airlines charges the same for all seats on a flight – unlike other airlines.

Psychological – Strategy intended to manipulate the customer's judgment process. Two common forms of psychological pricing are odd pricing ($9.97) and Prestige Pricing. There are also psychological price breaks such as – $9.99; $19.99; $24.99; $99.95; etc.

Price lining – The strategy of pricing different products in a product line at various price points, depending on size and features, to make them affordable to a wider range of customers – good, better, best. (Sears has been using price lining for years; State Farm Insurance has introduced this strategy.) Also, targeting a specific market segment based on price – a retailer who practices price lining only carries goods that sell within a defined price range.

Prestige or Image – A strategy where prices are set at a high level, recognizing that lower prices might inhibit sales rather than encourage them and that buyers will associate a high price for the product with superior quality – certain cars, appliances and clothing brands.

Value – A strategy where the selling price of a good or service is based on the company's assessment of the highest value of the product to the consumer – what the consumer is willing to pay for it; what the market will bear. Many times, it is predicated on supply and demand.

M. Larry Litwin, APR, Fellow PRSA - The Public Relations Practitioner's Playbook for (all) Strategic Communicators (AuthorHouse – 2013)

208 Tips to Succeed: New managers: Being boss and friend – but be careful

- **Don't get too close too quickly.** The easiest way to gain approval from employees is to shower them with attention and approach them as friends. But with the right mix, it's possible to be a boss and friend.
- **Be in power with, not over.** When you are in power over them, they feel intimidated and defensive. This means erasing the title and remembering who you were before you walked in your first day as a manager.
- **Find sources of honest feedback.** You have to realize as the new boss that people might try to butter you up. So when you ask your favorite employee what she thinks of your leadership skills and she has nothing but glowing things to say, be skeptical. It can be lonely at the top if you don't latch on to mentors and subordinates who aren't afraid to tell you what they think – for real.

Gannett News Service

209 Tips to Succeed: They call it – Workplace politics

Politics is among this book's author's Nine P's of Marketing – as in office politics. Here are seven tactics for successfully navigating office politics:

1. **Over communicate.** Let people in on what you're working on, or planning to do. For example, if your project affects another department or someone else's responsibilities, it's smart to give those people a heads-up. Nobody likes to be surprised.

2. **Get a mentor.** Look for someone at a higher level, with experience in the organization and who knows the personalities of the "senior team."

3. **Ask open-ended questions.** A lot of business decisions, unfortunately, are made on assumptions. Using open-ended questions, really listening to people's answers and taking notes can help avert making misguided decisions.

4. **Review constantly.** Always compare notes with colleagues and others about what's going on at work – from discussing a new company policy to rehashing what the boss said in a staff meeting. Having everyone on the same page helps organizations move ahead more quickly.

5. **Get buy-in.** This goes hand-in-hand with over communicating. If you're working on a project, get the opinions of staffers it may affect.
6. **Give –and take – due credit.** Give people the credit they're due, and you'll garner the support of your peers. "Credit hogs" are setting themselves up to fail. (While men tend to do a good job of broadcasting their contributions, he said, women often don't give themselves enough credit. So women, acknowledge the work of your peers, but also let management know of your own contributions.)
7. **Keep style in mind.** How you dress influences how you're perceived. Appearance is often the first gauge someone uses to decide whether or not to help you. For women, dress is especially important. (It's an unfortunate fact of life that a man can get away with being pretty badly dressed ... it's more difficult for a woman. A common mistake in attire for both genders, especially among younger workers, is dressing too casually–that includes flip-flops, shorts and shirts that bare your belly.)

Verbal communication skills, including talking face to face with colleagues instead of relying on email, and learning the finer points of public speaking, can also help polish your image.

John McKee - Author - 21 Ways That Women in Management Shoot Themselves in the Foot

210 Tips to Succeed: Don't get caught – Quid Pro Quo

Quid Pro Quo = money exchanged for an official act–expecting something in return for a political donation. Not only is it unethical, but illegal.

Simply put – someone gives something expecting something in return. Politicians call it "pay to play." (See Technique 195.)

211 Tips to Succeed: Want to sit at the corporate table?

Don't tell your boss what he/she *wants* to hear – tell him/her what she *needs* to hear!

212

Tips to Succeed:
How to make an editor angry

There are some PR practitioners who would try just about any trick in the book to make sure an editor takes a look at their news release. So here is a list of the top five ways to make an editor angry when presenting your news story.

1. Write a news release that is excessively long:
   Unless you're the President and have just proposed a new version of the Constitution, think brief. Your news should be short and sweet. Any additional information can be sent to the editor once you've obtained interest.

2. Get the editor's attention and then tell them they have to use the release word for word:
   Many news releases will get published verbatim, but don't test the editor's journalistic integrity by making it mandatory.

3. Send a huge photo email attachment when emailing a release:
   Editors receive hundreds of unsolicited news releases emailed to them everyday. Why waste their time with a huge file unless they ask you for it?

4. Send your release in a fancy package so that it commands attention:
   Most editors will simply use your apparent disregard for the number of trees destroyed to make the unnecessary package as reason to disregard your release.

5. Call the editor and ask to read the entire release over the phone:
   If you have to read the release the editor will label you as a lightweight. Say goodbye to the credibility of your release.

The bottom line is that editors want to see the news in a news release. If you don't have news in your release don't try to tap dance your way to their hearts. Start over and send it to them when you have some real news to tell.

Rowan (N.J.) University PRSSA Newsbriefs -
March 30, 2005

213 Tips to Succeed: 10 essential tips to ensure your news release makes the news

1. Make sure the information is newsworthy.
2. Tell the audience that the information is intended for them and why they should continue to read it.
3. Start with a brief description of the news, then distinguish who announced it, and not the other way around.
4. Ask yourself, "How are people going to relate to this and will they be able to connect?"
5. Make sure the first 10 words of your release are effective, as they are the most important.
6. Avoid excessive use of adjectives and fancy language.
7. Deal with the facts.
8. Provide as much contact information as possible: Individual to contact, address, phone (fax), email, website (address).
9. Make sure you wait until you have something with enough substance to issue a release.
10. Make it as easy as possible for media representatives to do their jobs.

214 Tips to Succeed: Crafting your resume

Recruiters usually spend less than 20 seconds looking at your resume. Monster.com says most resumes don't get a second look. Only about three percent of candidates are called for an interview.

No one seems to be immune to a pathetic resume. Even seasoned professionals can improve their image on paper.

The most common offenses: being too generic and not convincing enough about your accomplishments.

For instance, if you say you doubled sales in a short amount of time, say so. But be specific. Which sounds better? "Worked diligently to surpass sales quota on an ongoing basis" or "exceeded $1 million quarterly sales quota by at least 25 percent for six consecutive quarters"?

Eleanor Farmer, resume writer and business coach from Merchantville, N.J. says, "Do not use a generic resume. Customize your resume to the company and job to which you are applying."

Let them know why they should hire you. Use an applicant statement on the top of page one just under your personal information. That statement should tell something about the value you would bring to the company. For example:

Applicant Statement: Rowan University Professor Anthony J. Fulginiti, APR, Fellow PRSA, describes me as: "Mature beyond her years, articulate, well tailored and polished, loyal, has a passion for the profession, outstanding writer, and a skilled organizer and strategic thinker." I promise to bring those features to Burwyn Associates to increase the firm's double bottom line.

If your resume is more than one page, use footer on right hand side. For example:

Alana Kramer
Resume, page 2
kramer@njtown.net

For Resume Writing Suggestions, contact:
M. Larry Litwin, APR, Fellow PRSA - larry@larrylitwin.com

215 Tips to Succeed: Maintaining a strong professional relationship

Life is about finding ways to get along with people, not ways to separate yourself. You really find out who your friends are when you are down.

Rep. Robert Andrews (D-N.J.)

216 Techniques to Succeed: The power of the referral

Many salespeople are wondering about the best way to go after new business. The prevailing wisdom is that you have to develop a cold list, start from scratch and build your business that way. This is so far from the truth that it's laughable. An unqualified list will yield two to three appointments out of a hundred approaches. A referred list, when called by a professional salesperson, can yield initial appointments at the rate of 25 per 100 approaches—sometimes even more. That raises the question: Why don't we leverage referral prospecting as much as we should?

Warren Wechsler's *Total Selling Times* - Fairfield, Iowa

217 Techniques to Succeed: Using a boilerplate

A boilerplate is a short piece of text, usually no more than a single short paragraph, describing a company, person, product, service or event. It is standard wording about an organization that usually appears near the end of organization- or company-issued news releases (above the hash [end] mark or -30-). Here is a sample boilerplate:

The Atlantic City Convention & Visitors Authority serves as the destination's principal marketing arm, stimulating economic growth through convention, business and leisure tourism development. The Authority oversees the management of the Atlantic City Convention Center and Boardwalk Hall on behalf of its parent agency, the New Jersey Sports and Exposition Authority.

218 Techniques to Succeed: Office romances and workplace efficiency

It is widely accepted that workplace romances cannot be avoided. So, to avoid the perception that an employee is getting preferential treatment because of an office romance, or to avoid accusations of sexual harassment, favoritism or discrimination, companies should have:

- Consensual Relationship Agreements. Some firms have them for employees who date as well as married couples in the same workplace.
- Other types of written agreements in which romantically involved workers acknowledge the following:
  - the relationship is voluntary and consensual
  - they agree to abide by the employer's anti-harassment policy
  - they will behave professionally and not allow the relationship to affect their work
- and to avoid behavior that offends others at work.

Companies should use them only when a relationship has already started to cause a problem or when the employer becomes aware of a relationship – especially one involving employees reporting to one another.

Companies wanting to discourage office romance are legally free to do so as long as company policy doesn't focus on one particular group. For example, don't punish only the women for engaging in office romance.

The workplace is a natural place to meet and even find your beloved. If you discover yours there, discuss how the relationship can affect your work. Communication – the key to a romantic relationship – will also be the key to a successful working relationship.

Andrea Kay - Author - Greener Pastures: How To Find a Job in Another Place
www.andreakay.com andrea@andreakay.com

219 Techniques to Succeed: A good reputation sells itself

Remember, the public relations (strategic) writer is "relating" the image, not "selling" it.

220

Techniques to Succeed:
The art of rhetoric – learning how to use the 3 main rhetorical styles

Rhetoric (n) - The art of speaking or writing effectively.

According to Aristotle, rhetoric is "the ability, in each particular case, to see the available means of persuasion." He described three main forms of rhetoric: Ethos, Logos and Pathos.

To be a more effective writer, you must understand these three terms. Understanding them will help make your writing more persuasive.

ETHOS
Ethos is appeal based on the character of the speaker. An ethos-driven document relies on the reputation of the author.

LOGOS
Logos is appeal based on logic or reason. Documents distributed by companies or corporations are logos-driven. Scholarly documents are also often logos-driven.

PATHOS
Pathos is appeal based on emotion. Advertisements tend to be pathos-driven.

Rhetorical appeals can be achieved through:
- Visual Information Structure – Includes how the text looks on the screen. This is achieved through the appearance of such things as the titles and the headings.
- Color – Includes the color of the text, the background and the graphics. The contrast of the colors of each of these items is also important.
- Graphic Images – Includes the other information in the document aside from the text. This is achieved through such things as icons, buttons and photos.

Read more at www.rpi.edu/dept/llc/webclass/web/project1/group4/

221

Tips to Succeed:
25 words that hurt your resume

Words don't tell potential employers as much as deeds So, you're experienced? Before you advertise this in your resume, be sure you can prove it.

Often, when job seekers try to sell themselves to potential employers, they load their resumes with vague claims that are transparent to hiring managers, according to Scott Bennett, author of *The Elements of Resume Style* (AMACOM).

By contrast, the most successful job seekers avoid these vague phrases on their resumes in favor of accomplishments.

Instead of making empty claims to demonstrate your work ethic, use brief, specific examples to demonstrate your skills.

In other words, show, don't tell.

Bennett offers these examples:
Instead of..."Experience working in fast-paced environment"
Try..."Registered 120+ third-shift emergency patients per night"

Instead of..."Excellent written communication skills"
Try..."Wrote jargon-free User Guide for 11,000 users"

Instead of..."Team player with cross-functional awareness"
Try..."Collaborated with clients, A/R and Sales to increase speed of receivables and prevent interruption of service to clients."

Instead of..."Demonstrated success in analyzing client needs"
Try..."Created and implemented comprehensive needs assessment mechanism to help forecast demand for services and staffing."

The worst offenders

It's good to be hard-working and ambitious, right? The hiring manager won't be convinced if you can't provide solid examples to back up your claims.

Bennett suggests being extra-careful before putting these nicesounding but empty words in your resume.

- Aggressive
- Ambitious
- Competent
- Creative
- Detail-oriented
- Determined
- Efficient
- Experienced
- Flexible
- Goal-oriented
- Hard-working
- Independent
- Innovative
- Knowledgeable
- Logical
- Motivated
- Meticulous
- People person
- Professional
- Reliable
- Resourceful
- Self-motivated
- Successful
- Team player
- Well-organized

Laura Morsch - CareerBuilder.com - CNN.com

222 Techniques to Succeed: Make resume point quickly, but don't stop short–one page may not be enough

Some rumors just won't go away. Take the one that your resume is only supposed to be one page long. Since the late 1980s, I have given speeches and workshops to get workers to stop fretting about length and focus on content. I even wrote a book on it. But the rumor prevails.

So here, from my you-may-think-it's-true-but-it's-not file, is why you should erase this crippling belief from your mind.

Whenever someone brings up the one-page resume rumor–which is usually the first thing when I'm trying to help him or her develop a new and improved version – I ask, "Why do you think that?" Responses are always the same: "Employers only spend 10 seconds reading your resume."

Ten seconds? I don't know about you, but I can only read about 30 words in 10 seconds, let alone a one-page resume. What could an employer possibly glean from a 10-second read?

What these busy managers who are inundated with hordes of resumes are more likely to do, is glance, not read. They take a quick scan of the document to decide if it's worth actually reading at a calmer moment in their day.

To get them to that point with your resume, a short document is not the solution. Shoot for creating an enticing one.

In addition, if you've got experience, a one-page resume can't do you much justice. Let's say the employer is looking for someone with 10 years in public relations. If you're worth your salt, a one-pager does not leave room to summarize your knowledge about media and community relations and expertise in employee communications over 10 years.

Glance they do. That's why you need to highlight the most relevant information someone in your industry cares about with lively language in an easy-to-read format that helps the reader quickly see you're a contender. Even with the tendency to scan, if you can say boring things in an interesting way, zip up descriptions of yourself and share facts that show you're a star, the manager might even forgo email to read for three minutes.

One way to get and keep their attention is to offer a bird's-eye view of yourself in the first section of your resume where they will probably glance first. This is where you describe your experience, mention that you're self-motivated and can evaluate complex legal cases and express ideas succinctly and have a reputation for prosecuting difficult patent cases. You'll get into details of where you did all this in the experience section and later, show examples of how you made a difference.

If it captures your individuality, downplays potential liabilities and gives proof you have what it takes to do the job you want, then make your resume more than one page. So what if it takes two or three pages to separate you from the pack? If you don't get noticed, what's the point?

It's unfortunate that so many people are conditioned to create a short resume, believing the employer will give only a 10-second read. It would be much wiser to develop a document that easily captivates an employer upon first look so that he will give you the time of day.

Andrea Kay - Gannett News Service

223 Tips to Succeed: PR (strategic) counselors are heard, but not seen

- We work behind the scenes
- We get our just rewards watching the people we work with get theirs
- We help our bosses succeed–we lead them to become strong leaders
- We advise
- We counsel
- We see the big picture
- Quite simply: It is our job to have relations with the public

Larry Ascough - National School Public Relations Association

224 Tips to Succeed: Ease those public speaking jitters

Public speaking is many people's number one fear. These tips should help:
- Determine whom your audience is and what you want to say to them.
- Research your topic and find out what people want to know about it.
- Outline what you want to say.
- Practice your presentation – in the room where you will be giving the speech, if possible. Tape the rehearsal and play it back.
- Shortly before your presentation, make sure the equipment and props are ready.
- Take a short, brisk walk before your presentation. Breathe deeply and slowly. Drink water.
- Have confidence you will do well.

Mayo Clinic Healthquest

225 Tips to Succeed: A publisher's view of journalism

Journalism is the first "rough draft" of history. Sometimes you wish it weren't so rough.

Philip L. Graham - Publisher - The Washington Post from 1946 to 1963.

226 Techniques to Succeed:
When output = outcome synergy is achieved

SYNERGY'S COMPONENTS

- Advertising
- (Sales) Promotion*
- Public Relations*
- Direct Marketing
- Cause Marketing
- Sponsorship (Partnering) Marketing
- Positioning (Place)*
- Personal Selling*
- Price*
- Product itself*
- Packaging*
- Policy*
- Politics*
- Mind Share (Brainstorming)
- Brand Identity
- Interactive (Web)

Litwin's 9 P's of Marketing
M. Larry Litwin, APR, Fellow PRSA - The Public Relations Practitioner's Playbook for (all) Strategic Communicators (AuthorHouse – 2013)

227 Tips to Succeed:
Job hunting – consider using an agency

- Target one or two agencies that are advertising positions you are qualified for and then call them — don't send your resume.
- Talk to the representative whose client has the openings you are interested in. Talk to the consultant about your experience and explain where your relevance lies.
- Don't send your resume out to each of their listings. Automated recruitment processes should be avoided because it doesn't help you build rapport and make you stand out from the other hundreds of candidates sending in resumes.

David Carter - www.job-hunting-tips.com

228 Tips to Succeed: For entrepreneurs pondering a change

Some things you should know about starting and growing your business:

- Don't expect to become rich. If you want to make a lot of money in the next five years, go get a job. If you have the passion to see your ideas and actions succeed or fail, then become an entrepreneur.

- Know you will fail. It is not a matter of if you will fail, just when. Business is about the good times and the bad times. Develop resiliency to ride the rollercoaster up and down. Celebrate the good times with your family and team. Transition through the bad times by learning what you can, then moving on for better days.

- Be humble. You meet the same people on the way up as you do on the way down in your business career. You are totally responsible for your success and failures.

Barry Moltz - Author - You Need to Be a Little Crazy: The Truth About Starting and Growing Your Business www.barrymoltz.com

229

Tips to Succeed:
What amount of success is satisfying?

Question: How much is enough? Your answer may tell you that you need to make some changes in your life.

The authors wish to redefine our ideas about success and they argue that too many businesspeople try to group all their own ideas about success in just one professional basket, which places them on an endlessly revolving wheel where they chase more titles, deals and money. The result is an empty feeling because they can't grasp the unobtainable.

This leads us back to the question: "How much is enough?" The authors interviewed many people who passed through the Harvard Business School, and who, by most standards, would be called "successful," but they discovered that many of them weren't satisfied with their lives.

They felt as though something was missing. They sensed that there was far more to being successful than what their lives represented to them at the moment, but many could not say what that "something" was. The book says that kind of success is one-dimensional.

Success should be defined in four ways:
- Happiness. Being content with one's life.

- Achievement. Setting and reaching goals.

- Significance. Doing things that positively affect colleagues, family and friends.

- Legacy. In which a person's values and achievements are used to help others succeed in the future.

Success should be multidimensional — not built simply on work and money. If they were the answer, more people would be satisfied.

How do we define success? That depends on:
- Who we are.

- What we do for a living.

- How much we have of life's material possessions.

- How full or shallow we are in our personalities.

Laura Nash and Howard Stevenson - Harvard
University Business School - Authors - Just Enough
Newstrack Executive Information Service - www.News-Track.com - 800-334-5771

230 Tips to Succeed: Assertiveness skills help you de-stress

One way to de-stress at work is to improve your assertiveness skills. Here are some suggested strategies:

- Determine if you're passive or aggressive. Assertiveness is between passivity and aggressiveness. Gather information from others to figure out if you come across as passive and submissive or aggressive and intimidating. You want to fall in the assertive range.
- Learn how to say no. The ability to say no can relieve your stress at work. If saying no to work is difficult for you, begin slowly by working on not saying yes right away.
- Compromise for win-win solutions. Look for ways to create compromises that will work for everyone involved. If your boss wants you to have a project done in one week and that seems impossible to you, tell her the benefits of finishing within two weeks.
- State what you want. A major problem that leads to stress is not stating your goals. You then feel out of control of your work situation, but in reality you did not really try to be the leader of your own career.
- Ask for help. Look to others for assistance in decreasing your stress level.

Larina Kase - Doctor of Psychology, career coach and former counselor at the University of Pennsylvania - www.extremecommunicator.com

231

Tips to Succeed:
Speaking helps maximize growth

Participating as a speaker at business events can provide opportunities for you and your business.

You could gain more clients, greater name recognition and connections, which could offer you many long-term benefits.

However, it's important to carefully choose which events are worth taking the time to create and prepare a presentation.

Here are a few tips on when and where to share your expertise:

- Think outside your industry. Consider opportunities to present to people other than your own peers.

- Think business groups: Many organizations, such as chambers of commerce and Rotary clubs, have monthly programs that focus on education as well as networking. Take advantage of the chance to tell people about your work.

- Consider the time. When do you get your biggest influx of client calls? If your business is seasonal, consider doing presentations just prior to that time.

Speaking engagements work a lot like advertising. The more people hear and see you, the greater the chances of them buying whatever you're selling. Pick these opportunities carefully and you will be speaking your way to business success.

Valerie Schlitt - VSA - wwwvsanj@netcom.com

232 Tips to Succeed: The basics of conducting a scientific survey

HOW-TO-DO-IT

1. Decide what you want to learn from the survey.
2. Ask why you want to learn this.
3. Ask yourself whether you could get this information without doing a survey.
4. Decide who your public or audience is going to be.
5. Determine the type of survey method you will use.
6. Establish confidence levels for your survey.
7. Develop a timeline from start to finish for your survey.
8. Decide how the information will be analyzed and disseminated to your publics or audience (especially those surveyed).

233

Techniques to Succeed: Rather be somewhere else? Your customers will too!

Commitment – true acceptance and dedication to a goal – makes a huge difference in the outcome of any course of action, whether in business, reaching personal objectives, or the quality of personal relationships.

Not all entrepreneurs love what they do. After all, they're their own boss, right? If they're not happy, can't they just change direction? It may not be that easy.

You may not be able to change your business – at least not immediately, but you can change your attitude.

What happens when you lose interest in your own business?
- First, the quality of your work suffers. Customers leave, but your overhead remains.

- You stop developing your skills, so you lose ground against your competitors.

- Most importantly, your lack of enthusiasm shows whenever you try to market your products or services. Even when new customers come to you they sense your indifference and leave.

Being passionate about your work is a competitive advantage. Customers and employees sense you're doing something you truly believe in, and they respond accordingly.

What can you do to reignite your enthusiasm for your business?
- Evaluate why you've lost interest.

- Decide whether you want to stay in this line of work.

If you decide to stay in business – and most of us will – here are other steps to take:
- Give yourself a goal.

- Develop a plan.

- Expose yourself to new ideas.

- Embrace your commitment.

Rhonda Abrams - www.rhondaworks.com/

234

Tips to Succeed:
Juggling at work? How to stay sane

Ever feel like you are juggling so many things that at any minute you will drop all of them and lose it? Constant multitasking at work can cause intense stress and pressure.

There are solutions:
- Stop juggling. You need to commit yourself to not multitask. Instead of juggling, think of yourself as bowling: one ball at a time. Once that ball is finished, you can move on to the next one. This helps you to feel that you can devote yourself 100 percent to the task at hand without constant distractions and the feeling that you aren't doing a good job.

- Juggle better. The key to multitasking is prioritizing. As a rule, the activities to multitask are the trivial, routine, or automatic duties that do not need all your attention and energy. You could check your email while you are on hold on the phone. You can spellcheck a document while listening to your voice mails.

The right solution depends on what works for you.

Larina Kase - Doctor of Psychology, career coach and former counselor at the University of Pennsylvania - www.extremecommunicator.com

235

Tips to Succeed: 10 steps to shamefully successful self-promotion

1. Develop a strong belief system: Create better customer service, increase self-esteem and personal growth by promoting every aspect of your business.
2. Develop gutsy goals that make you stretch: Create a "crazy" file for those gutsy marketing ideas that could make your business stand out among your competition.
3. Seek out and act on opportunities: Sometimes the most important strategies appear to be so simple we tend to ignore them.
4. Stay active in your community by networking and volunteering: Work on your business in the community – not just in your business.
5. Take your expertise to another level: Have revolutionary thinking! Do more to service your clients with follow up, follow through and added conveniences.(What sets you apart from the others?)
6. Build a strongly connected group of strategic alliances: Look for opportunities to co-market and re-connect with similar business and/or your competition.
7. Break the mold then shamelessly promote your uniqueness: Share your marketing "commercial" and explain why people should do business with you.
8. Get out in front of your target audience on a regular basis and don't ever stop reminding them about your business: Ask and reward satisfied clients for referrals — in writing. Use them in your marketing materials.
9. Embrace technology and market yourself on the Internet: The opportunities to market your business worldwide are endless today. Don't miss this huge window of opportunity of a website for your agency or other business. Don't overlook a personal website.
10. Apply for and achieve awards: Create an award-winning portfolio and seek out opportunities everywhere. This is a great way to promote your business to the media.

Shel Horowitz - www.frugalmarketing.com/libraries.shtml

236 Techniques to Succeed: The dreaded social kiss

Social kisses can be awkward – to both women and men. But they seem to be spreading everywhere – including business functions. In fact, they have become almost a universal greeting.

Peggy Post, author of the 16th edition of her great-grandmotherin-law's book, Emily Post's Etiquette, seems a bit concerned that social kissing has become "almost a universal greeting." At least when reserved strictly for those close to you, though, she approves of it as a method for greeting.

Emily Post's Etiquette suggests, "The social kiss is a charming way to greet family and friends…but not random people. Ms. Post's advice: "Do what you are comfortable with. There's no law that says you have to lay a social kiss when greeting anyone, and if you see one coming at you, just make sure to follow these basic rules. Try to kiss on the right cheek. Always aim to the right. That provides a sense of order, and helps you avoid smacking heads."

It is not improper to gently take the hand of the other person just before the kiss. It is also wise to take the cue from the other person – which does not mean that just because he or she expects a social kiss, they are going to get one.

It is important in business, though, to master the technique, to avoid awkwardness.

237 Tips to Succeed: Speaking in front of groups

1. If you have to use notes, don't use them in the first 60 seconds of your speech.
2. Number every page.
3. Never blow or tap on the microphone.
4. If you speak a little louder than usual, you will expend energy that will make you less nervous.
5. Don't use words in a speech that you wouldn't use in a normal conversation.
6. Be understandable.
7. Be memorable.
8. Move people to action.
9. Motivate them to tell other people about your message.
10. The more often you speak to large groups, the more comfortable you will feel.

Media Training Worldwide www.topica-publisher.com

238
Techniques to Succeed: For the self-employed or soon to be

While you're never going to eliminate the ups and downs of owning your own business, you can take steps to make the ride a little less bumpy and a lot less scary:

- **Discover your "bread and butter" business.** What pays your bills each month? Often the part of your business that covers your monthly overhead seems boring: The customer you've had forever, the product that keeps selling. Nurture these! Return the call from the long-time customer before you call the new prospect. Advertise the product that sells itself as well as the new one you're excited about. Remember what pays the bills.

- **Pay yourself a set "salary" every month.** Instead of spending wildly when times are good, give yourself a set monthly "draw" or salary every month, and put the rest of your income away. Draw from that savings account when times are tough.

- **Open a "tax account."** Sooner or later, tax time rolls around. Instead of waiting until the end of the year or the quarter and then having to frantically rustle up cash, put 20 to 40 percent of every dollar you earn directly into a tax account.

- **Take advantage of retirement plans.** One of the best tax advantages for the self-employed are tax-sheltered retirement plans.

- **Recognize there are cycles.** Generally, neither the good times nor the bad ones last forever, so try to keep perspective.

- **This is your life – live it!** While the first couple of years in business may be more intense than other years, you're always going to have too much to do and plenty of stress. It's tempting to tell yourself you'll get around to spending time with family, taking a vacation or exercising when work "lightens up." If you're really an entrepreneur, then this is the life you're going to lead.

Rhonda Abrams - www.rhondaonline.com

239

Tips to Succeed: Rules followed by the best writers

1. Prefer the plain word to the fancy.
2. Prefer the familiar word to the unfamiliar.
3. Prefer the Saxon word to the Roman.
4. Prefer nouns and verbs to adjectives and adverbs.
5. Prefer picture nouns and action verbs.
6. Never use a long word when a short one will do as well.
7. Master the simple declarative sentence.
8. Prefer the simple sentence to the complicated.
9. Vary your sentence length.
10. Put the words you want to emphasize at the beginning or end of your sentence.
11. Use the active voice.
12. Put statements in a positive form.
13. Use short paragraphs.
14. Cut needless words, sentences and paragraphs.
15. Use plain, conversational language. Write like you talk.
16. Avoid imitation. Write in your natural style.
17. Write clearly.
18. Avoid gobbledygook and jargon.
19. Write to be understood, not to impress.
20. Revise and rewrite. Improvement is always possible.

20 Rules for Good Writing from the Writers Digest School

240 Techniques to Succeed: The 30-3-30 Principle

Copy should always be prepared using the 30-3-30 principle. Is your copy aimed at the 30-second reader, three-minute reader or the 30-minute reader? To be effective, write for all three audiences.

241 Techniques to Succeed: Writers should use their heart and their soul

"Write your first draft from your heart. Write your second draft from the head...then polish it."

David Trottier - "The Screenwriting Center"

242 Tips to Succeed: Marketing yourself online

1. **Don't lie** – Whether on a resume, application or personal website, make sure facts about you are accurate.
2. **Be professional** – For college or job applications, use a simple email address with your name or initials that helps connect an email to you.
3. **Censor yourself, and friends (if need be)** – If you know a college or potential employer might Google® you or search you out on MySpace®, make sure the content posted by yourself or others is appropriate.

Des Moines Register

243 Tips to Succeed: Strategic counselors

1. Analyze conditions
2. Assess policies
3. Inform
4. Develop programs
5. Make recommendations
6. Persuade
7. Get people to act

244 Tips to Succeed: Survival of the fittest

- Assume a leadership role
- Gain experience – it's the best teacher
- Exude confidence – not cockiness
- Attitude – being positive is contagious
- Ask questions (the Aladdin factor) – get answers

245 Tips to Succeed: 25 Unwritten Rules of Management

1. Learn to say, "I don't know." If used when appropriate, it will be often.
2. It is easier to get into something than it is to get out of it.
3. If you are not criticized, you may not be doing much.
4. Look for what is missing. Many know how to improve what's there, but few can see what isn't there.
5. Viewgraph rule: When something appears on a viewgraph (an overhead transparency), assume the world knows about it, and deal with it accordingly.

6. Work for a boss with whom you are comfortable telling it like it is. Remember that you can't pick your relatives, but you can pick your boss.
7. Constantly review developments to make sure that the actual benefits are what they are supposed to be. Avoid Newton's Law.
8. However menial and trivial your early assignments may appear, give them your best efforts.
9. Persistence or tenacity is the disposition to persevere in spite of difficulties, discouragement, or indifference. Don't be known as a good starter but a poor finisher.
10. In completing a project, don't wait for others; go after them, and make sure it gets done.
11. Confirm your instructions and the commitments of others in writing. Don't assume it will get done!
12. Don't be timid; speak up. Express yourself, and promote your ideas.
13. Practice shows that those who speak the most knowingly and confidently often end up with the assignment to get it done.
14. Strive for brevity and clarity in oral and written reports.
15. Be extremely careful of the accuracy of your statements.
16. Don't overlook the fact that you are working for a boss.
    * Keep him or her informed. Avoid surprises!
    * Whatever the boss wants takes top priority.
17. Promises, schedules and estimates are important instruments in a well-ordered business.
    * You must make promises. Don't lean on the often-used phrase, "I can't estimate it because it depends upon many uncertain factors."
18. Never direct a complaint to the top. A serious offense is to "cc" a person's boss.
19. When dealing with outsiders, remember that you represent the company. Be careful of your commitments.
20. Cultivate the habit of "boiling matters down" to the simplest terms. An elevator speech is the best way.
21. Don't get excited in engineering emergencies. Keep your feet on the ground.
22. Cultivate the habit of making quick, clean-cut decisions.
23. When making decisions, the pros are much easier to deal with than the cons. Your boss wants to see the cons also.
24. Don't ever lose your sense of humor.
25. Have fun at what you do. It will reflect in your work. No one likes a grump except another grump.

Here some "extra" rules from Business 2.0

1. You can't polish a sneaker.(notice when something hasn't got any real substance).
2. You remember 1/3 of what you read, 1/2 of what people tell you, but 100 percent of what you feel. (Leaders generate emotions that move people in the desired direction.)
3. Treat your company name as if it were your own (possibly the same as #19 above.)
4. When faced with decisions, try to look at them as if you were one level up in the organization. Your perspective will change quickly. (Your boss has to weigh more considerations than you do in making a decision.)
5. A person who is nice to you but rude to the waiter is not a nice person.
6. When facing issues or problems that are becoming drawn out, "short them to ground." (Solve problems instead of talking about solving problems).

Bill Swanson - CEO - Raytheon

246 Tips to Succeed: Speaking: overcoming fears

Speaking in front of a group is one of the best ways to enhance your career yet the biggest fear most people have – even greater than the fear of death. Here are three tips to help you overcome that fear:

1. Get excited about the topic.
2. You have earned the right to speak on this subject. It's a good bet that you wouldn't have been asked to talk about the subject if somebody didn't think you were capable.
3. Be eager to project the value to your listener. Decide what the one thing is you'd like to say about this subject and how it could change their view of a situation.
4. After hitting the key points on the subject, you should give your audience a chance to ask you questions. Answer the questions quickly and directly – again, showing the audience that you're the "expert" on the subject.
5. It's important that you learn to become comfortable when presenting in front of others. Practice your presentation with some of your colleagues or practice with a coach. Practice will enable you to feel more comfortable speaking in front of others.

Anita Zinsmeister - President - Dale Carnegie Training of Central and Southern New Jersey

247 Tips to Succeed: Trade show prep

When all the costs are added up, showing off a company at a tradeshow can be expensive. So, how can you maximize your efforts? Here are several ideas:

- When you've signed the check for your booth, ask the show organizers for a PR/marketing sponsor opportunity kit. These usually feature special awards, and new product showcases that can add extra visibility and sponsorship packages.

- Since some tradeshows sell their pre-registered attendee list, or the previous year's list of attendees, a $75.00 to $150.00 investment is a small price to pay so you'll know who's attending to maximize your investment.

- Be creative. Make your space extraordinary to build traffic and potential sales.

- Tradeshow attendees often reserve blocks of rooms at hotels. Seeing that they receive your corporate premium at their hotel room is another super idea. It will cost between $1.50 and $3.00 per room to get your premium delivered, not including the cost of the premium itself.

Home Technology Products, December 2004/January 2005
Newstrack Executive Information Service - www.news-track.com - 800-334-5771

248 Tip to Succeed: 10 Tips from 'The Donald'

Entrepreneur Donald Trump says it takes more than luck to be a winner. He says, "To be winner – you have to think like a winner."

1. Stay focused
2. Think big
   - Sell only to those who pay their bills
   - Do the big jobs
3. Enjoy what you are doing – No, love what you are doing
4. Never quit
   - Go through the wall
   - Go over the wall
   - Go around the wall
   - Just get there
5. Be paranoid
   - At least a little paranoid
   - Watch out for people – It's either you or them
6. Don't lose your momentum
   - Know when you've lost it
   - Think of yourself as a one-person show
   - Don't believe anyone else is on your side
7. Always see yourself as victorious
8. Go against the tide – go with your gut
9. Hire the best people and trust (but watch) them
10. Work hard – Be lucky
    - "The harder I work the luckier I get!" - Golfer, Gary Player

Donald Trump

249 Techniques to Succeed: Pack without wrinkles

Whether you are going on a brief business trip or an extended vacation, you don't want to waste time at your destination ironing wrinkled clothing or spending money to have them pressed.

BEFORE YOU PACK:
- Hang each outfit and cover it with a plastic dry cleaning bag
- Fold each one over
- Place it in the suitcase on the hanger

When you unpack your suitcase, simply hang the clothes up and you are ready to go. If any of the clothes do wrinkle, hang them in the bathroom with a hot shower running for a few minutes.

www.cruisediva.com

250

Tip to Succeed:
Don't overlook top workers

The economy is picking up, which means people have more ability to jump from one company to the next.

Many companies overlook retention and are surprised when top talent walks out the door.

Often, managers spend much of their time on problem employees and leave their best employees alone to do their work. It's important to check in and pay attention.

Here are some tips for keeping talent:

- Be sure your best people feel that their jobs are rewarding and challenging to them.
- Be sure their compensation is satisfying. Give them a raise, more stock options, or a spot bonus, before they come to you and ask for it.
- Take the moments you do have to coach them. For example, instead of racing off to your next meeting, walk them to their next meeting and give them feedback.
- If they are frustrated, nip it in the bud, and solve the issue together. Some

telltale signs that your best people may be out the door:

- They seem more distracted.
- They aren't communicating with you as much.
- They are complaining about things they didn't complain about before.

Susan Bethanis - Executive Coach and author of
Leadership Chronicles of a Corporate Sage
www.corporatesage.com

251 Technique to Succeed: The importance of *thank-you* notes

As the inside cover of The Public Relations Practitioner's Playbook for (all) Strategic Communicators notes, "Public Relations is as simple as a thank-you note."

You can never thank someone too much, or thank too many people in a day. Based on research, here are the seven most effective opportunities to send "thank-you" notes to help develop new business:

1. **When someone offers suggestions.** It's a wonderful gift when you are given a suggestion on how you might do something better. Here's how to start this type of note: "Thank you for your suggestion. You make my job easier and so much more enjoyable when you provide input."

2. **When people try something you recommended.** When others buy into something new, solely based on your suggestion, they're going out of their "comfort zone." This calls for a note that could read, "Thank you for your trust in me."

3. **When customers do business with you, every time.** Write a short, personalized "thank you" on an interesting card, letterhead, or even a postcard that says, "I appreciate your business, thank you."

4. **When people compliment you.** When someone compliments you about something, it's an opportunity to jot off a little note of thanks. Compliments are given so rarely, so take the lead to say "thank you" when you get one.

5. **When someone recommends you.** This is the best form of advertising you can ever get. It's so easy to take the time and go back to our advocate, and say, "thank you for referring me to ___. I will keep you informed on what develops."

6. **When people are patient.** People help us when they give us time to learn how to best work with them. This often requires their patience. A note for this could say, "Thanks for your patience. I appreciate the opportunity to better work with you."

7. **When someone says "no" to you.** You've just presented your ideas to a co-worker or even a customer, and it was completely

rejected. It's still an opportunity to write a short note. Thank others for their time, their consideration, and their honesty.

We should thank people because it's the right thing to do. Period. Taking the time to do this builds good relationships, and good relationships build good business.

www.selfmarketing.com
M. Larry Litwin, APR, Fellow PRSA - The Public Relations Practitioner's Playbook for (all) Strategic Communicators (AuthorHouse – 2013)

252 Tips to Succeed:
That all important *thank-you note*

Just a note to let you know the percentage of people who send you *thank-you* notes.

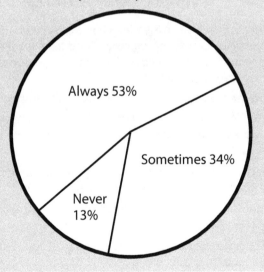

Always 53%
Sometimes 34%
Never 13%

253 Techniques to Succeed: A proven, simple, 2-way communication model

```
          Sender>>>Message>>>Receiver
    ^                                     v
    ^                                     v
    ^              Noise                  v
    ^                                     v
    ^              Noise                  v
    ^                                     v
    ^              Noise                  v
    ^                                     v
    ^                                     v

          < < < < < < < Feedback < < < < < < <
```

254 Techniques to Succeed: Teamwork – a key to success

Delivering high performance is easier when everyone on the team takes responsibility for working together. Good team leaders know how to motivate others and keep everyone moving in the same direction. Here are some suggestions:

- **Empower when possible.** Give team members the opportunity to make decisions.
- **Delegate when appropriate.** Ensure that all team members have the same workload.
- **Teach when knowledge or skill is lacking.** When you see that training is needed in a particular area, take time to train.
- **Provide guidance when you are needed.** Always be available for questions.
- **Get out of the way when you are not needed.** If you see that your team is handling their workload efficiently, don't hover over them.

www.dalecarneigie.com

255   Tips to Succeed: Tips for tipping
Tip = To Improve Service

- Hotel maids: $2.00 per day
- Shuttle driver: $1-$2 for helping you with one bag; $5 for heavy luggage.
- Doorman: No tip for opening hotel door; $1-$2 for carrying bag or opening cab door
- Wine steward: 10%-20% depending on service
- Concierge: $10-$20 for assistance such as acquiring hard-to-get show tickets
- Limousine drivers, masseurs, caddies: 20% unless a tip is included in the bill
- Theatre ushers: They generally get tips in Europe

Eileen Smith (from Emily Post's Etiquette) - www.courierpostonline.com

256   Tips to Succeed: Preventing identity theft

- Buy a shredder and shred all mail and other material that contains personal information.
- Never give out personal information, such as Social Security number, to anyone unless you know and trust them.
- Lock your mailbox.
- Don't carry more than two credit cards.
- Never carry your Social Security card.
- Consider opting out of free credit card offers by calling 888-567-8688 or online at www.optoutprescreen.com.

Associated Press

257 Techniques to Succeed: The 3-minute drill

The next time your boss asks you to solve a company problem, try the 3-minute drill – keeping in mind that every 30 seconds = 75 words:

PREPARE AN EXECUTIVE SUMMARY:
1. Situation Description (the problem in 60 words)
2. Analysis (the issues in 60 words)
3. Goal (the destination in 60 words)
4. Options (at least three in 150 words)
5. Recommendations (from the options in 60 words)
6. Justification (unintended consequences – pluses and minuses in 60 words)

James E. Lukaszewski, APR, Fellow PRSA - The Lukaszewski Group - www.e911.com [See details in Chapter 6 – The Public Relations Practitioner's Playbook for (all) Strategic Communicators (AuthorHouse – 2013)]

258 Tips to Succeed: Consistency

If you always tell the truth you don't have to wonder or worry about what you said. Your strategic message will be the same to everyone who asks.

259 Techniques to Succeed:

Six career secrets you won't learn in school – to help you win at the business world's game:

Develop a marketable corporate person:
Think of yourself as a publicist with the task of promoting you. Learn to capitalize on your skills, succinctly assert your achievements and project a corporate persona – or your most mature, professional and competent face.

Establish profitable relationships:
Business networking is a valuable tool to gain information, increase your visibility in your field and make connections that will help you move forward in your career. Seek out new contacts and potential mentors whom you like and admire and whose interests you share. On the home front, don't expect your boss to figure out what you're all about. Determine her priorities, find out what she wants from you, and brainstorm ways to surpass her expectations.

Master transferable skills like goal setting, effective communication and time management:
You might not know exactly what you want to do with your life, but transferable skills will serve you well no matter what future path you decide to pursue. Make your time count now by working with your boss to set specific, reasonable and attainable goals for your present position that will help you advance to the next level.

Stay motivated despite trying circumstances:
There's no doubt that the business world can be frustrating, but remember that you can choose your response to your environment. If you make a conscious decision to begin each day with a positive outlook, negative conditions at work can't take that away from you. Aim to increase your self-awareness so you can better understand your emotional hot buttons.

Get people to cooperate:
Always keep in mind that other people don't care what you want–they want to know what's in it for them. By approaching negotiations with an attitude that allows both parties to win, you'll be more effective at eliciting cooperation and ultimately getting what you want.

Be proactive about your career growth:
Approach your performance review strategically by soliciting feedback on your progress, identifying new goals and growth opportunities and hammering out a long-term promotion plan. When asking your boss for a raise, be prepared with a list of contributions that have positively impacted the bottom line.

When you're struggling to survive in a corporate job, it might be an achievement just to make it through the day. But if at any point you feel like taking these steps is not worth the effort, just consider how much time you are likely to spend in the business world. Assuming you work from age 22 to age 65 for 235 days a year, you'll be on someone else's clock for about 80,000 hours, or one tenth of your life. Isn't it only fair that you do everything you can to create a rewarding job experience?

Alexandra Levit - Author - They Don't Teach Corporate in College: A Twenty-Something's Guide to the Business World- (Career Press 2004) – www.corporateincollege.com and CareerBuilder.com

260 Tips to Succeed: Effort-Benefit Ratio

When you make people work, they stop reading. Communicate with clarity – clearly, concisely, consistently, calculatingly and completely (specifically and simply).

261 Techniques to Succeed: Know the Product Life Cycle

A concept which draws an analogy between the span of a human life and that of a product, brand or retail store (outlet) suggesting that, typically, a product's life consists of a sequence of five stages:

- Introductory – Product/brand is born and introduced.
- Growth – Demand develops for the product and/or brand.
- Maturity – Product/brand gathers "steam" as it ages.
- Decline – Competition or other factors have a negative effect on demand and bite into market share.
- Withdrawal – Product/brand (or retail store) dies or goes out of business.

The concept is used as a tool to form marketing strategies appropriate to each of the stages. Also, the history of a product from its introduction to its eventual decline and withdrawal.

262 Tips to Succeed: Your Goal: Achieve the 6 C's (Assessing your writing)

- Clarity: Say what you mean, mean what you say
- Correct: Avoid errors to avoid confusion
- Connection: Engage your reader
- Compelling: Motivate an action
- Conviction: Live the branding
- Consistency: Stay on message…always

Roger Shapiro - Mitchell Rose A Communications Consultancy - Lawrenceville, N.J.

263 Tips to Succeed: Reaching new heights

"It's not your aptitude, but your attitude, that determines your altitude."

Zig Ziglar (motivational author)

264 Techniques to Succeed: More on business dining etiquette

In today's business world, a tremendous amount of business is conducted at a dinner table. Whether at home or in a restaurant, it is important to have a complete understanding of how to conduct yourself when entertaining or being entertained.

Anxiety while dining can be reduced by following guidelines on how to order your meal, what utensils to use and how to use them, and knowing proper table etiquette.

A. Knowing guidelines on what to order will help relieve dining anxiety.

1. When possible let the host take the lead.
2. Ask for suggestions/recommendations.
3. Do not order the most expensive or the least expensive item on the menu.
4. Avoid foods that are sloppy or hard to eat.
5. Avoid alcohol even if others are drinking.

B. Choosing the correct silverware is not as difficult as it may first appear. Knowledge of a formal table setting will allow you to focus on the conversation rather than what utensil to use.

1. Know the basic table setting.
2. Eating utensils are used from the outside in. Dessert forks/spoons are placed at the top of the plate.
3. Everything to your right you drink. Everything to your left you eat.
4. When you don't know what utensil to use, watch what your host does and follow suit.
5. When you have finished, leave your plate where it is in the place setting. Do not push your plate away from you. Lay your fork and knife diagonally across your plate and side-by-side. The knife and fork should be placed as if they are pointing to the numbers 10 and 4 on a clock face.

C. Proper table manners will increase your confidence and promote your ability to show your skills in handling social situations. Be aware of:
1. Napkin Etiquette
2. Passing the Food
3. Eating

The Career Center - Florida State University
www.career.fsu.edu/ccis/guides/etiquette.html

265 Tips to Succeed: As a public relations counselor...

Build relationships

Keep a cool head

Be available (when the media comes calling)

Zack Hill - Senior Director of Communications - Philadelphia Flyers Hockey Club

266 Tips to Succeed: If the problem is you, climb out of that work rut

Perhaps it's not the place or the job – maybe you are the problem. Before you jump ship, it may be time to assess whether you're really putting everything you've got into the job you have.

- Maybe it's time to challenge yourself
- Come up with new ideas to create new excitement
- Treat the business as if it were your own.
  – Develop a plan
    - Where do you want to be in one or five years?
    - What duties would you like to have?
    - What skills do you need to accomplish those goals?
    - What are the obstacles in your way?

- How can you eliminate them?
  - Who are the key people you need to help you?
  - How much money do you want to be earning?
- At the same time, review your work over the last several years.
  - When did you start to feel bored or too complacent?
  - What factors were involved?
  - Did you feel as though some people were not helping or even trying to sabotage you? Treat the business as if it were your own.
  - Once you see where the traps are, you can work to avoid or overcome them so that they don't bog down your efforts to revitalize your job.

And finally, don't be afraid to ask for what you want. Ask the boss to work on a new project. Ask to train in other departments. Ask to attend a seminar, or to be taken off a dead-end task. Not all your requests may be granted, but continue to seek the changes you need to jump-start your career and fire up your enthusiasm.

Anita Bruzzese - Author - Take This Job and Thrive
(Impact Publications) - Gannett News Service

267 Techniques to Succeed: Be skeptical of venture ads

The Better Business Bureau deals with 10,000 complaints every year from consumers who say they have lost money to business opportunity ads such as "be your own boss" and "earn money quickly." The bureau has these suggestions when looking at such advertised ventures:

- Look at the ad carefully and be skeptical of promises of lots of money in little time for little work.
- Get earnings claims in writing.
- Scrutinize franchise offers by studying the disclosure documents and looking for a statement from previous purchasers.
- Interview each previous purchaser or investor.
- Check on complaint records.
- Find out if the company involved is well known.
- Consult experts such as an attorney or accountant before you sign anything or give any money.
- Do not give in to high-pressure tactics.

- Follow the first critical step in the public relations process – research, research, research.

Remember – if something appears too good to be true, it probably is.

www.bbb.org

268 Tips to Succeed: Leaving phone messages on voice mail

Always leave your name and phone number at least twice when leaving a voice-mail message – once at the beginning and once at the end. If you leave more than one phone number for call back, repeat all numbers. Speak slowly and clearly.

269 Tips to Succeed: Using visual aids

1. Use visual aids sparingly
2. Use visual aids pictorially
3. Present one key point per visual
4. Make text and numbers legible
5. Use color carefully
6. Make visual big enough to see
7. Graph data
8. Make pictures and diagrams easy to see
9. Make visuals attractive
10. Avoid miscellaneous visuals

270 Techniques to Succeed: Balance your life

Don't get out of balance in your life. Our lives are made up of seven vital areas.

- ✓ Health
- ✓ Family
- ✓ Financial
- ✓ Intellectual
- ✓ Social
- ✓ Professional and
- ✓ Spiritual

We will not necessarily spend time everyday in each area or equal amounts of time in each area. But, if in the long run, we spend a sufficient quantity and quality of time in each area, our lives will be in balance. If we neglect any one area, never mind two or three, we will eventually sabotage our success.

Much like a table, if one leg is longer than the others, it will make the entire table wobbly. If we don't take time for health, our family life and social life suffer. If our financial area is out of balance, we will not be able to focus adequately on our professional, etc. If we don't feel good about ourselves, our intellect and spirit suffer.

Is your life in balance?

Ed Ziegler - Director of Marketing - Rowan University - Glassboro, N.J.

271 Tips to Succeed: Lehrer writing approach

"I wake up every morning knowing I'm going to write. I know it's going to be typed and double spaced. The question is – 'What am I going to write?' My head does the thinking – my fingers do the writing. Sometimes, though, I think better with my fingers than I do with my head."

James Lehrer Journalist and Author - 2005

272 Tips to Succeed: Better writing through self-editing

"The most valuable of all talents is that of never using two words when one will do."

Thomas Jefferson

"The secret of play-writing can be given in two maxims: stick to the point, and, whenever you can, cut."

W. Somerset Maugham

"I love words but I don't like strange ones. You don't understand them and they don't understand you. Old words is like old friends, you know 'em the minute you see 'em."

Will Rogers

"It behooves us to avoid archaisms. Never use a long word when a diminutive one will do."

William Safire

"Men of few words are the best men."

William Shakespeare

"A sentence should contain no unnecessary words, a paragraph no unnecessary sentences, for the same reason that a drawing should have no unnecessary lines and a machine no unnecessary parts."

William Strunk

"Use the smallest word that does the job."

E.B. White

"Think like a wise man but communicate in the language of the people."

William Butler Yeats

273 Techniques to Succeed: En route to synergy

The right PR word!
By the right person!
At the most strategic moment!

274 Tips to Succeed: Make your website 'pop'

If you have a website and want it to "pop up" when someone searches for your name, product or service, you need to ensure that you set up your online presence properly. Search engines look for pages that have not only relevance, but the promise of rich content.

Here's how to get better results:

- Ask people to put a link to your site on their site. Besides direct traffic, the real benefit is that it raises your popularity. Ask for a text link with a good description.
- Put links to other relevant sites on your pages. This shows that you are enriching your site with outside resources and that you play well with others.
- Write good copy, and cover all of the high points on your opening page. Make the title of the home page relevant by including your business name, and perhaps product.
- Find a forum or mailing list where you can contribute occasionally. Anytime you contribute, don't pitch your product, but make sure you include a tagline with your site's full Web address and a short description.
- Put an FAQ (frequently asked questions) section on your site. It is likely rich with keywords that search engines will be looking for.

Terry Wilson - www.terryific.com

275 Techniques to Succeed: Maximize your workers' potential

Employers can get their employees to reach their potential through energizing and motivational techniques. Here are some key techniques:

- **Communication.** When managers and employees communicate honestly and frequently, there are positive effects.
- **Support.** When managers are mentors and cheerleaders, employees feel support.
- **Energize.** Successful managers inspire visions from their employees. Let them dream, test and run with an idea.
- **Empower.** Great managers approach employees with trust and an assumed sense of capability.

www.firstcalleap.org

276 Techniques to Succeed: Moderating a focus panel

ROLE OF THE MODERATOR
- Direct the discussion, ensuring that key topics are covered – yet remain flexible enough to allow for exploration of relevant issues that may come up spontaneously. Above all, the moderator must remain neutral.

MODERATING
- Establish a "safe" atmosphere, which encourages open, honest, thorough and valid participation. Participants should know that you are interested in their honest opinions – both positive and negative – and that there are no right or wrong answers.
- Be sure to cover the ground rules and get "head-nod" agreement on them. Groups may add their own rules to the list – if the moderator agrees.
- Encourage participation from all respondents – particularly those who are less likely to speak up.

- To gain early involvement by all members of the group, ask each participant to introduce him/herself.
- If everyone in the group seems to be saying the same thing, ask if anyone sees something differently.
- Do not reiterate participants' responses to clarify comments. If the moderator repeats back to the participant what has just been said, the moderator may not have understood the point exactly and may introduce an element of bias. Instead, ask the participant to clarify his/her own point.
- Remain neutral. Be careful not to nod your head in agreement or say "uh-huh" to those individuals whose opinions you agree with.
- Stick to time. You can move the discussion along by saying, "In the interest of time, we need to move to the next question."
- When you have several people who want to speak, you can "stack" speakers by saying, "First, we'll hear from Steve, then Jan and then Nancy."
- Move from a dominating speaker to another speaker by physically turning your body.
- Gesturing with your palm facing up encourages someone to speak.
- Don't be afraid of the "pregnant pause." It will encourage someone to speak.

Jennifer Wayan Reeve, APR - Director of Programs Colorado
Association of School Boards - Denver, CO 80203

277 Tips to Succeed: Starting or expanding your business?

Decide what you like to do. With your own business, you'll be spending a lot of time doing it.

- Know how much time you'll have to dedicate to your business. Running your own business doesn't always mean weekends off. So, be sure you have the time and energy to really make it successful.
- Identify technical skills or knowledge you have. You have to know what you're doing, and if you don't already know it, you must be completely willing to immerse yourself in learning.
- Determine what niche your business will fill. Just because you like something or are good at it, doesn't mean there is a market for it. Do some research to confirm or determine if there is a need for your product or service.
- Do your homework. Find out who your competition is, and how you will create demand for your product or service.

Andrew Glatz - Sun National Bank - www.sunnb.com

278 Tips to Succeed: Do for yourself

Tim's rules:
- Have fun
- Have it for yourself
- Share it
- Laughter might not be the best medicine, but it is preferred and the least expensive
- Tell yourself, each day, you are going to have fun – at work and at home – and no one is going to stop you

It's a ripple effect and you can be the "official" starter!

Tim Gard - www.timgard.com

279 Tips to Succeed: Take time to smell the roses

"Life is what happens to you when you are busy making other plans."

Yoko Ono

280 Techniques to Succeed: Beefing up your credit report

Here are some suggestions for maintaining or improving your credit history:

- Pay your bills on time. Payment history is the single most important factor in determining your credit score, making up 35 percent of the total number. Missing even one payment can knock 50 to 100 points off a good score.

- Pay down your debts and consider charging less. Lenders like to see plenty of room between the amount of debt reported on your credit cards and your total credit limits. Charging less can also improve your score, even if you pay off your credit cards on a monthly basis.

- Don't be afraid of credit counseling. In 1998, the Fair Isaac Corp. changed its scoring formula to remove references to credit counseling in consumers' files after learning that receiving credit counseling was becoming less predictive of credit risk. Be sure to research, and only become involved with legitimate organizations.

- Stay out of bankruptcy. Bankruptcy can knock 200 points or more off your credit score. After filing, consumers are usually only able to secure credit through high-interest lenders, which can often lead consumers back down the path of bad credit.

Centers for Financial Education, a division of Consumer Credit Counseling Services of New Jersey - www.crediteducation.com

281 Techniques to Succeed: Event Planning – 10 key points

1. Decide event's purpose (goal and/or objectives).
2. Organize your volunteers.
3. Be ready for anything.
4. Create a timeline (Gantt chart – See Page 222 in *The ABCs*).
5. Create an incentive to attract event participation.
6. Communicate (early on) with participants.
7. Make it a learning experience – determine what participants are going to "take away."
8. The event, if properly planned, will run itself. (Planning is everything).
9. Evaluate event and total plan at conclusion of event (exit survey).
10. Have fun!

282 Tips to Succeed: Do you have a brand? – Evaluate your 5 P's

Your brand consists of a complex set of characteristics and dynamics that play out in thousands of scenarios each workday.

You can use your brand to positively influence your image to others and enhance your career using these five P's:

Persona – The emotional connection and reaction you elicit from other people as a result of your personal style.

Product – The sum of your qualifications, experience, technical and/or functional expertise, ideas and results you've delivered over time.

Packaging – The presentation of your personal appearance, surroundings and tangible results of projects and assignments on the job.

Promotion – The way you inform your market about your value and impact.

Permission – The sense of legitimacy, confidence and core belief that you have important contributions to make.

Susan Hodgkinson - The Leader's Edge"

INDEX

30-3-30 Principle, 232

A

ABCs of strategic public relations, 192
Abrams, Rhonda, 70, 90, 117, 143, 229
Accountant, Hiring an, 176
Ads
    Ads in General, 74
    Ads on the Web, 73
Advertising
    Advertising, Agency, 81
    Advertising, Example, 151
    Advertising, Ogilvy's Tenets, 95
    Advertising, Reverse Psychology, 104
Ailes, Roger, 185
Alcantara, Rick, 181
All Business.com, 131
Allen, Scott, 127
Altitude, 247
Andrews, Rep. Robert, 212
Anxiety, 128
Applicant Statement, 157, 211
APR, What Does it Mean, 145
Aptitude, 247
Architectural PR, 120
Aristotle, 214
Ascough, Larry, 217
Atlantic City PR Council, 79

Audience
    Audience, Making the Best Impression, 185
    Audience Power Structure, 193
    Audience Segmentation/ Fragmentation, 146
Audiences, 68, 193
Azusa Pacific University, 65

B

Background Only, 182
Balance Your Life, 252
Beebe, Jordana, 103
Behavioral Change, 81
Belt and Suspenders, 80
Best Evidence, 168
Bethanis, Susan, 239
Better Writing Through Self-Editing, 253
Boilerplate, 212
Bookkeeping, 132
Boss and Friend, 207
Branches of Government, 129
Brand, Personal, 232, 259
Brand Recognition, Example, 151
Branding, 78, 79
Brands, Store vs. National 108
Bruzzese, Anita, 115, 163, 177, 186, 250
Budgeting, 76, 79, 80

Burgio, Ralph, Inside Front Cover, 167
Burnett, John, 81
Burnout, 133
Burson-Marsteller, 174
Business
    Business Angels, 77
    Business Coach, 106
    Business Dining, 77
    Business, Doing Business with Government, 127
    Business Entertaining, 134
    Business Letter, 90, 91, 131, 144
    Business Plan, 158
    Business Techniques, Through Osmosis, 98
    Business Travel, 80
    Business Trips, 70
    Business, Starting or Expanding, 172
Busse, Richard, Esq., 115
Byrnes, Jonathan, 172

C

Callahan, Dan, 135
Campaigns, Why They Fail, 151
Casperson, Dana May, 73
Career Center, 91, 111, 159, 249
Career Move, 97
Carnegie, Dale, 68, 83, 108, 113, 121, 158, 235, 242
Carrero, Andrea, 69
Carter, David, 90, 219
Cash, Stretching Your, 96
CBAs of Strategic Public Relations, 192
Cell Phone Etiquette, 86, 97

Chan, Janis Fisher, 132
Charette Design, 120
Clean Desks, 102
Cleaning Up, The Work Space, 186
Client Reluctance, 67
Cold Calling, 89
Commerce Bank, 78, 98
Communication Audit, 85
Consistency, 244
Consumer Reports, 95, 107, 108, 154
Convince, 89
Corporate Espionage, 109
Counselor, Public Relations, 217, 232, 249
Courtney, Roslyn, 162
Cover Letters, 90, 131
Crack Egg Persuasion Model, 96
Craig, Robin, 173
Credit, 71
Credit Card Protection, 86, 87
Credit Killers, 88
Credit Report, 88, 95, 258
Credit Score, 107
Crisis Communication, 93, 94
Crisis, Recovering From, 174
Cuddy, Claudia, ix, 92
Customer Relations, 112
Customer Relationship Management, 161
Customer Satisfaction, 78
Customer Service, 78, 112, 141, 225, 227

D

Dale Carnegie, 68, 83, 108, 113, 121, 158, 235, 242
Debit Card Safety, 103

Debt, Getting a Handle On, 100
De-clutter Your Space, 131
Delahaye Medialink Worldwide, 94
Dining Etiquette, 100, 188, 248
Direct Marketing Example, 151
Do for Yourself, 257
Doctor Visits, Employee, 101
Dollar Bill Test, 92
Double Bottom Line Theory, 105
Drafts, 232
Dratch, Diana, 184
Dressing for Business, 190
Dressing for Work, 122, 123, 125
Drip, Drip, Drip, 104

E
Ebert, Nila, 15
Editors and Reporters, Understanding Them, 169, 209
Effort-Benefit Ratio, 246
Eisenhower, Gen. Dwight D., 200
Elevator Speech, 72, 143, 234
Elon University, 188
Embedded Ads, 145
Employees, Retaining Them, 113
Entrepreneurs, 220
Espionage, Corporate or Industrial, 109
Ethos, 214
Etiquette
    Etiquette, Business Dining, 100, 140, 248
    Etiquette, Business, 77, 83
    Etiquette, Cell Phone, 86, 97, 179
    Etiquette, Dining, 100, 188

Etiquette, email, 124, 132
Etiquette, iPod®, 173
Etiquette, Phone, 66, 150
Etiquette, Work, 111
Excuses, Don't Make Them, 109

F
Failures into Successes, 117
Family Business Institute, 118
Family Businesses Have Rules, Too, 118
Farish, Dr. Donald, 110
Farkas, Lyna, 74
Favor, Getting One, 116
Ferrazzi, Keith, 129
FICA, 196
Fifth P of Marketing, 172
Fingerprint, 121
Fired, Getting, 114
First Impressions, 71
FirstCALL, 105
Five O'Clock Club, 97
Florida State University, 111, 159, 247
Focus Panel, 255
Four (New) P's of Marketing, 99
Fridays Before Holidays, 165
Fried, John J., 198
Fronting Your Brand, 114
Fulginiti, Anthony J., 192
Fuller, Tracey, 113

G
Gard, Tim, 257
Getting on the Air, 109
Gisclair, Jessica, Esq., 188
Gitomer, Jeffery, 161

Glatz, Andrew, 158, 257
Goldbeck, David, 80
Goldbeck, Nikki, 80
Google®, Advice From, 125
Gossip, Office, 129
Graham, Philip L., 218
Grunig's Four Models of Public Relations, 194
Gunning Fog Index, 130

H
Hallmark®, 166
Handbook Errors, 138
Handshake, Proper Business, 136, 195
Haney, Jim, 77
Health Tips, 251
Hill, Vernon, 112
Hill, Zack, 249
Hit the Ground Running, 68
Hodgkinson, Susan, 259
Holiday Cards, 166
Holiday Party Overload, 139
Home Entertaining for Business, 134
Home in vs. Hone, 137
Horowitz, Shel, 227
Hueston, Fred, 74

I
Identity Theft, Prevent, 243
Identity, 146
Image, 79, 84
Industrial Espionage, 109
Ingram, Leah, 125
Integrated Marketing Communication Achieves Synergy, 151

Internet Security, 144
Interviewing Preparation, For a Job, 148, 153
Interviews, 67
Investing, 148
Investor Tips, 126

J
Jackson, Patrick, 105
Jefferson, Thomas, 253
Job, Getting One, 156
Job Hunt, 154, 219
Job Market, Getting Ready, 107
Job Search, 154, 219
Johnson, Joseph, 126
Jones, J. William, 94
Journalism, First Draft, 218, 232
Juggling at Work, 226

K
Kahn, Roger, 84
Kalmer, Bill, 142
Kersten, Denise, 72, 73
Kase, Larina, 110, 128, 147, 222, 226
Kay, Andrea, 155, 212, 216
Kopec, Joseph, 85
Kraushar, John, 185

L
Landers, Ev, 22, 169
Lawsuits, Avoid Them, 135
Leaders, 65
Leadership, 162, 163, 164
Leaving Messages, 251
Lee, Nora, 112
Lee, Tony, 176
Lehrer, James, 252

Levit, Alexandra, 91
Levy, Maury Z., 90, 183
Lin, Feng, 82
Litwin's Nine P's of Marketing, 166
Loan Mistakes, 162
Logos, 213
Lubetkin, Steve, 170
Lukaszewski, James, 244
Lynch, Robert, 167

M
Malloy, Steven, 68
Management Rules, 233
Managing, Better, 83
Marketing, Yourself, 232
Marzi, Marie Poirier, 197
Maslow's (Abraham) Theory of Motivation, 201
Maugham, W. Somerset, 253
Mayo Clinic, 93, 218
MBA, Earning an, 167
McKee, John, 208
Media
    Media, Challenging It, 167
    Media, Dealing With It, 168
    Media Interviews, 170
    Media Mistakes, 168
Messages, Leaving, 251
Mihal, Heather, 71
Misner, Ivan, 173
Mission Statement, 167
Moltz, Barry, 220
Moriarity, Sandra, 81
Muney, Dr. Alan, 101
Mutual Fund Terminology, 119
My Business Relationships.com, 116

N
Names, Bad With, 82
Nash, Laura, 221
National Association of Broadcasters, 109
Nelson, Noelle, 83
Networking, 159, 171, 175, 178, 179
New Boss, Meeting the, 177
News Releases, 210
Newsome's Principles of Persuasion, 196
Newstrack, 65, 99, 161, 164, 172, 221, 226
Nierenberg, Andrea, 156, 175, 178, 179, 204
Nine P's of Marketing, 166
Not for Attribution, 182

O
Off the Record, 182
Office Romances, 213
Older People, Communicating With, 93
Ogilvy, David, 95
On the Record, 182
Ono, Yoko, 258
Open, Honest, Thorough, Valid, 185
Organizational Learning, 182
Output equals Outcome, 187
Outside the Box Thinking, 184

P
Pachter, Barbara, 84, 97, 101, 122, 134, 190
Pack Without Wrinkles, 238
Password, 144
Pathos, 214

Pay-to-Play, 198
Pendaflex®, 165
Perdue, Frank, 114
Personal Brand, 232, 259
Personal Code of Ethics, 185
Persuade, 89
Persuasion Model, 96
Pfeffer, Jeffery, 182
Phishing, 103
Phone Bills, Slash Them, 154
Photo Opportunities, 197
Pinged, Getting, 198
Pitches, 74
Pitino, Rick, 164
Planning, 113, 165
Planning Rule, 199, 200
Political Advertising, 205
Politics, Workplace, 207
Positive Vibes, 158
Post, Emily, 228, 243
Practitioners, Public Relations, 232
Preparation, 190
Presentations, 173
Press Releases, 209, 212
Pricing Strategies, 206
Primacy - Recency, 196
Product Life Cycle, 247
Product Placement, 145
PRSA Code of Ethics, 160
P's of Marketing, 166, 172
Public Relations
    Public Relations, Example, 151
    Public Relations Agency, 81
    Public Relations Counselor, 217, 232, 249

Public Speaking, 218, 229, 235
Publishing, 200, 201
Punctuality, 199

Q
Quid Pro Quo, 208

R
Raz, Tahl, 129
Reading Ease, 82
Recency-Primacy, 196
Reeve, Jennifer Wayan, 256
Reeves, Scott, 141
Referral, 212
Relations, Workplace, 121
Relationships, 163
Releases, 209, 212
Reporter, Don't Blame, 172
Reporters and Editors, Understanding Them, 169
Reputation, 213
Research, 224
Restaurants, Picking Good Ones, 157
Resume, 211, 215, 216
Rhetoric, 214
Rogers, Will, 253
Rosenthal, Neil, 122
Roses, Smell the, 258
Rosner, Robert, 65
Rove, Karl, 103
Rowan University, 110, 162, 167, 187, 252

S
Safire, William, 253
Schaefer, Christine Mazza, 138
Schlitt, Valerie, 223

Schulman, Steve, 104
Seat at the Table, 208
Self-employment, 230
Self-promotion, 227
Selling Yourself, 191
Shakespeare, William, 253
Shaping Your Life, 110
Shapiro, Roger, 6 C's of Communication, 247
Silber, Lee, 191
Skimming, 103
Smell the Roses, 258
Smile, 191
Smith, Eileen, 243
Social Kiss, 228
Song, Mike, 124
Speaking, 229, 235
Speaking, Public, 218, 226, 235
Special Events, 259
Stainer, Maria, 75
Staver Group, The, 133
Stevenson, Howard, 221
Strategic Advisor Wanted, 174
Strategic Counselor, 217, 232
Stress, 128, 147, 222
Stress, Reducing, 110
Strunk, William, 253
Stumbling Blocks into Stepping Stones, 117
Sullivan-Williams, Lizziel, 107
Survey Techniques, 172, 224
Surveys, 172, 224
Survival, 233
Survival of the Fittest, 233
Swanson, Bill, 235

Sweet-Belle, Stacey, 171
Synergy, 151, 219, 254

T
Team Player, 68
Teamwork, 242
Telemarketing, Example, 151
Television, On-camera Interview, 152
Television Tips, 92
Thank-You Note, Inside Front Cover, 204, 240, 241
Theory of Motivation, Maslow's, 201
Think Backwards, 201
Thirty-Three-Thirty Principle, 232
Three-minute Drill, 244
Tipping, 243
Tisch, Jonathan, 98
Trade Show Prep, 236
Travel Tips, 202
Traveling, Less Stress, 184
Triple Bottom Line Theory, 105
Trottier, David, 232
Trump, Donald, 237
Truth, 244
Tumminia, Dr. Philip, 162
Two-Way Communication Model, 242

U
Uszynski, Al, 189

V
Venture Ads, 250
Visual Aids, 251
Voice Mail, 251

W

Wagenheim, Marc, 166
Walsh, Jim, 146
Web, 69, 73, 181
Weber, Karl, 98
Website, 69, 254
Wechsler, Warren, 212
Wells, William, 81
White, E.B., 253
White, Jo Anne, 184
Wilson, Terry, 254
Work Rut, 249
Workers' Potential, 255
Workplace
    Workplace Enthusiasm, 108
    Workplace Politics, 207
    Workplace Problems, 105

Writers Digest School, 231
Writing, 69, 209, 231, 232, 247, 252, 253

Y

Yeats, William Butler, 253
Your Personal Brand, 232, 259
Yourself, Do for, 257

Z

Ziegler, Ed, 187, 252
Ziglar, Zig, 247
Zinsmeister, Anita, 83, 235

More Third-Party Endorsements

"In a word, Larry Litwin's books are 'amazing.' I got hooked after hearing the buzz about The PR Playbook."

Callie Peterson
University of North Dakota

"Larry has always been the consummate professional. Do you know what makes a professional of this caliber? Talent, of course, but style even more! With all his skill there's always a smile! Larry Litwin is certainly a role model for everyone–students, media moguls and public relations professionals. I'm honored to be his peer."

Sharla Feldscher
President, Sharla Feldscher Public Relations, Philadelphia, Pa.
Philadelphia Public Relations Association's Hall of Fame Honoree

"Litwin's books are a lifesaver – professionally *and* personally. Read them and you will soon agree."

Nadia S. Liquori
Public Relations Counselor
Girl Scouts of the USA

**For information and ABCs' updates and additions:
www.larrylitwin.com**

All Tips and Techniques are on the Companion CD available at www.larrylitwin.com